ALTMAN

ALTMAN

KATHRYN REED ALTMAN and
GIULIA D'AGNOLO VALLAN
INTRODUCTION BY MARTIN SCORSESE

CONTENTS

INTRODUCTION

BY
MARTIN
SCORSESE

Robert Altman and I crossed paths fairly often over the years, but I felt like I got to know him intimately through his films. His signature. His human imprint as an artist, as recognizable and familiar as Renoir's brushstrokes and Debussy's orchestrations. It seems increasingly precious as the years go by, particularly now, when individual expression in moviemaking is so precarious.

I suppose that my first Altman film was *M*A*S*H*—it was for many people. It took us all by surprise. The irreverence, the freedom, the mixture of comedy and carnage, the Korean renditions of American hits and the voice over the loudspeaker as running commentary or counterpoint, the creative use of the zoom lens and the long lens, the multiple voices on the soundtrack—he was like a great jazz musician, taking us all along on a grand artistic journey.

He changed the way we looked at people and places and listened to voices, and he really changed our understanding of exactly what a scene was. Bob made so many wonderful pictures, but finally it's all the work taken together that is such a source of wonder.

Bob and I would cross paths from time to time every few years or so, and it was always memorable. He was there at the New York Film Festival in 1973 when *Mean Streets* was shown, which was a big event for me in so many ways. We met, and I remember that he was so gracious, so reassuring, and entirely complimentary. He really went out of his way for me. It was inspiring, and it meant the world to me.

OPPOSITE Robert Altman looking over a location in the Mar Vista neighborhood of Los Angeles during the filming of *Short Cuts* in 1992.

Ten years later, we ran into each other at an official function on a yacht. We struck up a conversation, and we discovered that we both had pictures, made at the same studio, that had been pulled—*The King of Comedy* for me, *HealtH* for him. There we were, both at a crossroads. Given the way things were going in the industry, neither of us could get a picture funded. We were marked men. For a while, at least.

Bob's solution to the problem was very simple: He just kept working. He persevered. Mind you, this is when he was almost sixty, a time of life when many other people would have given up. He was just getting his second wind—or was it his third? Or maybe his fourth? Bob started in the world of industrial film-making, then moved into television with episodes of *Alfred Hitchcock Presents, Whirlybirds, Peter Gunn, Bonanza,* and *Combat!*, among others. He was able to shift to features in the late sixties, which led to *M*A*S*H* and that amazing period in the seventies when he made one remarkable picture after another. Then he went into the period I was discussing before, what I guess he might have called his "journeyman" years in the eighties.

This was inspiring to me, and it should be a model to all young film-makers. He probably figured, "Look: This is the business we're in, this is the way it is—you gamble, and sometimes you win, and sometimes you lose—but you keep playing with whatever you have." He just plowed ahead, working under all kinds of conditions. He shot adaptations of plays by David Rabe and Sam Shepard and Christopher Durang—some on Super 16, like the beautiful *Come Back to the 5 & Dime, Jimmy Dean, Jimmy Dean* by Ed Graczyk. He did television—some one-act plays by Pinter, a tremendous adaptation of *The Caine Mutiny Court-Martial.* He did some wonderful work in Europe, including *Vincent & Theo.* And it seemed that his "years in the wilderness" only increased his motivation to steal his way back into the system. Which he did in the nineties, with *The Player.* Imagine breaking back into Hollywood, like a guerrilla fighter, with a picture that cast as tough and sharp and cynical an eye on the movie business as *Sunset Boulevard* had forty years earlier—and perhaps even less forgivingly than Billy Wilder's classic. *The Player* was made with the energy of a young man and the wisdom of an older one.

No matter what the circumstances, Bob's films remained his and his alone. I never cease to be amazed by the sheer range of his work, and the apparent ease of it. It seemed like he could take on absolutely any kind of material, from *The Long Goodbye* to *The Gingerbread Man,* from *Thieves Like Us* to *Gosford Park,* from *Kansas City* to *Vincent & Theo,* and pull off two things at once: do justice to the material and incorporate the film into his own universe. He did it with apparent ease, and with such evident grace. I was astonished by *Gosford Park,* the way that he simply went off to England and confidently made this movie, with all these characters coming alive, the movement so fluid, the drama among the people so exact, the sense of place and weather so sharp. (Bob made extraordinary use of weather in picture after picture—the snow in *McCabe & Mrs. Miller,* the desert heat in *3 Women,* the falling rain in *The Caine Mutiny Court-Martial,* to name just a few examples.) And there are all those little moments, grace notes that finally aren't so little, and that are the heart of Bob's pictures—for instance, Alan Bates as the butler, standing around a corner, listening secretly to Ivor Novello (Jeremy Northam) playing the piano and tapping his foot to the rhythm.

There are so many of Bob's pictures that I cherish: *Nashville,* of course—there's no other picture like it, a true American epic; *Thieves Like Us* and *California Split,* two remarkable pictures that must have been made almost back-to-back; *Cookie's Fortune,* of his wonderful "group" movies, and *The Gingerbread Man,* an unusual thriller in which the atmosphere is the star; *Kansas City,* a truly great musical film; and, of course, *McCabe & Mrs. Miller,* probably one of the most beautiful American films ever made. It's a favorite of mine, for many reasons. First of all, there's the sense of authenticity—there's such a powerfully evocative sense of life on the frontier, of the little town in the process of being built, and you feel like you're really living with the characters. And then there's Warren Beatty's McCabe, like no other character I know of in movies: a dreamer who's talked himself into believing that he's some kind of tough guy but who isn't at all; and Julie Christie's Mrs. Miller, who is much harder than McCabe but who softens herself for him, to protect his sense of masculinity. And it's still remarkable to me that Bob was able to pull off that ending: the quiet, the falling snow, the fire and the people running to put it out, and, in the end, two souls fading into oblivion.

We always stayed in touch. I asked Bob to join the board of the Film Foundation in 1998, and I was extremely pleased when he accepted. And I'm proud to say that he asked me to work with him on *Tanner on Tanner*. It was quite an experience. The atmosphere was so relaxed and convivial—I remember just showing up, sitting down to have a drink at a table, and suddenly I was in an episode, improvising with Steve Buscemi. There was absolutely no separation between art and life: I didn't know when we were shooting and when we weren't, what was part of the picture and what wasn't. After Steve and I did our improv a couple of times, we thought it had gone pretty well, so we asked Bob what he thought. "Gentlemen," he said, "that . . . was . . . . . . adequate." It was all very relaxed, but he was absolutely clear. So we worked at it, we got it to the point where he was happy, we talked it through, and then we shot it. I have such warm memories of the whole experience. We shot for the entire day, and when I got back to my hotel I didn't feel exhausted or drained—I felt like I had spent a good day in the company of friends. That was the last time Bob and I saw each other.

I had so much admiration for Bob Altman—I still do. This man who came out of the system and developed his own individual voice along the way, his own vision, unique and true—it was there at the beginning and it was there at the very end, in the beautiful *Prairie Home Companion*. Bob represented the real spirit of independence and freedom in moviemaking. He had the audacity to treat cinema as an art form. From time to time I find myself remembering Bob, thinking about his pictures . . . and realizing just how lucky we were to have him.

Martin Scorsese is the director of more than twenty-five films, including *Taxi Driver* (1976), *Raging Bull* (1980), *Goodfellas* (1990), and *The Wolf of Wall Street* (2013). He has been nominated for twelve Academy Awards® and won for Best Director in 2006 for *The Departed*.

BY
KATHRYN REED
ALTMAN

I met Bob in 1959. At the time, he had three children, and I had one. We married that year and soon had two more together. We started taking pictures of our life, as people do. I think we started with the original Polaroid and moved on to the Instamatics, then right on up to the disposables. Then, of course, came digital cameras and cell phones.

The photos in my albums are mostly family photos and photos given to us by friends. I started making the albums in the mid-sixties. I purposely didn't want any publicity photos or 8-by-10 glossies! I just wanted a family history. I started putting the photographs into albums because I was determined not to end up with drawers full of undated photos, as so many of my friends had. I covered every year that Bob and I were married.

It was an ongoing project. I was always working on an album no matter where we were, be it Malibu, New York, or on location. I'd pack up all the photos that I had already organized chronologically and ship them to wherever we were going to be living. It really became a sort of hobby. There were times when I'd be years behind in the albums, but I'd always catch up somehow. Bob really enjoyed them, too, but he loved to tease me about cropping the photos at unusual angles. My reply was always the same: "If I don't crop them, we are going to need to add on another room just to house all these photo albums!" I actually liked cropping them. I thought it was rather creative, and it didn't end up looking like your typical photo album.

We lived in Malibu, California, for many years, and that is where the photo albums had a permanent place on the shelf. Wildfires constantly threatened Malibu, and there were a number of times when we were forced to evacuate. We'd have a few minutes to grab what we could and get in the car. No matter which family members were there at the time, the first thing out of their mouths to me was always, "Don't worry, we've already put the photo albums in the car!" The albums were more important than even the silver, the jewelry, or the keepsakes. They really have become a family heirloom.

When I was first approached about this book, I almost had to pinch myself. Never in all the years of laboring over these albums did I ever think that these family photos would one day become part of a book that would grace the world's libraries and living rooms. As I sat down and started perusing the photographs, especially those from various film locations, I was reminded of all the exciting times when the company—cast and crew—would be settling

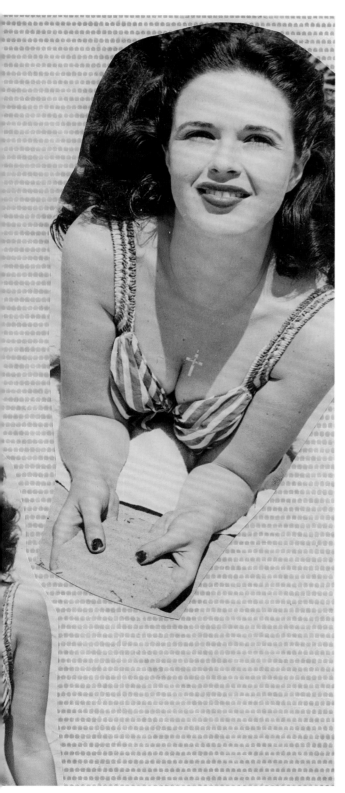

into their new surroundings. It was always very important to Bob that his actors were comfortable and happy with their accommodations. He would go to great lengths to see to that. We would have lots of get-togethers, from kick-off parties to wrap parties, and would watch dailies together every night to see what had been shot the day before. This, of course, was before the advent of digital cinema, when it became possible to view the footage immediately. Bob encouraged, without insisting, that all of his actors come to dailies. It was always very festive, with lots of food and drink. Everyone was welcome. The actors became comfortable with each other, with Bob, and with their work.

That comfortable feeling permeated our temporary homes and made for an atmosphere of one big happy family. From the beginning, this naturally became my job—setting up camp. And I loved it. It was very much like summer camp—intense, lots of new friends—and then it was over. And each project was so different from the last. Yet the style was the same. Bob had a real style in the way he did everything. He liked to pursue new subjects with each of his projects, subjects he hadn't previously addressed or investigated. This is what made each new film an exciting event. We met so many different people, be they crew members, cast members, or locals. I tried to capture that in my albums, the sense that our "family" grew to include so many new friends over the years. Many people came and went; some stayed on for years. It's interesting to me to see the faces woven throughout the pages.

When Bob died in 2006, that was the end of my project. I had completed thirty-three albums spanning forty-seven years of our life together. I am happy to say that our children are extremely appreciative and really enjoy them. As for this book, I sometimes wonder how Bob would have reacted. Ultimately, I think he would have been very pleased and quite proud. Perhaps he would've taken back his cracks about my cropping of the photos!

I've had the extreme pleasure of being assisted on this project by a very talented and brilliant young woman. She patiently helped me turn decades of memories into written pages, and written pages into readable ones. I've been fortunate to have had her as a collaborator, and I am forever grateful to our granddaughter, Signe Lohmann.

Kathryn Reed Altman met and married Robert Altman in 1959 and was an active participant in his professional life. She lives in New York City and Los Angeles.

LEFT Kathryn on the beach in Atlantic City, New Jersey, 1944. She was working as a showgirl at the time and is practicing "cleavage" during a break. These photos were taken by an acquaintance named Charles Herman.

PREFACE

BY
GIULIA
D'AGNOLO VALLAN

"There are so many books about Robert Altman." That was my first thought when I was approached about this one. My second thought was actually an image: a scrapbook. I had not seen Kathryn's albums at that time, nor even glanced at the 11,500 photos that were part of the Robert Altman Collection at the University of Michigan Library in Ann Arbor. But what immediately appealed to me was the opportunity to work within a more intuitive, nonlinear format than the one offered by a conventional biography.

Having watched Altman's movies while growing up in Italy, he had always seemed to me a "European-style" American director. A public intellectual of sorts, fearless in his determination to explore and engage so many different worlds—each of his films like a new, self-contained, occasionally exotic universe. And yet all part of a single, coherent philosophical vision rooted in an almost anthropological attraction to humankind. No matter how diverse they may be, all his films are, as he said, "chapters of the same book." The multiple elements, textures, and narratives that are the basis of this volume seem a good way to trace that "same book," the vision and the process that lie beyond the individual pictures.

The incredibly vast selection of photos (mostly heretofore unpublished), contact sheets, documents, clippings, and even objects contained in the Ann Arbor collection allowed us to show Altman at work, literally immersed in his process. When given the right materials, I have favored a similar approach in all of my previous books, which were often designed in close collaboration with the filmmakers. Over the years, I had only met Altman a few times, and briefly, for a couple of interviews (the last one to talk about *Gosford Park*) and when we invited *Dr. T and the Women* to the Venice Film Festival. But I was sure that a collage-like structure made even more sense for a book about him, as it mirrors the loose architecture of his pictures.

A wide cast of characters seemed also fitting. The choice of asking so many writers to participate was not an accidental one: Altman had the reputation of heavily altering film scripts, when not forgoing them altogether. Yet he engaged with great writers through his entire career and was admired by them.

Both Kathryn and I are very grateful to the people who have contributed to our project. Rarely have I found convincing someone to write or give an interview for a book so easy. This is a testament to the fact that the "Altman family" existed, and exists, well beyond the confines of the frame. And of his mark on American cinema, as the many up and downs of his long, adventurous, career parallel and reflect/illuminate the evolution of that industry.

A great deal has been written and said about Altman. Yet, while watching and re-watching his films during the past two years, I often found myself discovering threads I had not seen before, dots I had not connected. Some of those ideas have filtered into these pages, and I hope they may offer new insights to his work as a whole.

Scrapbooks are by definition made of fragments. Their nature is intrinsically suggestive, as well as imperfect and incomplete. This volume claims no exception. I apologize in advance for the omissions. My work is indebted to the very generous access Ron Mann gave me to the incredibly extensive and painstaking research made for his film *ALTMAN*, as well as to the writings of Altman biographers and interviewers, such as Mitchell Zukoff and David Thompson. I would also like to acknowledge Matthew Seig's invaluable insights and my friend Bill Krohn, whose film writing and feverish passion for cinema are not only deeply inspiring but also great fun.

Giulia D'Agnolo Vallan is a film writer and curator. She has published numerous books on American cinema, including monographs on Robert Aldrich, John Landis, William Friedkin, Clint Eastwood, George Romero, and John Carpenter. She has served as the co-director of the Torino Film Festival and is presently the US Programmer of the Venice Film Festival. She lives in New York City.

1

THE EARLY YEARS

BY GIULIA
D'AGNOLO VALLAN

Robert Altman was born on February 20, 1925, in Kansas City, Missouri, to a prominent, upper-middle-class family of German origins. In some of his early interviews, Altman recalled his regular childhood visits to the local Plaza Theater, where he and his friends would buy a single ticket so that one of them could go in and sneak the rest of the group through the rear entrance, or crawl through pipes and corridors that led right into the men's room. *King Kong, Viva Villa!,* and *Gunga Din* are films he vividly remembered from those years. But at that time movies were just fun. It was only after World War II that Altman started looking at films in a different way—as a means of expression that he might like to explore himself. David Lean's *Brief Encounter* and John Huston's *The Treasure of the Sierra Madre,* as well as early works by Bergman and Fellini, very much impacted that perception.

LEFT Robert Altman, producer–director of *Nightwatch*, checks an angle, 1964. At this stage of his career, Altman had already produced and directed several episodes and pilots of prominent series for every TV network in the US.
ABOVE Altman, B-24 copilot, 1945–1946, 307th Bomb Group, 13th Air Force.

OPPOSITE Altman and his sisters, from left: Barbara Hodes and Joan Sarafian, c. early 1930s.

RIGHT "Bobby" Altman, c. early 1930s.

BELOW Altman (front row, kneeling, second from right) with other members of the 307th Bomb Group while stationed in the Pacific.

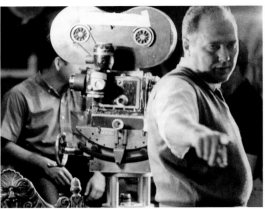

After attending the Catholic St. Peter's School and the Jesuit-run Rockhurst High School, Altman enrolled at the Wentworth Military Academy in Lexington, and in 1943 enlisted in the U.S. Air Force. Trained in Missouri and California, he was stationed on the island of Morotai in the East Indies (now Indonesia), near the Pacific front, where he copiloted a B-24 on dozens of bombing missions. It was during that period, in his letters to a cousin of his father who worked for the Hollywood agent Myron Selznick, that Altman started talking about becoming a writer. Once the war was over and he returned to the United States, he moved to Los Angeles.

There, with new friend George W. George, he wrote the story treatments for Edwin L. Marin's crime melodrama *Christmas Eve* (1947) and Richard Fleischer's tough noir *Bodyguard* (1948), his first official screen credit. But making it in Hollywood (which included a tiny appearance in Danny Kaye's *The Secret Life of Walter Mitty*) did not prove easy, and Altman thought he would have a better chance to pursue his writing career through the stage, in New York. He was on his way there when, during a stop in Kansas City to visit his family, he learned of the existence of the Calvin Company, which was looking for directors. Despite his almost complete lack of experience, he was hired for $250 a month.

At that time one of the biggest industrial film companies in the United States, Calvin was Altman's film school—professionally speaking, his most formative experience. It was there that he learned to write, cast, do production design, shoot, edit, and even score his films. They were short or medium-length films, mostly 16 mm, commissioned by a variety of businesses such as DuPont, Goodyear, and the International Harvester tractor company, for which Altman thought up a very funny story involving a mailman, his young apprentice, and a man who keeps postponing his honeymoon to Niagara Falls because he is spending all his money on Harvester agricultural machines. Under head of production Frank Barhydt (whose son Frank Jr. would become one of Altman's screenwriters), he made about sixty of those films in about six years. Daring camera movements, overlapping sound, a taste for formal experimentation, a passion for documentary, and a desire to subvert linear storytelling—all trademarks of Altman's later work—were developed at Calvin. In order to further explore his handling of actors, the young director volunteered at the Resident Theatre, the Kansas City Jewish Community Center's amateur theater program.

Between the end of the forties and the mid-fifties, Altman went back to Los Angeles a few times looking for work in the local entertainment industry, to no avail. So he kept returning to Kansas City. It was there that he also found the opportunity to take his first steps in the world of television drama, as a producer of the series *Pulse of the City*, and as a director of *The Delinquents*. Shot in a gritty, "realistic" style, over a two-week period for a budget of about $60,000, this was Altman's oblique take on the fifties teen craze reflected in a lively slew of drive-in exploitation films as well as mainstream Hollywood successes such as Nicholas Ray's *Rebel Without a Cause*. United Artists released *The Delinquents* in 1957. The same year, Warner Bros. would release Altman's second feature,

TOP LEFT Brochure for the Calvin Company, c. early 1950s.
TOP CENTER Altman during his years with the Calvin Company, c. early 1950s.
ABOVE Photograph of Altman, likely taken in the U.S. while he trained to be a pilot, c. 1944.

OPPOSITE
TOP LEFT Publicity poster for *The James Dean Story*, 1957.
TOP RIGHT Poster for *The Delinquents*, 1957.
BELOW Script for Altman's first feature film, *The Delinquents*.

The James Dean Story, a documentary about Dean's life and death told through interviews interwoven with a rather experimental use of dramatic reenactments and still photographs.

Through these films, Altman finally found the Hollywood break he had been looking for, although his Midwestern roots and his long training far from the entertainment industry's official enclaves of New York and Los Angeles definitely heightened his natural antiestablishment instincts and his determination to pursue a wholly original creative path. An avid, curious reader, Altman kept a special place in his heart for Sherwood Anderson's modernist masterpiece, *Winesburg, Ohio*, hinting in several of his films at its great gallery of peculiar characters and small-town setting. Even once he established himself in Los Angeles and started working there, he would keep and cultivate that outsider, off-center perspective.

A thirty-something professional, skilled in most aspects of the filmmaking process, Altman was better suited to penetrating the heart of the entertainment business through the more structured world of dramatic television than the wild jungle of low-budget independent productions of the time. Ten years would pass before he would get to do another feature, but even within the rules and constraints imposed by the grid of mainstream TV production he somehow managed to leave his artistic mark, while at the same time honing his craft by collaborating with some top studio technicians. Television also gave him the opportunity to meet actors he would eventually use in his film career, such as Michael Murphy, Robert Fortier, and John Considine.

His first TV directing credits in Los Angeles were for two episodes of *Alfred Hitchcock Presents*, "The Young One" and "Together." He also directed nineteen episodes of Lucille Ball and Desi Arnaz's series *Whirlybirds* that aired in 1958–59. It was on one of those that he met his future wife, Kathryn Reed, who had come to the set as an extra. Among the many other series Altman worked on into the sixties are Don Fedderson's *The Millionaire*, Warner Bros.' *Hawaiian Eye* and *The Roaring 20's*, United Artists' *Troubleshooters*, Blake Edwards's *Peter Gunn*, and the popular westerns *Maverick* and *Bonanza*. As a director, he was able to smuggle into most of the episodes unusual visual solutions, interesting performances, and a palpable preoccupation with realism—a remarkable feat considering the tight production schedules and the fact that most were filmed on studio lots.

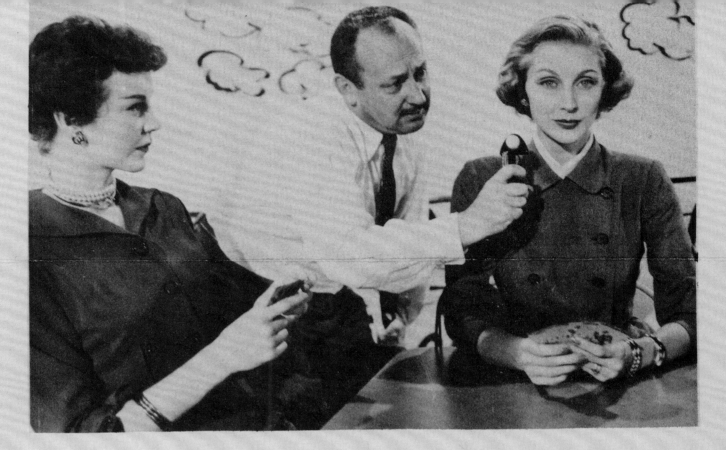

Stop the game girls! Cameraman Sid Zukor takes a light reading before filming Ricky Van Dusen and Marie Mahar.

Bob Altman, our director, gives Carolyn Cross some heavy instruction on how to look "at home" in front of the cameras while the crew stands-by.

Photos of an assignment at the Calvin Company, c. 1950s.

OPPOSITE The staff of the Calvin Company, c. 1950s.

TOP Cameraman Sid Zukor takes a light reading.

BOTTOM Altman directing Carolyn Cross in an editorial fashion show for Kansas City–based dress designer Nelly Don c. 1950s.

Style 574 (5574) – rayon gabardine

KANSAS CITY BOB

FRANK BARHYDT

BELOW Altman halfway up a crane during the shooting of *Better Football*, a Calvin Company training film for high school students, 1954.

Bob left Kansas City in 1957. I left in the early seventies. We started working together in the late seventies. Kansas City, and all it entailed, was a strong bond, primarily because of my parents.

In 1987, Bob directed two one-act plays for television, and because he thought he would be doing more, we wrote a script called "Blondie" set in Kansas City, our hometown. Things changed at the network, and "Blondie" was shelved. Then came *The Caine Mutiny Court-Martial*, *Tanner '88*, *The Player*, and *Short Cuts*, all projects I had a role in, ranging from extra to producer to writer. "Blondie" came up from time to time over the years, but so did many other ideas that never became movies. Bob sometimes left out the specifics of what he had in mind. *Short Cuts* was presented to me like this as we were driving to the Santa Anita race track one day: "Ever read Raymond Carver?" "Some," I said. "Why?" "I think you should read a lot more." Then he went back to talking about his racehorse, Farewell Promise.

After *Short Cuts*, Bob called one day and said, "I know what your next movie is going to be. It's called 'Kansas City, Kansas City.' It's 'Blondie' with jazz."

Returning on the first scouting trip, we discovered that what had been the heart of the city had been downsized almost out of existence. Somehow I had missed the news that the Calvin Company had been torn down. It was the largest industrial film company in the country from the forties to the seventies, and where my father had spent most of his working career. Bob worked at Calvin in the fifties, leaving and returning a few times, then making it final in 1957.

At one time, Calvin employed hundreds of people and made hundreds of movies on the largest soundstages outside New York and Los Angeles. All the steps from set building to film processing were done in-house. To me it was like magic. To my father and Bob, not so much. Calvin had all the politics of a Hollywood studio.

If it had been standing and safe, I'm sure Bob would have enjoyed using the old building for production offices, the screening rooms for dailies, and the soundstage for the Hey Hey Club. The symmetry would have been irresistible.

Driving by the Altman house in Kansas City had a symmetry as well. Sitting on the front porch was a boy eight or nine years old, his elbows on his knees, holding his face in his hands. A pose suggesting he'd been left behind or excluded from some activity. Bob was delighted. He saw himself. "There I am! That's me!"

I was that age when I met Bob. He came from Los Angeles in the early fifties, looking for a job after a time trying to work as a writer in Hollywood. My father hired him as a writer at Calvin. Bob's experience in the dog-tattooing business (as an ID in case a pet ran away or was stolen) probably made him more interesting to my father than his movie credit for *Bodyguard*. Calvin was his film school. It's where the Altman style began to develop.

The movies Calvin made were usually thirty minutes. They had a story, and they were supposed to entertain as well as educate and promote the message of Caterpillar Tractor, Phillips Petroleum, or DuPont. Or in the case of Wilson Sporting Goods, teach rules for high school and college sports—baseball, basketball, and football. Bob wrote, directed, edited, experimented, and invented his own techniques for dozens of these films.

On the soundtrack of *The James Dean Story*, someone wrote a long description of the movie and the music. I think it was Bob. The sentiments are his: "This is a film in which there are no actors, there is no fiction. It is, instead, the story of a young man in search of himself—a story of a lonely boy growing into a lonely manhood, of a quest for discovery and meaning, of a great talent and zest for creative expression." Bob was describing himself.

After reading *The Old Man and the Sea* in *Life* magazine, Bob came to the house to discuss it with my father. He was talking about what a great movie it would make and how he knew how to direct it. Years later I asked him if he remembered that day. He remembered writing a letter to Ernest Hemingway but never hearing back. The zest for creative expression was unforgettable.

My sister Sally and I could easily relate to Bob. He seemed ageless. More friendly and playful than most adults. One Halloween he happened to be at the house, and he reinvented my Halloween costume. He did the makeup using colored chalk and wrapped a turban on my head; my mother produced a tunic. My father took a photograph. On it he wrote: "Altman's work, 1953."

Sally had a crush on Bob, of course. My younger sister was too young to talk about it, but maybe she did, too. Sally and I thought Bob was the most exotic person we knew. He'd been a bomber pilot in World War II. He was in his twenties, and he always seemed to be doing exciting things: sports, parties, shows, live music. He worked in local theater, and his wife was an actress. He lived on a lake.

He was self-assured enough to remove a fishhook from my foot once at Lake Lotawana, likely after a lot of drinking, if he was the Bob I knew. He pushed the hook through and out the other side—painlessly, as I remember. My mother, a nurse, thought this was a very skillful procedure.

There were many experiences involving Bob that have been useful professionally, one having to do with the pilot friend of his that I vaguely knew. Maybe Bob brought him to our house at one time. The pilot looked like a movie star and, like Bob, was a ladies' man. In addition, something about him was unforgettable. Years later I asked about his pilot friend, and it turned out Bob had a very useful anecdote that came back in *Short Cuts*. The pilot became Stormy Weathers, a jealous husband, who could not accept rejection. Except that in real life it was the pilot's ex-wife or girlfriend who spent a weekend in his place, while he was away, cutting up all his clothes, smashing anything breakable, and melting all his records.

I didn't see Bob for fifteen years after he left Calvin in 1957. When my wife and I moved to California, and after I saw *McCabe & Mrs. Miller*, I made an appointment to see him at his office in Westwood. I wanted to know how people got into the movie business. "What do you want to do?" I said "Write." He said, "If you ever write anything, I'll take a look at it." He also said if he didn't like it, he would say so. I asked naively if there was anything like a stylebook—in other words, rules to follow. He laughed. "Screenwriting is not writing, in the literary sense; it's thinking."

His offer to read what I wrote kept me from showing him anything for a long while, which was good. When I did, in 1977, we started working together.

The notes on the *James Dean* soundtrack go on to say: "If there are supporting roles in his picture, the parts must be credited to the people of Fairmount, Indiana, where Dean lived as a boy; to the nine million faces of New York City, where he struggled for recognition as an artist and as an individual; and to the men and women of Hollywood who shared in the development of his career." These are Bob's sensibilities, and this is Kansas City Bob, as Kathryn sometimes called him: turning the spotlight away from himself, downplaying his genius, but revealing it just the same.

FRANK BARHYDT is a writer whose father was head of production at the Calvin Company, where Altman made industrial films in the 1950s. As a screenwriter, Barhydt worked on several films with Altman including *Quintet* (1979), *HealtH* (1980), *Short Cuts* (1993), and *Kansas City* (1996). He also appeared as an actor in Altman's TV series *Tanner '88* (1988) and in the film *The Player* (1992).

OPPOSITE Contact sheet of on-set photos from an episode of *Kraft Suspense Theatre* entitled "Once Upon a Savage Night," directed by Altman, 1964.

TOP LEFT Altman pointing out a shot on the set of *Combat!*

TOP RIGHT Fabian from the *Bus Stop* episode "A Lion Walks Among Us." Called a "negative influence on youth," it was only broadcast once.

The series where his presence was felt the most are probably *Bus Stop* and *Combat!* An anthology series based on the William Inge play, which Joshua Logan had brought to the screen in a 1956 film starring Marilyn Monroe, Twentieth Century Fox's *Bus Stop* came with the ideal Altman setting: a small village in the Rockies with a very active bus stop. That combination gave him the opportunity to build on the sense of community generated by recurring characters in an offbeat environment, as well as to introduce new ones who came and went on the bus. In "The Covering Darkness," Altman's first episode for the series, the cast included Robert Redford and Barbara Baxley. His most controversial one—and his only work ever to ignite a congressional inquiry—was "A Lion Walks Among Us," adapted from a novel by *New York Times* journalist Tom Wicker. It starred Italian American teen idol Fabian as an attractive drifter who comes to town, commits a vicious murder, and almost seduces the whole population into believing his innocence. Worried about the violence and overall psychotic undertones of the piece, several advertisers pulled out after its first broadcast on December 3, 1961. After the *New York Times* described it as "an hour of dark and sordid ugliness," and *Newsweek*, *TV Guide*, and the *Los Angeles Times* echoed its judgment, Senator Thomas Dodd of Connecticut, a crusader against negative media influence on youth, scheduled an inquiry into *Bus Stop* without having seen the show in question. Fox then banned "A Lion Walks Among Us" from any future broadcast and buried it in its vaults. But the director of the infamous episode gained attention and some illustrious supporters, among them director William Wyler and novelist James Jones.

Altman was creatively involved in *Combat!* from the very beginning. He wrote and produced several episodes, was involved in their casting, and directed nearly half of its first season (1962–63). War would become a recurring theme in his work (*M*A*S*H*, *Streamers*, the television film *The Caine Mutiny Court-Martial*), and in *Combat!* he was determined to portray it as realistically as possible. The series revolved around a U.S. Army platoon in Europe during World War II. Vic Morrow was the lead, and it was shot on MGM's Lot 2, which came with a French village surrounded by forest and lakes. Cameraman Robert Hauser provided often handheld, daringly naturalistic camera work. Darker, moodier, and looser in dramatic structure than most TV shows at the time, *Combat!* reflected Altman's unheroic, unsentimental view of war as a grinding, brutal by-product of humanity. Several of his episodes are noteworthy ("The Volunteer" was screened out of competition at the Venice Film Festival), although to this day the most famous is "Survival," a script so grim that it was initially rejected by executive producer Selig Seligman. Altman waited for him to go out of town and then shot the hallucinatory episode anyway, featuring

Morrow, separated from his platoon, wandering alone in the forest like a ghost. When Seligman returned, he punished the director's insubordination by firing him from the series. But "Survival" was critically well received and garnered Morrow an Emmy Award nomination.

Between 1963 and 1964, Altman also did three one-hour films for *Kraft Suspense Theatre*. Shot on location in Chicago and hauntingly scored by John Williams, his "Once Upon a Savage Night" was expanded and given a limited theatrical release as *Nightmare in Chicago*. But he was getting impatient with the world of television production and was determined to move on to features.

His first production company, located on Westwood Boulevard, was called Westwood Productions. The first two films he wanted to make there were an adaptation of John Haase's *Me and the Arch Kook Petulia* and a World War I pilot drama, *O Death, Where Is Thy Sting-a-ling-a-ling?* Vic Morrow's former wife, Barbara Turner, and novelist Roald Dahl were hired to write the scripts.

While trying to gather financing for the two projects, Altman kept busy by writing, producing, and directing a few very amusing "homemade" shorts: *The Kathryn Reed Story* (conceived as a birthday present for his wife), *The Party*, and *Pot au Feu*, a lesson on how to make the perfect marijuana joint, disguised as a parody of a cooking show. Legend has it the latter helped him get *M*A*S*H*.

It was at this time that Warner Bros. asked him to direct the adaptation of a book for which he had tried to buy the rights himself, Hank Searls's *The Pilgrim Project*. Altman liked the opportunity this story of U.S.–Soviet rivalry in space afforded him to explore the human and psychological dimension of the astronauts' experiences, so he accepted the job. The film would be called *Countdown*, with James Caan and Robert Duvall leading the cast. It was a low-budget

When loneliness drives a desperate virgin spinster to possess a wild, teen-age boy,

you've got the "post-Graduate" you've been waiting for!

When does loneliness overtake reason? For Frances, a society spinster in her thirties, it's "That Cold Day In The Park." The day when frustration is overwhelmed by the promise of fulfillment she sees in a wet, shivering teen-age boy. If she can possess him, she will desire him. And, as she reaches out to do both, the camera peeks without shame into the deepest crevices of human emotion. Sandy Dennis is superb. She makes "That Cold Day In The Park" the "post-Graduate" you've been waiting for. Book it now. And count on a long, hot summer at the box office.

Commonwealth United presents
A Factor-Altman-Mirell Production starring

Sandy Dennis in
That Cold Day in the Park
Co-starring Michael Burns
With Susanne Benton, John Garfield, Jr., Luana Anders
Produced by Donald Factor and Leon Mirell, Directed by Robert Altman
Screenplay by Gillian Freeman, Based on a novel by Richard Miles
Music by Johnny Mandel. Color by Eastman Color
Released by Commonwealth United

United

studio production, but Altman enjoyed shooting it and tried to give it his realistic touch. A crisis apparently ensued when Jack Warner saw the dailies and did not appreciate the overlapping, not always clearly understandable dialogue. But *Countdown*'s poor showing in theaters was eventually due less to friction between Altman and the studio than to the fact that Warner Bros. decided to release it in a double bill with John Wayne's *The Green Berets*. Altman's introspective sci-fi piece, where human relations came before Cold War concerns, could not have called for a more different audience than Wayne's defiantly pro-American military, pro-Vietnam War film.

The Max Factor cosmetic empire was partly responsible for Altman's next film, *That Cold Day in the Park,* based on Richard Miles's novel of the same title. A coproduction of Factor's son Don (a friend of the director's agent, George Litto) and released through Commonwealth United Entertainment, it was shot in Vancouver on a set built in a warehouse, where Altman created the big apartment in which a lonely, rich woman, Frances Austen (Sandy Dennis, an Oscar winner for Best Supporting Actress in *Who's Afraid of Virginia Woolf?*), locks up a seemingly mute hippie boy (Michael Burns) she has rescued from the rain in the park. Before settling for Dennis, Altman had tried to cast Ingrid Bergman, but reportedly the Swedish star hated the script and the character. Later in his career, the director would describe this early film as "naïve" and "pretentious," but his atmospheric, suspenseful direction, paired with László Kovács's hauntingly fluid cinematography, bring a distinctive, austere grace to the rather sinister premise. *That Cold Day in the Park* would be Altman's first exploration of female subjectivity.

Although not many people saw the film at that time, Altman, having successfully completed his first truly personal movie, was ready for the next step. He never could have anticipated that it was going to be such a big one.

OPPOSITE
TOP LEFT Clipping from Hollywood industry trade paper, *Variety*, from 1963, in which Altman compares Kraft's television programs to their cheese.
TOP RIGHT Publicity poster for the *Kraft Suspense Theatre* episode "Once Upon a Savage Night."
BOTTOM Contact sheet of on-set photos from the *Kraft Suspense Theatre* episode "Once Upon a Savage Night."

TOP LEFT A newspaper clipping from 1971 recounting that the methods that got Altman fired from *Countdown* were what made *M*A*S*H* a success.
TOP RIGHT Advertisement for *That Cold Day in the Park*, directed by Altman, 1969.

SOMETHING AKIN TO LOVE

MICHAEL MURPHY

Although he never talked about it, Bob was a bomber pilot during World War II. He flew more than fifty missions over the South Pacific—almost twice the number flown by most of his peers. Garrison Keillor researched this period in Bob's life, and one of the stories he tells is how Bob, a lieutenant, had a reputation for generally spending as much time drinking, gambling, and carousing with enlisted soldiers as he did with his fellow officers. This kind of fraternization, as anyone who has been in the service well knows, is very much frowned upon. It is, in fact, a breach of military regulations and can easily result in serious trouble for an officer. But Bob being Bob, a guy who never felt the need to give orders and didn't take kindly to those who did, couldn't have cared less. Besides, he liked living on the edge.

This small biographical glimpse says a lot about the man Robert Altman was. Although, in time, he would become a successful, powerful, and brilliant film-maker, he remained utterly democratic in the way he treated those around him. He was the embodiment of the saying "When you're the boss you don't have to *be* the boss." I can attest to this through personal experience.

It was 1962, as I recall, and, just out of college, I was trying feverishly to get an acting job in Hollywood. I was spending a lot of time playing scenes in the many offices of casting directors, producers, agents, and, yes, "talent scouts." As these folks were usually on the phone or otherwise engaged while I was emoting my way through *Detective Story* or a Doc Simon comedy, this process was becoming somewhat grim.

Bob, meanwhile, was making a name for himself working at MGM on a World War II series called *Combat!* A meeting with him was arranged for me through a mutual friend, who thought I might stand a chance of getting a job because they "used a lot of young guys" on the show. So, off I went to meet Mr. Altman, not a credit to my name but filled with youthful enthusiasm. Little did I know that it was to be my lucky day.

Bob had a very funky office under a stairwell at the studio. It was so completely unpretentious that it surprised me. I don't think he even had a secretary (as we called them in those days), for I seem to remember just knocking on his door, walking in, and there he was. And from the minute I crossed that threshold I knew I was in the presence of someone truly special, someone very different from those I was used to meeting while making my depressing rounds in Hollywood.

MICHAEL MURPHY is an actor who collaborated with Robert Altman on a dozen films, miniseries, and TV episodes dating back to an installment of the show *Combat!*, "Survival," which originally aired March 12, 1963. He was the star of Altman's 1988 HBO series *Tanner '88,* and appeared in such films as *McCabe & Mrs. Miller* (1971), *Nashville* (1975), and *Kansas City* (1996).

We sat talking, getting to know one another, for perhaps an hour—a very long time for that kind of meeting. Finally he said, "Well, great, let's do something together." *Let's do something together!* It seemed such a generous way to put it. I was completely dazzled.

Then, a few days later, a script arrived on my doorstep. It appeared that I was all set to play Tank Driver #1 in an episode of *Combat!* I had a few lines, and it was to be directed by Bob. No audition, no nothing! I couldn't believe it.

I went to work on that show a couple of days later, and it was to be the beginning of an extraordinary friendship that would last until Bob died. (Or "stepped off the planet," as he sometimes referred to life's final exit.)

There are many stories to tell about this extraordinary guy—many, many stories. What's on my mind today, however, is a time long ago, when a young, inexperienced, but very hopeful actor was treated with the utmost kindness, consideration, and something akin to love—*because Bob did love his actors!*—even though he was only Tank Driver #1.

BELOW Still from an Altman-directed episode of *Combat!* Altman gave Michael Murphy his first work as an actor in this series.

COUNTDOWN

BELOW *Countdown* was TV writer Loring Mandel's first produced feature screenplay. NASA cooperated with the making of the film, which was mostly shot on soundstages at Warner Bros., with the Mojave Desert as a stand-in for the lunar landing scene.

RIGHT Robert Duvall hands a flag to fellow astronaut James Caan as the Americans race to beat Russia to the moon.

"MOONSHOT"

8/5/66

FINAL

PLEASE RETURN THIS SCRIPT TO PRODUCTION MANAGER
WHEN PICTURE IS COMPLETED   FORM 55A

Received from Stenographic Dept.

1 SCRIPT

8/5/66

FINAL   *Title*   "MOONSHOT"

*Signed*_____

CHANGE
10/5/66
1.

FADE IN:

1. INT. APOLLO CAPSULE (SIMULATOR)   DAY

The SCREEN IS BLACK. We are looking through one of the small round portholes at the black sky, lit by only a few unblinking stars.

There are three men in the capsule, all wearing space suits but not helmets. The oldest of the three is CHIZ, very close to forty years old, just under six feet tall, his face tough and eroded, deeply lined. Chiz is a tightly-controlled hard-driving man who smiles rarely (but when he does it's a warm open grin) and is accustomed to being obeyed without questioning. Another of the three men is LEE, in his early thirties, as tall as Chiz but built tauter and more graceful. Lee's features are just irregular enough to be interesting, and he is quick to smile. He has great curiosity, and his eyes rarely stop searching. Lee seems usually to be relaxed but he is an innately cautious man who must accept a commitment both intellectually and emotionally before acting upon it. The third man is RICK, about the same age as Lee, perhaps slightly shorter. Rick is the lightweight of the three, because he has always been willing to go along without searching his own motives. Enjoying the work, the flying, the glory of being an astronaut, Rick is the ultimate in the casual man. If he seems wilder or quicker with comment, it's because he is the most cynical about himself and the world. When Lee jokes, he smiles. When Rick jokes, his face is drained of emotion.

As we see the interior of the capsule, we HEAR the voice (on FILTER) of DUNC, a land-based astronaut...a dry voice for a wry character.

                    DUNC'S VOICE: (FILTER)
          Apollo Three, Houston. Do you read?

                    LEE:
          Roger, Houston. Apollo Three.

Slowly a hair-thin band of light appears, spreading in an arc along the horizon.

                    DUNC'S VOICE: (FILTER)
          Apollo Three, all systems are Go down
          here, gentlemen...

There is a pause. Lee is looking at the horizon. The arc is widening, the ribbon of light thickening and separating into colors: red, orange, white, blue. And in the center of the arc, a brilliant white oval sun begins to rise. Lee looks down at the instrument panel.

                                        (CONTINUED)

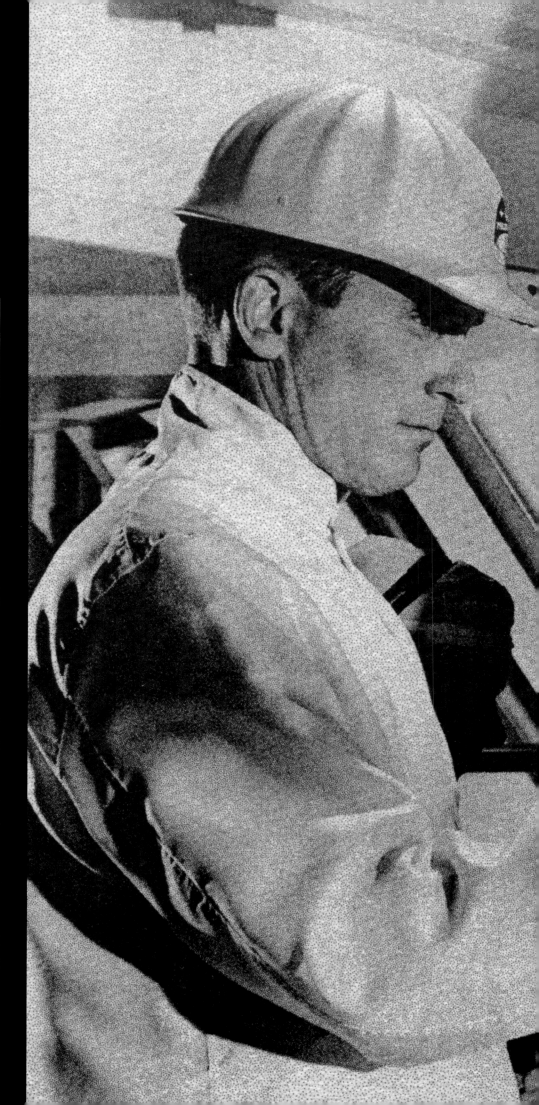

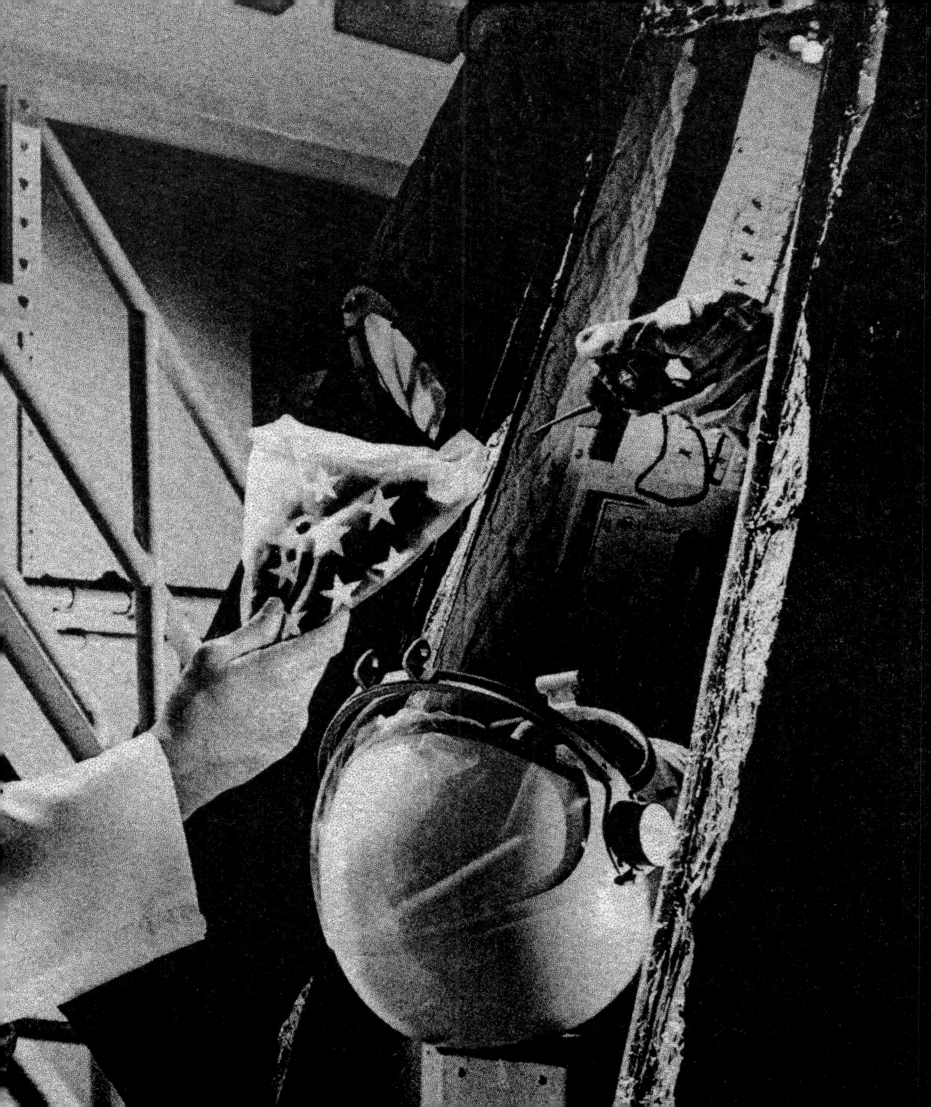

Dennis glances outside her window while Altman looks on from behind the camera. Production designer Leon Ericksen built the interior of her character's apartment allowing for extra space so that Altman's camera could easily go everywhere.

THE EARLY YEARS

BY
KATHRYN REED
ALTMAN

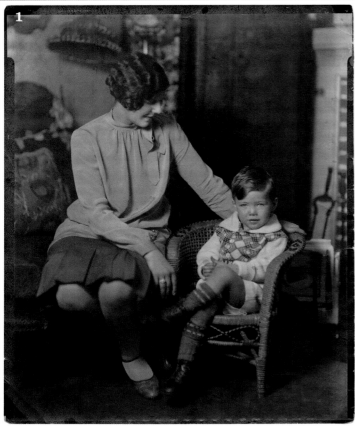

=========== Mother
========= 1927

1 Bob and his mother, Helen. He was two and a half years old.

=========== Bob and Bobby
========= 1927/1962

2 Bob at two and a half. **3** Our son Bobby at the same age. I secretly put this together, and we gave it to Bob for Father's Day. He just loved it, and it was always on his desk. People would ask him if he had twins at home!

=========== Halloween
========= 1938

4 This picture was taken on Halloween in Kansas City when Bob was thirteen years old. It was presented to him, while he was shooting *Kansas City*, by one of these fellows in the picture. In case you can't identify Bob, he's the one holding the purse! He loved this picture. So do I.

=========== Calvin Company
========= 1959

5–7 These are all pictures from the Calvin Company, where Bob learned his trade. He worked there off and on all through his twenties. An industrial film company in Kansas City, Missouri, they made training and other films for clients like Caterpillar Tractor and the big oil companies. It was quite a big business in those days. I didn't even know that such things existed. Bob got a job there after the war. What was great about this place was that everybody did everything and learned all the crafts. He came and went a few times before making the permanent move to Hollywood. It was a great training ground for him. He just took to it. In those days, there were no film schools, no places you could go to learn how to make movies. It was an

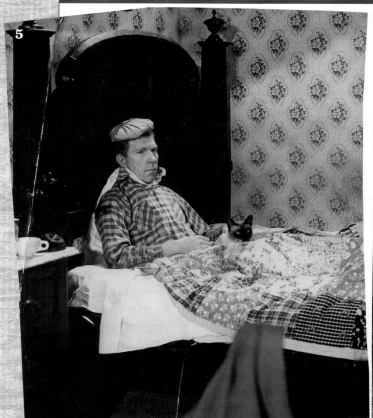

Dee Sharon and Evelyn Cedar
1959

8 These are the two girls I worked with as extras: Dee Sharon and Evelyn Cedar. The one on the left is Dee; she was dating Tommy Thompson, who was an assistant director. I had known Tommy from working on sets, and then he started dating Dee. Tommy and I had the same sense of humor. Tommy once said to Dee, "Boy, this director who I'm working with, Kathryn would really like." And so then he requested me on that TV episode; Tommy was in charge of the extras. So that's how that went.

The day came to go to work on the series Bob was directing, called *Whirlybirds*. I had a hangover, and I just felt crummy. And on the bus Dee kept telling me, "Oh, you're really going to like him," blah, blah, blah. And so we got there and the bus door opened and at the foot of the stairs stood Tommy and Bob, Bob with no shirt and a wet rag on his head. It was hotter than hell in Agoura Hills that day. And I walked down the steps and Tommy said, "Hi, Kathryn," and introduced me: "Kathryn Reed, this is Bob Altman." Bob looked at me and said, without missing a beat, "How are your morals?" He didn't say "hello" or anything. And that's when I said, "A little shaky. How are yours?" and just kept walking.

on-the-job kind of thing. I don't know how other filmmakers learned at that time; I never thought of it before. But the Calvin Company was certainly Bob's learning ground. And these pictures depict scenes from a couple of the films he made there. I don't know how many he did, but they are all documented.

5 One of the actors who worked in a lot of these became a very close friend of Bob's. His name is Owen Bush, and here he is in one of these industrial films doing God knows what—your guess is as good as mine. I don't know what the army film **6–7** was about either, but Owen is also in this one. What I remember about Owen Bush is that he was a wonderful character actor, and he decided to come to California just about the time I met Bob. I'd only known Bob maybe a month or so, and he said, "My friend Owen Bush is coming to California to try to make it as an actor." We were walking down Fountain Avenue in front of El Palacio, a beautiful old Spanish building on Fountain and La Cienega where Bob lived, and we were leaning on the wall just talking, and he said, "He's a really unusual guy." He was trying to explain to me what Owen's personality was like, so we ran through this whole little scenario. He said, "Now you be me and I'll be Owen Bush. Just start talking." So I started with, "Well, Bob, it sure is good to see—" but before I could finish, he, as Owen Bush, cut me off, saying, "Yeah, yeah, great to see you, Bob, really great to see you." Then I continued, "Nice weather we're having to—" but again he jumped in, friendly and agreeable

as ever: "Oh yes, Bob, great weather here in California. Really great!" Oh, I'll never forget it. It was hilarious how Bob had me acting out this little scene. Of course, when I met Owen, he was a lovable, delightful guy, a real Midwestern hick kind of a guy in the very best way. That's all I can think of when I see these photos—and also his wife, Ruth. I'm sorry I don't have more Calvin Company pictures, but it was all before I met Bob.

9

11–23 These photographs were taken during the time when the adoption agency called and told us that our son Matthew **21** was available to be picked up. It was right in the middle of Bob's first feature film in California. Other than that, he had made a feature in Kansas City, before I knew him, called *The Delinquents*, for which he raised local money and pulled the feature together with friends and relatives. That was the movie Hitchcock saw that brought Bob to California, where he started directing television. He stayed in television until this time, summer 1966, when he shot a feature under a new directors program at Warner Bros.; it was called *Countdown*. There was an actor named Bill Conrad, who was in many television shows in the fifties and sixties. Jack Warner signed Bill to a program to develop new directors with low-budget feature films within the confines of Warner Bros. Bill chose Bob and four others to direct various projects, although I don't recall who or what they were. Bob had been directing a lot of the prominent television shows at the time.

Anyway, *Countdown* was from a book by Hank Searls. He and Bob became friendly. He was a really nice guy and thought Bob did a great job, but then Jack Warner came back after being out of town. As Bob told it—and this is a famous line of Bob's, which he said in dozens and dozens of interviews—"When Jack Warner looked at the dailies, he said, 'That fool [meaning Bob] has people talking at the same time.'" And he threw Bob out of the editing process and wouldn't let him finish the film. Warner closed up Bob's office and wouldn't let him back on the lot, and he changed the ending somewhat. And that was that. It really upset Jimmy Caan, who was the lead, and Robert Duvall, Michael Murphy, Charles Aidman, and Joanna Moore, the mother of Tatum and Griffin O'Neal. Anyway, it was an experience.

In the middle of it, when Bob was in pre-production, just before shooting, that's when we got the notice that the child we had waited to adopt was ready to be picked up. And Bob said something I'll never forget. He was standing at the breakfast bar talking to his office about *Countdown* when we got the call from the adoption agency. They said to "come and bring a change of clothes for the baby, and be here at such and such a time, and bring your son Bobby." **16**(top), **17**, **19**, **20**(right), **23** I was standing there cooking, and Bob got right on the phone with his office and told them that on Monday morning, or Tuesday morning or what-

Bob would always find something to do creatively between pictures that seemed to keep him going. He never had idle hands. During this one period he tried photography. This would've been starting in 1963. He bought all the equipment. He always bought all the equipment that went with whatever hobby he was involved in. He took a lot of pictures of the children, and he took a lot of pictures of Greece. He went over there regarding a project called *MacBird!* that never happened. He took some beautiful pictures there. And here is a picture of Bobby and me, **9** one of my favorites. In *The Kathryn Reed Story*, where you see me smoking cigarettes—the smoke's coming up at the very end of the film where it says, "And now all she wants is a Cadillac"—that's a Bob photograph, too. I don't know where that one is. But that was during that whole period.

10 The reason I love this page of photos is because Bob never really had the time to go alone anywhere with all three boys (Michael, ten; Stephen, eight; Bobby, five), although he did his best to spend one-on-one time with them when he could. On this day, he took all three of them to get haircuts. I took before and after photos with the Polaroid. It was just a really special day.

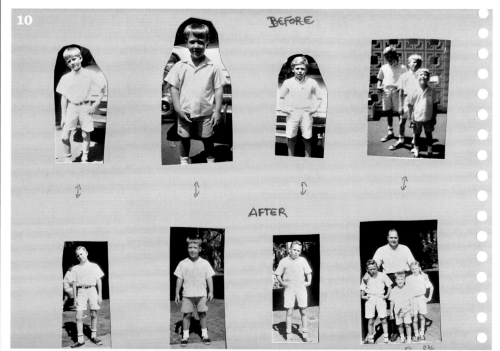

10

BEFORE

AFTER

ever it was, we had to go pick up our son Matthew, and that he'd be late for work. Meanwhile, I was waving at him in the background to get his attention, and I said, "Bob, Bob, Bob, wait! This may not be *the* baby." And he put the phone down on the bar and said, "Kathryn, we're not *shopping*. We asked for a hard-to-place, young-as-possible male child, and that's what we've got." Then he got right back on the phone and continued talking. Boy, did he ever pull me right back to my center!

There's an old Irene Dunne and Cary Grant movie, *Penny Serenade*. I remember they were going to adopt a baby, and they walked down this long corridor in a hospital. On each side were rows and rows of cribs, and they'd look in each crib and say, "Oh well, I don't know about that one," and then move on to the next. That must have been what I was thinking! I don't know what I was thinking. And we'd already gone through six months with psychiatrists, meetings, visits and forms, and pulling documents together.

Anyway, we had started the whole adoption process on January 6, 1966, just after the holidays, filling out tons of paperwork, doing interviews, and then just waiting. So we got the call, and we drove out to Inglewood to pick him up. It was July 15, and in the car were Bob, me, and Bobby, who was six and a half. The adoption agency had insisted that we bring

Bobby with us. It was a very emotional day to begin with—and then the clutch pedal broke off while we were driving. We were in the middle lane, so the car behind us had to push us into a service station that was luckily right there and also had a pay phone. Bob called his office, and Bob Eggenweiler and Pat Latona came rushing out to where we were, somewhere on Slauson or Crenshaw or something, to bring us a VW van. So we got into the van and continued on; they stayed behind to get the car fixed. It was a Monza, kind of a hotshot car at the time. When we finally arrived, we went into a little waiting room, and a woman came out and asked Bobby to please come with her into another room. Bob and I were sitting in this waiting room, and Bob was a nervous wreck because he had to be at work. And pretty soon the door opened and Bobby came back into this little waiting room—and he was holding Matthew, who was ten weeks old. It was the most touching thing. God, I wish we had a picture of that!

Bob later shot a party scene for *Countdown* at our Mandeville Canyon home. Two or three times he shot where we lived, and you just never knew what was going to happen. One night, it was three or four in the morning, and everyone was sitting around the kitchen. Our son Bobby Altman's lunch was sitting on the counter in a little brown bag all packed for

the next school day—and Bob Duvall ate it. He ate Bobby Altman's lunch! It became a running joke for years.

15 This picture in the middle is from a set from *Countdown*. Bob's telling the actors what to do, although nobody seems to be listening—they're all just reading the paper! Maybe that's what he's telling them to do.

11 Here's Bob lying in front of the headboard that he made out of beautiful beige- and ecru-toned tiles. It was nailed to the wall.

Mandeville Canyon flood
1969

24–31 Bob was casting *M*A*S*H* in Chicago, and Nelda, our new housekeeper straight from Jamaica **27**, had just started working for us. We were having heavy, heavy rains—and then the creek behind our house filled up, and all the mud came down the hillside behind us and took out our storage shed. We had a rectangular, conventional swimming pool that started at two feet and went to nine feet deep. The mud completely filled it to the top! And just as the mud was coming through the glass doors into our living room, a fire engine arrived.

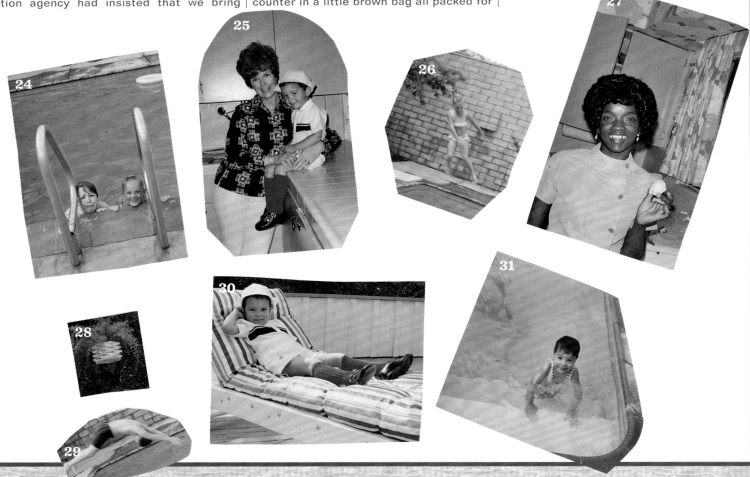

So the fireman driving the fire engine put Matthew, who was three and a half, on his lap, and we squeezed Doris Reed, my stepmother, in between the hook and the ladder somehow. Nelda was terrified. And it took almost two hours to get down the canyon, which was usually a ten-minute drive. Bob was on the phone saying, "Don't forget your jewelry!" I said, "I won't. It's on my hand." I mean, all I had was my ring. At the bottom of the hill was George Litto, our agent and friend, there to meet us in a car. Konni, my daughter, and Signe, my month-old granddaughter, met us there, too. We were in the parking lot of Paul Revere Junior High. Matthew, Konni, Signe, and I went with George to his house, and Bobby went to my mother's. He loved going there.

When I finally went back up to the house, the mud had stopped just before it got to our brand-new, gorgeous, mustard-gold-colored carpet. It had just stopped! Amazingly. But the side yards

were caked with mud that had hardened to clay and had to be chopped away. Matthew played out there for almost a year in the mud. It was just a fairyland for him. Then the pool guy came in with about six other guys, and it took them weeks to dig out the mud-clay from the pool by hand.

When the local Santa Monica

paper came out, there was a front-page photo of us with another family on the fire truck. The caption read "The Robert Altman Family," so it looked like that was the name of the other family. The information was all wrong, but Bobby ended up taking it into the third grade to use it as a current event.

*M*A*S*H*
1969

<u>32–37</u> *M*A*S*H* was filmed in 1969 on the back lot of Twentieth Century Fox. <u>33</u> Here is Bob in the editing room with Danford B. Greene, the editor.

2
THE SEVENTIES

BY GIULIA
D'AGNOLO VALLAN

(PART 1)

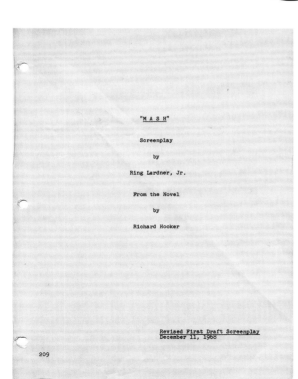

MASH gives a DAMN

Stanley Kubrick, Sydney Pollack, Sidney Lumet, George Roy Hill, and even Gene Kelly had already turned down *M*A*S*H* by the time agent George Litto suggested Robert Altman to producer Ingo Preminger. Blacklisted writer Ring Lardner Jr. had penned the adaptation of the novel by Richard Hooker (a pseudonym for surgeon-writer H. Richard Hornberger and sports journalist W. C. Heinz) about a U.S. Army hospital unit stationed near the front during the Korean War. Richard Zanuck and David Brown were interested in making the film at Twentieth Century Fox. But it seemed that most A-list directors were ticked off by the disjointed narrative, the crude, absurdist humor, the gore, and what they saw as dangerously ambivalent attitudes toward war, race, and sex.

OPPOSITE Donald Sutherland, Elliott Gould, and Altman on the Los Angeles set of *M*A*S*H*, 1969.

ABOVE Publicity artwork for Altman's *M*A*S*H*, 1970.
LEFT Ring Lardner Jr.'s Oscar-winning script for *M*A*S*H*.

41

What others perceived as shortcomings, Altman considered points of interest. He jumped at the opportunity to direct a studio film in which he could incorporate his own war experience as well as the work he had already done on his cherished, never-realized World War I project, *O Death, Where Is Thy Sting-a-ling-a-ling?* (aka *The Chicken and the Hawk*). With its $3.5 million budget, *M*A*S*H* was an inexpensive enterprise compared to the other two war movies in production at Fox, *Tora! Tora! Tora!* and *Patton*. It turned out to be not only the most groundbreaking of the three, but by far the most profitable.

Preminger hired Donald Sutherland and Elliott Gould to star as the stone-faced and often stoned army surgeons Hawkeye Pierce and Trapper John McIntyre. From his television years, Altman brought Michael Murphy and Tom Skerritt. He also went to scout experimental theater stages in San Francisco, where he cast several actors who had never been in a film before but were used to ensemble performances and improvisation.

Altman had shown his inclination for multiple plots and multiple characters in some of his TV work. But *M*A*S*H*'s episodic structure and its chaotic army-base setting provided the perfect opportunity to crystallize what would become one of the director's recurring forms. Sutherland and Gould were not yet stars, but they perceived that their characters were the protagonists of the picture and initially had a hard time accepting Altman's very loose directing style and the fact that Hawkeye and Trapper were not necessarily the main focus of his attention. Of the two, Gould would eventually adapt, and he ended up finding Altman's process congenial to his own. They would work together again several times. Like other actors later on, Sutherland never took to Altman's method, and their collaboration ended with this film.

After the elegant, chillingly claustrophobic duet of *That Cold Day in the Park*, *M*A*S*H* represented a radical stylistic shift for the director. Its look was deliberately unglamorous, even rough. (Fog filters were used to lessen the definition of the image, contributing to the blurry, unsteady look.) When cinematographer Harold Stine, whom he knew from *The Roaring 20's*, replaced the studio's director of photography, fired by Altman after one week of shooting, the director worked with Stine to further explore the combination of slow zoom and camera movements that would become part of his signature. Allowing Altman to get closer to an actor without visibly moving the camera, zoom

lenses suited his preference for catching performers in unguarded moments and shifting the focus of a scene on his whim.

If, visually speaking, *M*A*S*H* was a pretty unusual film, even when Hollywood was moving away from studio aesthetics toward techniques that would result in a more realistic, less polished feel, from the standpoint of sound it was a revolution. Inspired by Howard Hawks, Altman had used overlapping dialogue since his early years at Calvin. Foreground and background sound blended freely in *M*A*S*H*. Out the window went not only the Hollywood rule mandating clean, easily intelligible conversations, but also any hierarchical notion of a main (dialogue) track dominating what was going on everywhere else in the scene. Altman simply did not believe in that.

Within a few years, upon making *California Split* in 1974, the director would have his tech team create an in-house, eight-track recording machine, and he had actors equipped with individual radio microphones. Everything, including the background noises, would be recorded on multiple channels, allowing him to modulate things freely in post-production, as if he were mixing a piece of music.

Born in 1925, Altman had grown up with radio, a medium that remained very influential throughout his career and, to a certain extent, shaped his sophisticated understanding of sound. Sound would also become the way he often tied together the fragmented structure of a film. To achieve that effect in *M*A*S*H*, he made brilliant use of an autonomous voice-over narration composed of radio broadcasts, coming from loudspeakers stuck up around the base. The contents were lifted from Twentieth Century Fox's publicity archives and Korean War almanacs. To top off the unorthodoxy of it all, it was Altman's teenage son, Michael, who wrote the lyrics for the theme song of the film, "Suicide Is Painless."

The director may have wanted blurred images, an "ugly" look, but great care went into finding the perfect color for the blood in the very gory surgery scenes. In interviews he said he had brought to *M*A*S*H* the "silliness" of the war as he had experienced it on the Pacific front, where he was stationed not far from an Australian army hospital. He also wanted to make sure nobody would forget that war is carnage.

With his instinctive dislike for group thinking and political platitudes, Altman made a most unconventional antiwar movie: a film set during the Korean War, which clearly stood for Vietnam, but not a film against the Vietnam War itself. In mostly liberal, anti-Nixon Hollywood, he was creating a counterculture of his own.

Confronted with studio demands to cut down the film (and the gore in particular), Altman requested a preview. It was held in San Francisco, in

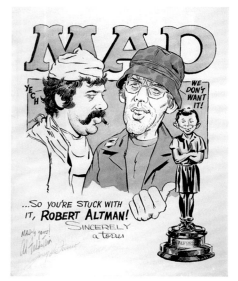

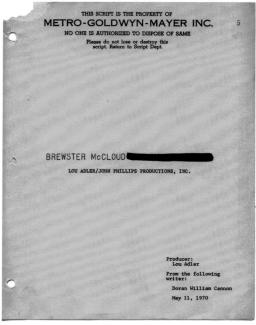

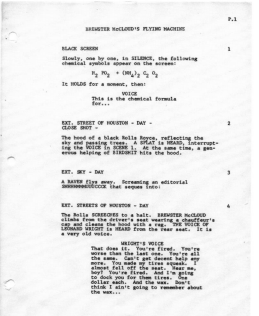

a three-thousand-seat theater. *M*A*S*H* was shown after the Paul Newman–Robert Redford vehicle *Butch Cassidy and the Sundance Kid*. In Altman's words, "The crowd went nuts." It opened in New York on January 25, 1970, and became one of the three top-grossing Hollywood films of the year. It also won the Palme d'Or at the Cannes Film Festival. Lardner won an Academy Award for Best Adapted Screenplay—even though he admitted disliking the film and publicly complained that Altman had betrayed his script.

Altman's passion always lay with human behavior, not complicated plots or "important" subjects. That passion, which became almost anthropological late in his career, found rather peculiar expression in his next film. Music producer and manager Lou Adler (among his talent pool, Sam Cooke and the Mamas and the Papas) brought him a script titled *Brewster McCloud*. The director liked the dark fairy tale of a boy who desperately wants to fly, living hidden in Eero Saarinen's TWA terminal at John F. Kennedy International Airport. Given the success of *M*A*S*H*, MGM decided to finance the picture, which went into production in June 1970. Bud Cort, who had a small role in *M*A*S*H*, was cast as the lead character. Also from that set came Sally Kellerman, René Auberjonois, and Michael Murphy. Altman moved Brewster's nest from the modernist building in New York to Houston's Astrodome. It was also in Texas that he found his leading lady, an actress who became emblematic of his flawless casting sense and—by appearing in seven of his features—of his work as a whole.

Shelley Duvall was not into films at the time, nor had she ever thought of acting in one. Some of Altman's collaborators who had met her at a party in Houston suggested he see her. He immediately loved the uniqueness of her presence, her rawness. Duvall became Brewster's girlfriend on the spot.

A wannabe Icarus possibly trapped in a baseball stadium and possibly connected to a series of grisly murders; a seedy cop named Shaft; Sally Kellerman mysteriously naked under her trench coat; an ornithologist who looks more and more like a bird—as rewritten (often while shooting) by Altman himself, *Brewster McCloud* did not have much of a plot. It was the first film to come out of Altman's new production company, Lion's Gate, named after the suspension bridge that leads into the city of Vancouver from the North Shore.

Unsure about the film, the management at MGM gave it a weak, end-of-the-year release. It disappeared quickly. But critics had started noticing Altman, and some of them, such as Judith Crist (*New York* magazine) and Andrew Sarris (*Village Voice*), praised the film's boldness and its deep melancholy. On some later occasions, Altman mentioned it as a favorite of his, or his most original movie. Some critics saw in the story of a boy desperate for wings a metaphor of the director's lifelong struggle for creative freedom and independence.

Confronted by the fact that expensive, traditionally made "big spectacle" films were turning one after another into huge financial flops (*Paint Your*

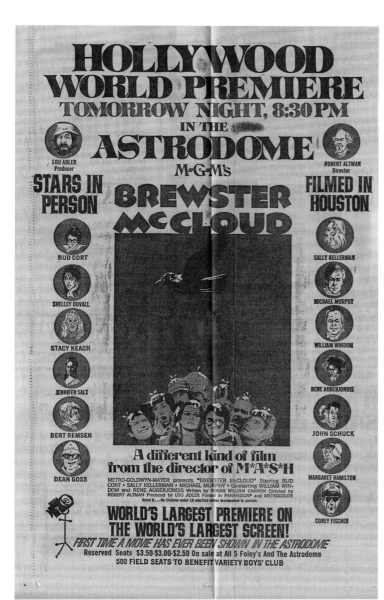

Wagon, Camelot, Star!, Hello Dolly—to name just a few), Hollywood was by necessity starting to be more open to independent-minded directors. A new generation of young filmmakers would soon be breaking down the studios' gates, changing the American film industry forever. At forty-five, Altman was older than "movie brats" Steven Spielberg, George Lucas, Peter Bogdanovich, Francis Coppola, and Martin Scorsese, and he had not gone to film school. His passion for cinema history was more intuitive, less encyclopedic, than theirs; his relationship with the golden age of the studio system, less reverential.

Still, taking advantage of the winds of change that were sweeping the industry, he engaged in a conversation of his own with Hollywood's past, and implicitly with its power structure, by tackling most of its traditional genres, one by one.

After the war comedy (*M*A*S*H*) and before the forties noir (*The Long Goodbye*), the Depression-era crime movie (*Thieves Like Us*), and the musical (*Nashville*)—all in a short span of five years—came the most sacred of all, the Western. Reportedly, genre legend John Wayne labeled as "corrupt" Altman's adaptation of Edmund Naughton's 1959 novel *McCabe*, whose icy Northwestern settings and most unheroic characters were in themselves a break from the classic "Tombstone" premise.

Later in this book, Jules Feiffer notes how each of Altman's films functions as its own perfectly coherent, utterly believable world. It is certainly true of the best ones. So it is not a surprise that, given a chance, the director would embrace the opportunity of building an entire town almost from scratch. Scripted by Brian McKay and Altman, *McCabe & Mrs. Miller* was shot forty miles west of Vancouver. There, production designer Leon Ericksen raised Presbyterian Church, the

highly uncivilized outpost of civilization where gambler John McCabe, fond of shooting people in the back, builds his brothel and soon will be joined by the opium-addicted madam, Mrs. Miller. Warren Beatty was cast first (as McCabe), and then Julie Christie, his lover at the time, came on board (as Mrs. Miller). While Beatty's involvement made the movie possible at Warner Bros., he proved to be less malleable than most actors Altman had worked with in the past. Not only did his status as a movie star give him extra power, his method was in open conflict with Altman's. The actor liked to fine-tune his performance slowly, take by take, shooting a lot of film. The director prioritized the immediacy of a first or second take and wanted to move on quickly.

Still, from this uneasy collaboration came some of the best work that both Altman and Beatty ever did. With its grim, harsh view of frontier life, so wonderfully internalized in Christie's vacant close-up in a Chinese-run opium den at the end, Altman had made the finest, most accomplished of his more "linear" films, and a film that influenced the look and texture of several Westerns to come. Ever the technical innovator, Altman had instructed director of photography Vilmos Zsigmond to flash the negative of the film before shooting so that the ensuing double exposure would give the images a sepia, worn-out tone. A big truckload of turn-of-the-century immigrant costumes sent by the Warner Bros. wardrobe department made for a more diverse, rugged ethnic population of the West. (Giving his actors needle and thread, Altman had them repair their characters' clothes.) Blessed by a super snowstorm that lasted several days, the long, suspenseful final hunt that leads to McCabe's death is proof that no matter how many rules he loved to break, Altman is a master of traditional film language. And once again, his choice of music was not traditional: three songs from Leonard Cohen's debut album.

Emerging reviewer Roger Ebert at the *Chicago Sun-Times* called *McCabe & Mrs. Miller* a "perfect" movie. In her *New Yorker* review, Pauline Kael described it as a "beautiful pipe dream of a movie" and "a figment of the romantic imagination."

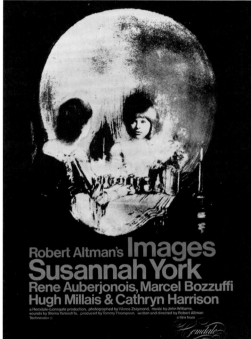

Part of what critics—Kael in particular—found exciting about Robert Altman was his willingness to shift gears, his unpredictability. With him, they never knew what would come next. Now, after the American Northwest, came Ireland—and a film that could have easily been born out of Mrs. Miller's opium reveries.

"A husband and wife are having an argument, and he is going in and out of the bathroom. At some point she looks up, and he is someone she has never seen before": based on this vision that hit him in a Los Angeles restaurant sometime in the mid-sixties, Altman had been trying to do *Images* for a while. It was the British company Hemdale that eventually put up the budget for the director's first European venture. The film reflected his interest in the work of Ingmar Bergman, *Persona* in particular, and American expatriate Joseph Losey, and *Images* created the template for the mysteriously opaque female character that Altman would further explore in *3 Women* and *Come Back to the 5 & Dime, Jimmy Dean, Jimmy Dean*.

British actress Susannah York (*The Killing of Sister George*) was cast as the lead after Altman spotted her in Delbert Mann's 1970 TV adaptation of *Jane Eyre*. To convince her to accept the role of a lonely, wealthy woman haunted by visions of past lovers, sex, and murder, he went to meet the actress in Corfu. Always encouraging actors to blend their own experience into their roles, Altman suggested that they would use the children's story York was writing at that time, *In Search of Unicorns*, in the film. Shot by Zsigmond and scored by John Williams in his pre-Spielberg period, *Images* is a hauntingly strange film, whose liquid, hypnotic style and oneiric themes Altman would return to on occasion. He called these his "interior" films.

Critical reception for *Images* was mixed. Confirming the devoted following that the director was building in Europe, Susannah York won the Best Actress award at the Cannes Film Festival that year. But the film was not widely seen in the United States due to the sparse release that Columbia Pictures gave it.

Nonetheless, Altman was clearly on a roll, creatively. His next project would bring him back to the United States and right to the heart of Hollywood. Never one to shy away from the opportunity to confront a "classic," he accepted an offer to direct *The Long Goodbye*, a Raymond Chandler novel adapted by Leigh Brackett, who had also scripted Howard Hawks's 1946 movie based on Chandler's novel *The Big Sleep*, starring Humphrey Bogart as detective Philip Marlowe. The key to bringing Chandler's moody, romantic, hard-boiled forties Los Angeles into the seventies was to play on Marlowe's anachronism, an anachronism that became even more pronounced when Elliott Gould was

MCCABE & MRS. MILLER

ROGER EBERT

McCabe rides into the town of Presbyterian Church under a lowering sky, dismounts, takes off his buffalo-hide coat, puts on his bowler hat, and mumbles something under his breath that we can't quite make out, but the tone of voice is clear enough. This time, he's not going to let the bastards grind him down.

He steps off through the mud puddles to the only local saloon, throws a cloth on the table, and takes out a pack of cards, to start again. His plan is to build a whorehouse with a bathhouse out in back, and get rich. By the end of the movie, he will have been offered $6,250 for his holdings, and he will be sitting thoughtfully in a snowbank, dead, as if thinking it all over.

And yet Robert Altman's *McCabe & Mrs. Miller* doesn't depend on that final death for its meaning. It doesn't kill a character just to get a trendy existential feel about the meaninglessness of it all. No, McCabe doesn't find it meaningless at all, and once Mrs. Miller explains the mistake he made in his reasoning, he rides all the way into the next town to try to sell his holdings for half what he was asking, because he'd rather not die.

Death is very final in this Western, because the movie is about life. Most Westerns are about killing and getting killed, which means they're not about life and death at all. We spend a time in the life of a small frontier town, which grows up before our eyes out of raw, unpainted lumber and tubercular canvas tents. We get to know the town pretty well, because Altman has a gift for making movies that seem to eavesdrop on activity that would have been taking place anyway.

That was what happened in *M*A*S*H*, where a lot of time didn't have to be wasted in introducing the characters and explaining the relationships between them, because the characters already knew who they were and how they felt about each other. In a lot of movies, an actor appears on the screen and has no identity at all until somebody calls him "Smith" or "Slim," and then he's Smith or Slim.

In *McCabe & Mrs. Miller*, Altman uses a tactfully unobtrusive camera, a distinctive conversational style of dialogue, and the fluid movements of his actors to give us people who are characters from the moment we see them; we have the sense that when they leave camera range they're still thinking, humming, scratching, chewing, and nodding to each other in the street.

ROGER EBERT was a Pulitzer Prize–winning film critic for the *Chicago Sun-Times* and champion of such Altman movies as *Nashville* (1975) and *3 Women* (1977), both of which he ranked as the best films of their respective years.

McCabe and Mrs. Miller are an organic part of this community. We are aware, of course, that they're played by Warren Beatty and Julie Christie, but rarely have stars been used so completely for their talents rather than their fame. We don't ever think much about McCabe being Warren Beatty, and Mrs. Miller being Julie Christie; they're there along with everybody else in town, and the movie just happens to be about their lives.

Because the movie is about a period in the lives of several people (and not about a series of events that occur to one-dimensional characters), McCabe and Mrs. Miller change during the course of the story. Mrs. Miller is a tough Cockney madam who convinces McCabe that he needs a competent manager for his whorehouse: How would *he* ever know enough about managing women? He agrees, and she lives up to her promise, and they're well on their way to making enough money for her to get out of this dump of a mining town and back to San Francisco where, she believes, a woman of her caliber belongs.

All of this happens in an indoor sort of a way, and by that I don't mean that the movie looks like it was shot on a soundstage. The outdoors is always there, and people are always coming in out of it and shaking the rain from their hats, and we see the trees whipping in the wind through the windows.

But it's a wet autumn and then a cold winter, so people naturally congregate in saloons and grocery stores and whorehouses, and the climate forces a sense of community.

Then the enforcers come to town: the suave, Scottish-accented Butler, who kills people who won't sell out to the Company, and his two sidekicks. One of them is slack-jawed and mean, and the other is a nervous blond kid with the bare makings of a mustache. On the suspension bridge that gets you across the river to the general store, he kills another kid—a rawboned, easygoing country kid with a friendly smile—and it is one of the most affecting and powerful deaths there ever has been in a Western.

The final hunt for McCabe takes place in almost deserted streets, because the church is burning down and everybody is out at the edge of town trying to save it. The church burns during a ghostly, heavy daylight snowstorm: fire and ice. And McCabe almost gets away. Mrs. Miller, who allowed him into her bed but always, except once, demanded $5 for the privilege, caught on long before he did that the Company would rather kill him than go up $2,000. She is down at the foot of town, in Chinatown, lost in an opium dream while the snow drifts against his body. *McCabe & Mrs. Miller* is like no other Western ever made, and with it, Robert Altman earns his place as one of the best contemporary directors.

cast in the role of the private detective. Robert Mitchum and Lee Marvin had also been considered for what would probably have been a more deferential take on the book. But Gould was definitely as far as one could imagine from Bogart or Dick Powell (who had played Marlowe in *Murder, My Sweet*).

Living across the hall from a group of pot-smoking, tanning-in-the-nude, free-spirited girls in Altman's bleached-out seventies California, this Marlowe is a fish out of water, a man with a code of honor that belongs to a different era. He engages in long conversations with his cat (which eats only one specific brand of food) and even drives a 1948 Lincoln Continental. Some critics suggested that Altman had projected himself onto this total outsider. Whether that's true or not, *The Long Goodbye* plays very much like a movie about Hollywood. Further texture and Hollywood subtext were inserted by casting Sterling Hayden, whose career had never recovered from the controversy over his testimony before the House Un-American Activities Committee. In interviews, Altman would say that Hayden's character, Roger Wade, reminded him of Chandler himself, as well as other writers, such as Ernest Hemingway or Irwin Shaw, in a disillusioned stage of their lives. European folksinger Nina van Pallandt became Wade's wife. Film director Mark Rydell was cast as the gangster Marty Augustine, who bashes a Coca-Cola bottle in his girlfriend's face. The box office for the film was initially disappointing but improved after United Artists adopted a new ad campaign conceived by Altman, aiming at younger, hipper audiences and featuring illustrations by *Mad* magazine artist Jack Davis. By end of 1973, *The Long Goodbye* had made some top ten lists.

Altman continued this stunning five-year streak with two more films. Edward Anderson's 1937 novel *Thieves Like Us* had been on his mind for a while when Elliott Kastner and Jerry Bick, producers of *The Long Goodbye*, suggested he make a movie out of it. Showing his usual tendency to think out of the box, the director promoted to the role of screenwriter Joan Tewkesbury, formerly a child actress, a dancer, a theater director, and recently the script supervisor on *McCabe*. Altman had taken several liberties with Chandler (notably having Marlowe kill his best friend at the end of the movie), but he instructed Tewkesbury that this was to be a faithful adaptation of Anderson's book, which had already been brought to the screen once, in 1948, as Nicholas Ray's *They Live By Night*. Radio offered him once more the opportunity to add an extra thread, in the form of a Romeo-and-Juliet commentary, to this story of tragic young

TOP LEFT Sterling Hayden (as Roger Wade) and Nina van Pallandt (as Eileen Wade) in *The Long Goodbye*, 1973.
TOP RIGHT *Mad* magazine–inspired advertisement for Altman's neo-noir *The Long Goodbye*.
BELOW Elliott Gould (and his feline roommate) in *The Long Goodbye*.

love framed by a Depression-era crime story set in Mississippi, giving the film a more lyrical accent than Arthur Penn's *Bonnie and Clyde*. Keith Carradine, who had been in *McCabe*, and Shelley Duvall played the protagonists. In its approach to genre, *Thieves* is probably the least revisionist of all of Altman's films. Although, once again, it was given a limited release (by United Artists), it was immediately embraced by critics. "It is the closest to flawless of Altman's films—a masterpiece," wrote Pauline Kael in the *New Yorker*. Today, it remains one of his least-known gems.

As filmmakers, Robert Altman and Steven Spielberg do not appear to share many interests. But what became Altman's next project was actually initiated for Spielberg. The writer Joseph Walsh was a friend of the young director, who had already made *Duel*, and in 1971, he brought Spielberg a very autobiographical story of gambling addiction, tentatively titled *Slide*. Reportedly the two of them worked together on the script for a while. After the project was shuffled between studios and Spielberg moved on to something else, what was going to become *California Split* landed with Altman, who had his own autobiographical affinities with the material and loved the idea of a film set in the gambling world. Again, behavior was at the center of his interest, and through the frenzied, intermittently sweet chemistry between George Segal and Elliott Gould he captured the absolute essence of that environment, down to the credo that winning or losing is not really the point—nor is money. Real gamblers were used, as well as about two hundred patients at the California rehabilitation center Synanon, who were paid ten dollars a day as extras in the big casino scenes. Paul Lohmann shot the film (the first of three he would photograph for the director) in a loose, impressionistic style. The new eight-track recorder was used to push the envelope in creating separate sound channels while shooting and mixing freely and creatively in postproduction.

California Split made the *New York Times*'s ten best list of 1974, the fifth Altman film in that miraculous five years to do so. Showered with critical praise but not ready to settle in it, Altman had plans for something even more adventurous.

TOP LEFT Poster for Altman's *California Split*, 1974.
TOP CENTER Elliott Gould (as Charlie Waters) on the set of *California Split*.
TOP RIGHT George Segal (as Bill Denny) in *California Split*.
BELOW Shelley Duvall (as Keechie) in Altman's *Thieves Like Us*, 1974.

LOVE AND COCA COLA

PAULINE KAEL

OPPOSITE Contact sheet of on-set photos of Keith Carradine (as Bowie), Shelley Duvall (as Keechie), and Altman during the making of *Thieves Like Us*.

In *McCabe & Mrs. Miller*, a rangy, bucktoothed young boy discovered undreamed-of pleasures at a snow-bound brothel and met a scrawny, scared girl, a widowed bride who had just turned whore. She had teeth and a grin to match his own, and when he left they said good-bye, like the affectionate innocents they were, and he called out that he'd be back the next year. A minute later, still harmlessly affable, he was shot down from a bridge, and his body slowly crushed the ice before disappearing in the water. Robert Altman has reunited the pair, Keith Carradine and Shelley Duvall, in *Thieves Like Us*; he's Bowie, one of three escaped convicts, and she is Keechie, whose drunken father runs the gas station the convicts hide in.

Bowie has been in prison for seven years, since he took part in a holdup when he was sixteen; Keechie has never had a boyfriend—not even one to walk her to church. They fall in love; it's two-sided, equal, and perfect—the sort of romantic love that people in movies don't fall into anymore. Keith Carradine takes the screen the way a star does, by talent and by natural right. In his bit role in *McCabe*, he made the audience yield to him so completely that his sequence almost threw the movie out of whack; he makes us yield here for the entire film. He has the rawboned, open-faced look of a young Henry Fonda or Gary Cooper; he's a beautiful camera subject, and the rawness saves him from the too-handsome-juvenile look of earlier stars. There has never been an ingenue like Shelley Duvall, with her matter-of-fact manner

and her asymmetrical, rag-doll face; if it weren't for her goofy, self-conscious smile, she could be the child of Grant Wood's *American Gothic* parents. Her Keechie carries candor to the point of eccentricity: She's so natural that she seems bizarrely original. Whatever it was that Altman saw in her when he put the twenty-year-old Houston girl, who had never acted professionally, into *Brewster McCloud* didn't quite come through that time, but it certainly peeped out in her small role in *McCabe*, and here she melts indifference. You're unable to repress your response; you go right to her in delight, saying "I'm yours." She looks like no one else and she acts like no one else. Shelley Duvall may not be an actress, exactly, but she seems able to be herself on the screen in a way that nobody has ever been before. She doesn't appear to project—she's just *there*. Yet you feel as if you read her every thought; she convinces you that she has no veils and nothing hidden. Her charm appears

---

PAULINE KAEL was a celebrated film critic at the *New Yorker* magazine from 1968 to 1991. Her biting wit and fiery opinions made her the most influential critic of her day. She was an early champion of Altman's *Nashville* (1975) and her support helped soothe the studio's second-guessing about the film.

31

31A

32

32A

to be totally without affectation. Altman must have sensed in that inexperienced twenty-year-old girl some of the same qualities that separate him from other directors: a gambler's euphoria about playing the game his own way, assurance without a trace of imitativeness.

In other Altman films, there is always something that people can complain about; they ask, "What's that there for?" In *Thieves Like Us*, there's nothing to stumble over. It's a serenely simple film—contained and complete. You feel elated by the chasteness of the technique, and the film engages your senses and stays with you, like a single vision. It's beautiful right from the first, pearly green long shot. Robert Altman finds a sureness of tone and never loses it; *Thieves Like Us* has the pensive, delicate romanticism of *McCabe*, but it isn't hesitant or precarious. It isn't a heady, whirling sideshow of a movie, like *The Long Goodbye*; it has perfect clarity. I wouldn't say that I respond to it more than to *McCabe* or that I enjoy it more than the loony *The Long Goodbye*, but *Thieves Like Us* seems to achieve beauty without artifice. It's the closest to flawless of Altman's films—a masterpiece.

Altman breaks the pattern of what American directors are commonly supposed to be good at; this picture has the relaxed awareness that we honor Europeans for and that still mystifies Hollywood. Like *Mean Streets*, it didn't cost enough for Hollywood people to understand it. *Thieves Like Us* is based on a neglected, long-out-of-print 1937 novel by Edward Anderson—the novel that Nicholas Ray's 1948 picture *They Live by Night* was derived from. (Edward Anderson won a literary prize with his first novel, *Hungry Men*, in 1935, and then, as far as I can determine, published *Thieves Like Us* and disappeared from the writing world. It is said that he was living in Texas when *They Live by Night* was made, but the novel, according to Avon Books, which is putting out a new edition, is in the public domain, and the publishers have had no contact with the author.) The Ray film, produced by John Houseman and starring Cathy O'Donnell

and Farley Granger as Bonnie-and-Clyde figures, retained Anderson's plot but strayed far from the book's tone; the Altman film stays very close to that tone, while moving the action from Oklahoma and Texas to Mississippi. The picture was shot in sequence in forty-three days, at a cost of $1,250,000. Altman didn't build thirties sets; he found the vegetating old towns that he needed. He took his crew to Mississippi and made the picture in the sort of freedom that Jean Renoir had when, as a young man, he took his family and friends out to make *A Day in the Country*. Before Altman was hired to direct, the producer, Jerry Bick, had commissioned a script by Calder Willingham. Although Willingham gets a screen credit, his script didn't have the approach Altman wanted, and Altman's former script girl, Joan Tewkesbury, then devised another script, in collaboration with the director, which stays on Edward Anderson's narrative line, retaining much of his dialogue. (He was a considerable writer.) The movie has the ambience of a novel; it is the most literary of all Altman's films, yet the most freely intuitive. *Thieves Like Us* is so sensuous and lucid that it is as if William Faulkner and the young Jean Renoir had collaborated.

Robert Altman spoils other directors' films for me; Hollywood's paste-up, slammed-together jobs come off a faulty conveyer belt and are half chewed up in the process. I think I know where just about all the elements come from in most American movies (and in most foreign movies, too), and how the mechanisms work, but I don't understand how Robert Altman gets his effects, any more than I understand how Renoir did (or, for that matter, how Godard did from *Breathless* through *Weekend*, or how Bertolucci does). When an artist works right on the edge of his unconscious, like Altman, not asking himself why he's doing what he's doing but trusting to instinct (which in Altman's case is the same as taste), a movie is a special kind of gamble. If Altman fails, his picture won't have the usual mechanical story elements to carry it, or the impersonal excitement of a standard film. And if he succeeds

aesthetically, audiences still may not respond, because the light, prodigal way in which he succeeds is alien to them. Three-quarters of a century of slick movies have conditioned audiences' expectations. But *Thieves Like Us* might win him the audience that was put off by the elliptical poetry of *McCabe & Mrs. Miller* and the offhand pyrotechnics of *The Long Goodbye*. There's no predicting what he'll do next; *Thieves Like Us*, with its soft, unassuming grace, may be the only fully accessible movie he'll ever make. Its vision is just as singular as that of his other films, but the masterly aboveboard method could put him in touch with a popular audience; Griffith used to reach that audience (less corrupted then, of course) with comparable pastoral romances, such as *True Heart Susie*. *Thieves Like Us* is not just the easiest-to-like picture Altman has ever made—I think one would have to fight hard to resist it.

The scope is small, but *Thieves Like Us* is a native work in the same way that *The Godfather* is; we know the genre (Depression, bank robbers, Bonnie and Clyde), and the characters are as archetypal as one's next-door neighbors. Altman didn't have his usual cinematographer and production designer with him this time; working with Jean Boffety, a French cinematographer who had never done a picture in this country, and with a newcomer, Jackson De Govia, as production designer, he seems to have changed his style of improvisation—to have become calmer, more fluid. Everything in the Anderson book is refined in the movie, instead of what usually happens to novels—the coarsening that results from trying to make things fit a preordained plan, and settling for the approximate. The milky, semitransparent cinematography makes the story seem newborn. Altman uses the novel as his base, but he finds his story through the actors, and, as Renoir did, through accidents of weather and discoveries along the way. He finds spontaneous comedy; the novel isn't funny, but the movie is. The lovers are far less conventional in the movie than in the book. (With Shelley Duvall, you wouldn't be conventional even if you wanted to.) Bowie isn't a psychopath or a crazed dreamer, like his two robber friends; he's still a kid, and his essential healthiness becomes the core of the picture. He wants what Keechie represents, but he's caught, living a life that doesn't make sense to him. When he says to a wandering dog, "Do you belong to someone, or are you a thief like me?" we know that for him "thief" means "stray." Identifying with Bowie, we react to each eruption of violence as he does—with a moral chill. Anderson, too, had basically seen him as gentle and straight, but the picture takes its cue from the rapport of Carradine and Duvall, omitting other elements in his character and moving away from the links to *Bonnie and Clyde*.

At first, the two convicts who escape with Bowie—T-Dub and Chicamaw —sit around giggling, high on freedom, but then their characters start to take shape. Bert Remsen, who had given up acting, was working as casting director on *Brewster McCloud* when Altman put him into the picture; he appeared again, memorably, in *McCabe*, and now he's T-Dub, a veteran bank robber. T-Dub is a cheery, likable fool who becomes flushed with success and gets reckless; Remsen plays the role so warmly that T-Dub's careless idiocy is fully believable. John Schuck, who was Painless in *M*A*S*H*, has also turned up in two other Altman films, but there was nothing in his earlier work to prepare one for his major performance here, in the pivotal role of the heavy-drinking, half-mad Chicamaw. Schuck has always had a suggestion of a bulldog in his face, and now, grown corpulent and more powerful-looking, he gives a performance that in some scenes rivals the intensity that Bogart brought to his Fred C. Dobbs in *The Treasure of the Sierra Madre*. Schuck's comic, terrifying big scene, when he insists on playacting a robbery at home with small children and explodes in a murderous rage when they lose interest, and his last scene, in which he's deserted, yelling in torment on a country road, are classic moments. Altman often picks up part of his cast on location, or puts members of the crew to work; the writer Joan Tewkesbury turns up here as the woman in the train-station sequence. Louise Fletcher, who is Mattie, T-Dub's sister-in-law, had been a TV actress in the early sixties and had retired, but she is married to the film's producer and was on location in Mississippi. Altman asked her to play the small part of Mattie, and then, when he saw the presence she brought to it, he enlarged the role. Louise Fletcher has a full, strong body and great rounded arms; her Mattie is a no-nonsense woman who looks as if she had lived through what women in soap operas prattle about. She's a tough-broad earth mother with a coating of banal respectability—an authentic American-woman character.

You can see that Altman doesn't have to prove to anybody that he can re-create the thirties. The movie isn't a work of nostalgia; it's not a glorification of the past. It's localized in an era, and the people can be understood only in terms of that era. They are part of the age of radio, and Altman uses radio programs of the thirties for his score, and Coca-Cola for his motif. Everyone swigs Coca-Cola. Keechie is always reaching for a bottle; the old truck advertising Coca-Cola makes an appearance; and on the prison sign at the Mississippi State Penitentiary, at Parchman, there are Coca-Cola ads. I inquired, to find out if this was on the level, and was told that the crew was denied permission to film at actual prisons, where these ads are indeed on the signs, but that the reproduction is faithful. The prison at Parchman is, of course, a landmark in several Faulkner novels. For the last two years now, friends of mine have been shouting that Altman must do *The Wild Palms* or *As I Lay Dying*; they've been convinced that he is the man to bring Faulkner to the screen. Maybe he knew it all along, and maybe he was smart enough to know that he could do it best by using someone else's material for his text. (Perhaps this is also how someday someone will put Fitzgerald on film.) *Thieves Like Us* comes closer to the vision and sensibility of Faulkner's novels than any of the movie adaptations of them do. Altman didn't start from Faulkner, but he wound up there. If he did a Faulkner novel, he might not be able to achieve what people want him to. But *Thieves Like Us* is his Faulkner novel.

The *New Yorker*, February 4, 1974

LEFT A still from *Thieves Like Us*.

M*A*S*H

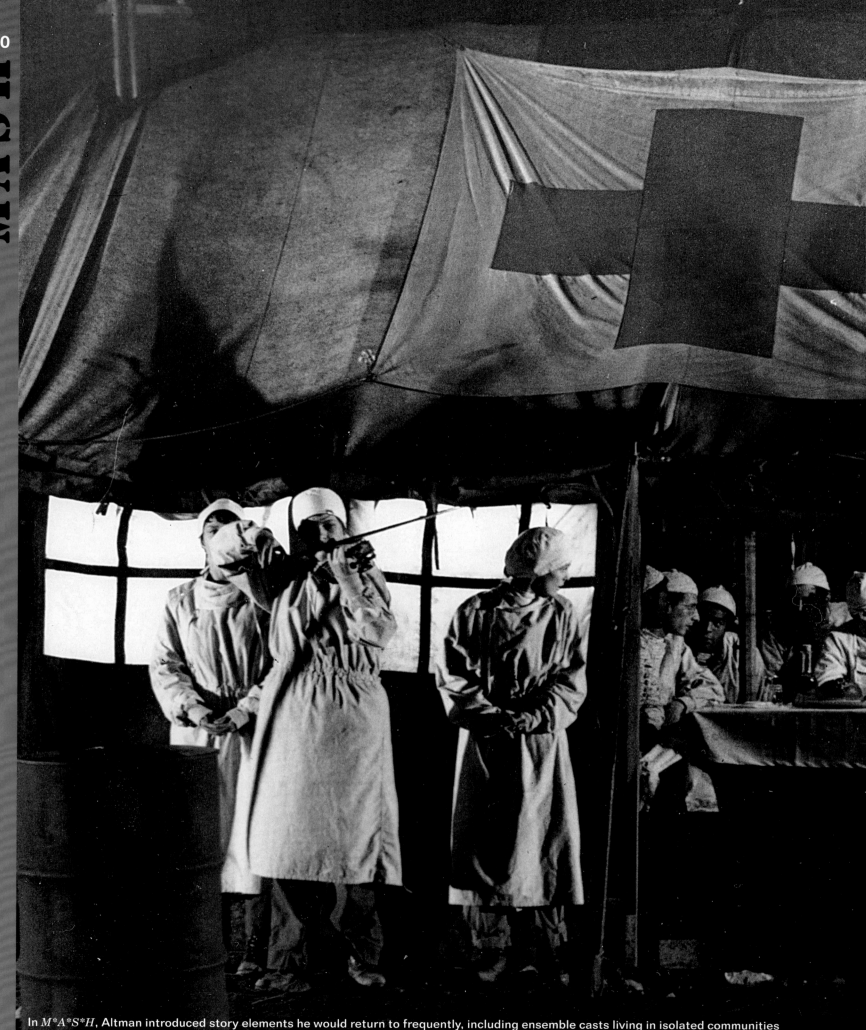

In *M*A*S*H*, Altman introduced story elements he would return to frequently, including ensemble casts living in isolated communities of his own making (*McCabe & Mrs. Miller*, *Buffalo Bill and the Indians*, *Popeye*, *Gosford Park*, *A Prairie Home Companion*) or within broader communities (*Nashville*, *Short Cuts*, *Prêt-à-Porter*, *Kansas City*), and an enthusiasm for engaging with and satirizing culture and politics

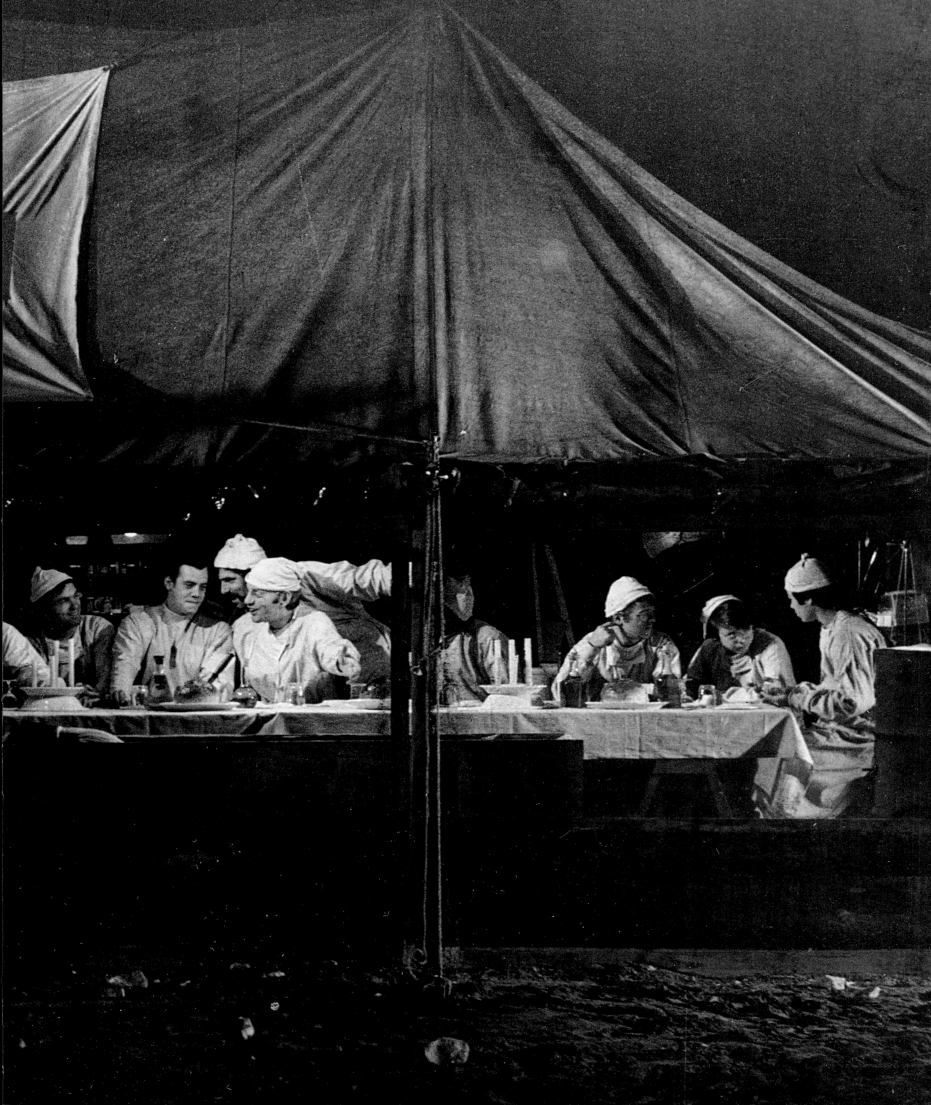

THIS SPREAD Photos of Altman on the set of *M*A*S*H*, including (opposite) the director capturing the legendary football game between the camp's ragtag squad and General Hammond's very serious one. Included in the scene were also some actual football players, such as Buck Buchanan, Fran Tarkenton, Noland Smith, and, in his film debut, Fred "The Hammer" Williamson.

ABOVE One of the *M*A*S*H* football game's cheerleaders.
BELOW Elliott Gould as Trapper John McIntyre.
OPPOSITE Still of Sally Kellerman as "Hot Lips" in the controversial shower scene.

BREWSTER McCLOUD

THIS SPREAD Robert Altman and his leading man Bud Cort shooting in Houston's Astrodome. Brewster's wings were designed by Leon Ericksen.

Still of some of Mrs. Miller's girls during the funeral scene.
OPPOSITE Altman behind the camera.

Contact sheets of on-set photos of Warren Beatty, Altman, and Julie Christie.

OPPOSITE Warren Beatty and Julie Christie were among the most celebrated and sought-after movie stars in Hollywood when Altman cast them in *McCabe & Mrs. Miller*.
ABOVE Altman and director of photography Vilmos Zsigmond lining up a shot.
BELOW Julie Christie received an Academy Award nomination for Best Actress for her performance as Constance Miller.

IMAGES

TOP Susannah York (as Cathryn).
BOTTOM A publicity photo for *Images*.
OPPOSITE TOP Cathryn Harrison and John Morley.
OPPOSITE BOTTOM René Auberjonois (as Hugh).

1973

THE LONG GOODBYE

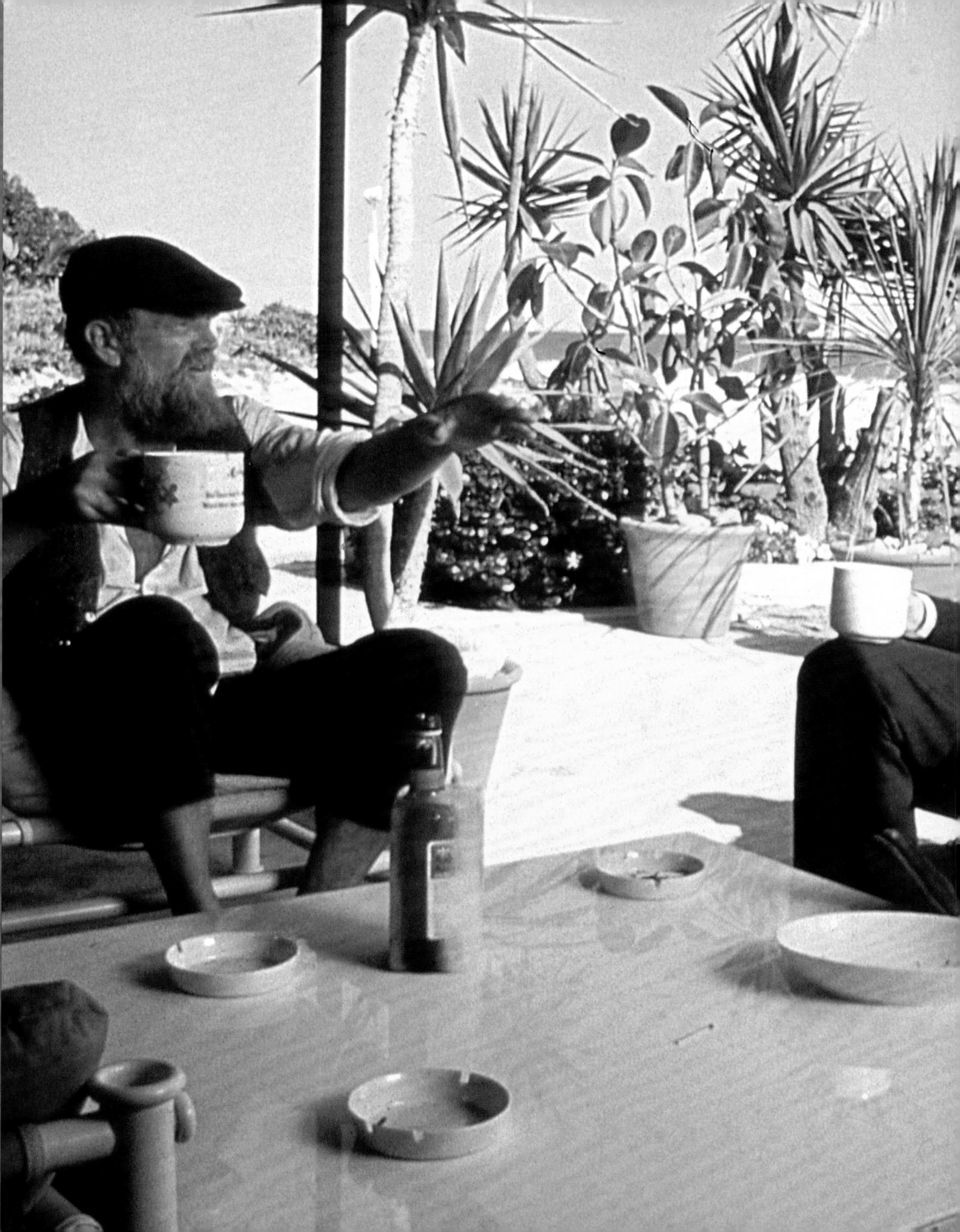

LEFT Sterling Hayden and Elliott Gould on set.
RIGHT Elliott Gould as punching-bag private detective Philip Marlowe.

ABOVE Elliott Gould plays the down-and-out gumshoe Philip Marlowe and Nina van Pallandt plays Eileen Wade.
BELOW Nina van Pallandt in makeup. The European folk singer made her Hollywood debut in Altman's film.
She would also work with Altman on *A Wedding*, *Quintet*, and *O.C. and Stiggs*.
OPPOSITE Contact sheet of behind-the-scenes photos with Elliott Gould, Altman, and Mark Rydell (as ruthless gangster Marty Augustine).

K TRI X PAN FILM

X PAN FILM

FILM KODA

THIEVES LIKE US

Altman on the Mississippi set. On the boat are John Schuck (left) and Keith Carradine (right) as inmates Chicamaw and Bowie.

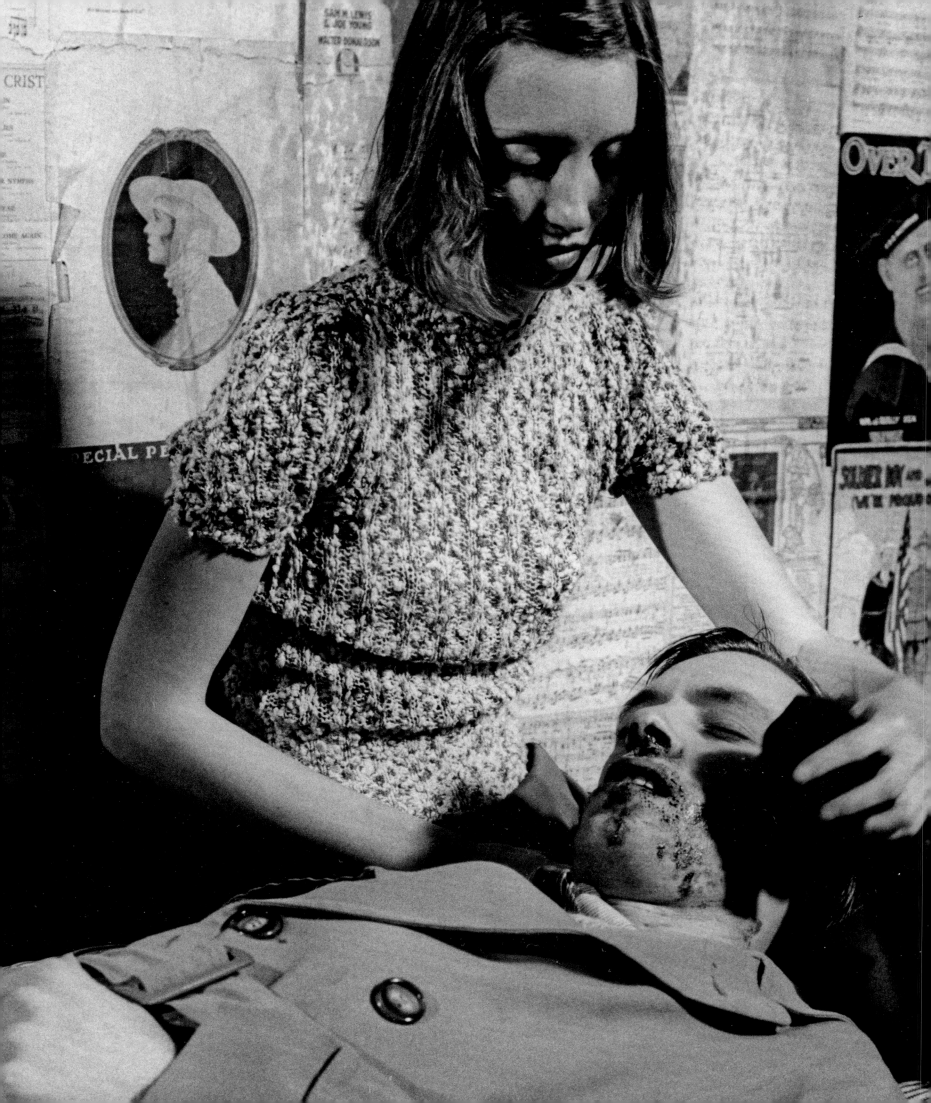

OPPOSITE Shelley Duvall and Keith Carradine as doomed young lovers Keechie and Bowie.
THIS PAGE Photos from the set of *Thieves Like Us*, one of Altman's most faithful adaptations. One of the few liberties he took from Edward Anderson's novel was the introduction of Coca-Cola bottles as a recurring motif.

CALIFORNIA SPLIT

Altman and George Segal on the set. Most of the extras on the film were former gamblers from the Santa Monica alternative community and rehab center Synanon.

KODAK SAFETY FILM

→ 25 → 25A → 26 → 2

KODAK SAFETY FILM

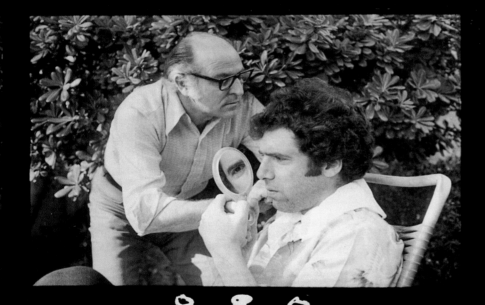

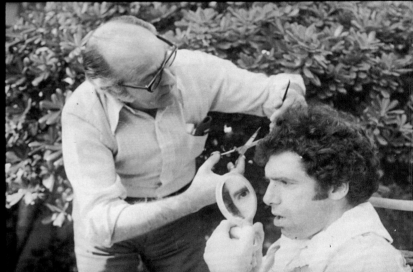

8 8 0 8 8 1

→ 30 → 30 A → 31 → 31

SAFETY FILM

Contact sheet of behind-the-scenes photos featuring George Segal, Alan Rudolph, and Robert Altman.
OPPOSITE ABOVE George Segal and Elliott Gould.
OPPOSITE BELOW Ann Prentiss and Gwen Welles.

McCabe & Mrs. Miller
1970–71

9 *McCabe & Mrs. Miller* was Bob's next film after *Brewster McCloud*. It was originally called *Presbyterian Church*, which is the name of the town in the book, written by Edmund Naughton and titled just *McCabe*, and that's what this picture shows. They modeled the set after it. The book was optioned by David Foster and Mitchell Brower. 1970 was a huge adjustment in our lives, as it brought a whole new career level and whole new lifestyle for us. I didn't really realize how huge it was until it was over. We just kind of rode with it, because Bob never acted like there was any difference about anything, whether it was fame or destitution. It all was just something to deal with, day by day. And this was exciting, because we sold our home of nine years and went to Vancouver to shoot *McCabe*. We had had a Vancouver experience in 1968 when he shot *That Cold Day in the Park* there, but we didn't make a permanent move. I just went to visit. Bob had rented a house up there with Danny Greene, the editor, who ultimately edited *M*A*S*H*. I would take the boys up for weekends. I think it was only like a four- or six-week shoot. So that's how we got to know Vancouver and became very interested in it, and I think that's what led Bob there for *McCabe*.

The story of *McCabe* is that they are building a town, called Presbyterian Church, all through the movie. They found this area above the Upper Levels Highway

Brewster McCloud
1970

1–8 *Brewster McCloud* was shot in Houston. It was right after *M*A*S*H*, and I had all the kids living with us, so I didn't get down there that much. We went down for one long weekend and were in the last shot, which was a big circus scene in the Astrodome. Matthew had on a little tuxedo. I was Big Bird. We had been waiting so long in line to come out that Matthew had fallen asleep, so I pulled him in a wagon. Michael was an organ-grinder. Bobby was a clown. Stevie was a penguin. This was before *McCabe*, so I really kind of felt like an outsider. Bob had been down there in Houston for a while and he was a real swinger, swinging all over the place with Brian McKay, his co-writer, and Lou Adler, his producer. It was very uncomfortable for me at that time. But anyway, then he had us go into wardrobe and be in this scene. We were only there for a long weekend.

I went down again when they wrapped, and Bob and I left from there to go on this fantastic trip: a week in Buenos Aires, where they were having a Latin press conference all about *M*A*S*H*. They wined and dined us. We had empanadas, which I'd never heard of, and they served us practically the whole bull from the ears to the balls, and very famous Argentine barbecues on the pampas. We bought a camera. I bought a red leather coat. He bought a sculpture that is now in our New York apartment. The bellboys in the hotel stole our camera. Oh, all kinds of stuff happened.

That took us right to England, which was my second visit. We stayed two nights there while Bob was trying to romance Vanessa Redgrave into being in some project. He left me in the Westbury Hotel to go have a meeting with her, and I'm watching TV with all this coverage of protests of Vietnam and this big parade in the street—and all of a sudden there's Vanessa Redgrave! And I look out the window, and coming straight for the hotel are these masses of people, and she's leading the whole thing, and Bob's right beside her! And I'm sitting in the damned hotel room! Boy, I was pissed off, I'll tell you.

The town of Presbyterian Church
1902

10

11

12–15 This is the house in London where we lived from 1971–72 when Bob was in pre- and post-production for *Images*. He actually shot in Ireland but did everything else in London. We lived in this house a full school year, like September to June. It later became the New Zealand Embassy, in a very chic section of town: Kensington. It just was really hot stuff. Each house is joined to the next all the way along. The kitchen was belowstairs, and that's where all the deliveries were made. The sidewalk is right in front, and there is a little driveway where you can pull your car right up to the house. From the bedroom, I could hear people walking, what they call foot traffic. I would hear what they had for breakfast or which subway they were going to—or the tube, as they call it. It was an interesting place to live.

While in London, we experienced what I call "the famous Mercedes episode." John Williams, the renowned composer, was doing *Fiddler on the Roof* for Norman Jewison at the time. It was a big movie. He did all of Norman's stuff in those days. John and his late wife Barbara Ruick had lived in this house for almost a year while he was doing the score, until they moved out and we moved in. But he had to stay around London for various

in West Vancouver that was being developed for a housing project, so the wiring and power were already in place, but that's as far as they'd gotten. So they just started building the set. They had all these talented guys our production designer, Leon Ericksen, had hired. Leon was a full-out hippie in those days. He had long hair—everybody had long hair. I remember he came into Bob's office one night and said, "So-and-so from the such-and-such department, I think he just ripped us off." And I thought, "What in the world does *that* mean?" Anyway, he hired all these skilled carpenters and painters and draftsmen, and they all lived right on the set as they were building it. They were all hippies who lived "off the land." We had a guy from Sri Lanka, his name was Omakash, and he hadn't sat down in a chair for seven years because he was a Sikh. So he lived there—he was a security guard—along with all these other guys and girls, and some children and babies Leon hired. They lived and worked and camped and built this town. It was really quite remarkable. And they filmed it all the while. It was quite organic, I guess you could say.

We had this house on Chartwell Place: a beautiful, huge house. Then we had another house where we spent Christmas, in West Vancouver, and where we met our friends Lori and Ira Young. Signe came up with Konni. My mother came up. And Michael Altman lived with us for a while.

10, **11** We came back to California for the Academy Awards for *M*A*S*H*, and we invited the Youngs to go with us. I borrowed a dress from Lori; here I am wearing it. That was a big night—the first of many.

12

13

14

15

reasons—number one being that he wrote the score for *Images*. So he was in and out, and he stayed with us. He speaks really softly—*beautiful* vocabulary tinged with humor. He called me the landlady—"Landy." And he was "the lodger." He still calls me "Landy." During that period, we got a new little Mercedes sports car that Bob had ordered from Germany. It was a two-seater with kind of a shelf up in the back. Jewison, who was a big, popular director, had a home outside London in an area called Putney. We didn't know them socially, but they invited us to dinner with John because John was a close friend of theirs. The only way all three of us could go in this car—and Bob was dying to drive it—was for me to lie down in the back. Somehow or other I got up onto that shelf area. I squeezed in or something. It was tight, whatever it was. And we went to Putney and had our evening, and we were all feeling no pain. So we went back home, and Bob was driving. We pulled into the driveway and he missed the brake, and the car nose-dived down in front of the kitchen window that was below the sidewalk level **14**. We could get out, but we couldn't back up. We got hysterical: We just laughed and laughed, and left it there at a 45-degree angle. And then we went upstairs and went to bed. We woke in the morning listening to people walking by saying, "Oh my God, look at that! Oh my dear, it's a new Mercedes! Oh dear!" I mean, it was just amazing!

16

===== *California Split* scout
===== 1972

16 We were getting ready to do *California Split*, and we went to Las Vegas to scout locations. Left to right, there's [associate producer] Bob Eggenweiler; me; Bob; Leon Ericksen, the genius production designer; [assistant director] Tommy Thompson; and Joey Walsh, who wrote *California Split*. And we were there watching the Mills Brothers, whom I'd known from high school days. We didn't end up shooting there, though. We shot it in Reno.

===== Cannes/*Images*
===== 1972

17–21 In 1972 we took *Images* to the Cannes Film Festival. It was our second time at Cannes. We had been there for *M*A*S*H* the year before and won the Palme d'Or.

This was the first time we chartered a boat for the two weeks of the festival. It was called the *Lulli*, and Ira and Lori Young joined us from Vancouver. We all stayed on the boat. It was exciting!

We went to Monaco to the Grand Prix. Monaco runs along the coastline of southeastern France near Italy, so the best place to watch the race from is a boat.

17, **19** This was our night of showing *Images*. Here's Marcel Bozzuffi, who was in *Images*. That's his wife, Françoise Fabian. He died too young. It was very sad. He was a terrific actor. And Susannah York won for Best Actress. The prize for that was a crystal punch bowl. Susannah couldn't be there; I think she was having her baby, because she was pregnant during the shooting of *Images*. Bob accepted it for her. **21** I've always loved this picture. Ira took it, with Lori's shoes in the foreground. She was just so stylish. I learned a lot from her about clothes and style and trends that were going on in those days.

18 Ira Young also took this picture of us in front of the famous Carlton Hotel.

17

18

The Long Goodbye
1972

22 This was taken on the set of *The Long Goodbye*. Matthew was six. They shot in a house in Malibu for two weeks, and then we lived in it for a year. It was a fabulous old Hollywood beach house, very glamorous but not what one would call "a family home," so that was another adjustment.

Thieves Like Us
1973

23 This was on location for *Thieves Like Us* in Jackson, Mississippi. Bobby Altman was fourteen. Thirty-three was Bob's lucky number. Jean Pagliuso took this wonderful photo.

24 After selling our home in Mandeville in 1970, we went from movie to movie and country to country. In 1973 we started looking for a house in Malibu, where we had taken summer places off and on through the years. One day while I was looking, I saw a house that was under construction. It was in its frame and had been designed and was being built by Vicki Pierson and her husband, Andy. We were looking at other houses on that street, and so we just walked through, but I thought that if we were ever to build, this is *exactly* what Bob would want, something he would really love. I just knew it when I walked through that frame and saw the ocean.

So one day when Bob and I were out looking at the few houses to which we had narrowed it down, we drove by this house and I said we had to stop and walk through it. He got out of the car, walked over to the house, walked through, and went right over to our realtor, Patty Brouillette. He looked at her and said, "Will they sell?" Patty said, "Probably."

We ended up buying the house for $300,000 and the lot next door for another $50,000.

We started thinking about building an addition in 1975, but it was probably almost 1977 before we got going on it, because of a problem with the California Coastal Commission. We were trying to get the permits, but they kept stalling and stalling. So one night we were at an invitational party that Warren Beatty gave. He used to live in the penthouse of the Beverly Wilshire Hotel for many years and had all his girlfriends in and out. So this one particular night, he gave a party to introduce Jimmy Carter to Hollywood Democrats. It was a lovely evening, and Carter was so accessible. And just as it was starting to end, Jerry Brown, our governor, came in with two or three people. The party was starting to break up and everybody was talking to each other, and Jerry was heading toward the elevator with his entourage. I said to Bob, "God, we should try to talk to him" [about the commission problems]. And Bob said, "Well, go ask him." I had had a couple of drinks, or I wouldn't have had the guts to do it. So I got over to the elevator, which was in the foyer of his suite, and I said, "Excuse me, Mr. Brown, blah-diddy-blah-blah." He had his coat over his shoulders, like a man on the go, and he said, "Send me a letter! Send me a letter!" So I thanked him and he left. So we did that the next day—and that did it!

BEFORE—
THE NEW WING
(MATTHEWS' FORT)

25 You can see in this picture, from the street, the lot where we eventually extended. We used another architect, Richard Dodson, who I think stayed very much in the motif of the house.

26, 27 We were staying at the Essex House in New York when Bob was casting *Buffalo Bill*. We stayed there for about a month, and I brought Bobby and Matthew back. They were fifteen and nine.

There had been a big spread in the Sunday paper about what to do in and around New York with children, and I had cut it out. I said to Bob, "I'll do everything else if you'll do the helicopter ride." He said, "Fine." But when it got right down to it, he couldn't do it. I had to do it. I was terrified. I had an Instamatic camera, and I was so scared that all I could do was take pictures the whole time 29, 30. The boys just loved it.

We had a great time. That was just after the big Muhammad Ali–George Foreman fight in Zaire. Ali had returned to New York and was also staying at the Essex. We had gone out to dinner that night, the four of us, and when we came back, the elevators were roped off. Unless you were a guest, you couldn't get through. Behind the rope, in front of the elevators, was Muhammad Ali, and he was standing there letting people photograph him. We were behind the rope, and Bobby looked up at some guy taking a picture right in front of him, tapped the guy's shoulder, and said, in the nicest way, "You have your lens cap on." Then Matthew said to Ali, *"He"*—pointing at Bob over his shoulder—*"he* bet against you." And Muhammad Ali smiled and said in the sweetest voice, "He diiiiidn't." He was so adorable. Bob just beamed.

In 1973 we were at the George V, that great Parisian hotel, with Irwin Shaw. It was on one of those publicity tours we took for *The Long Goodbye*. We started the European trip in Paris. The night before we were to leave for Munich, we stayed up all night with Irwin, James Jones, and others. We didn't make the plane for Munich, but we continued to Berlin and Gottesberg, and ended up in Stockholm. It was a great trip.

31 Ira Young took this great photo of Irwin Shaw and Bob. Shaw was a very colorful character. Very popular. Everybody loved him. He wrote *The Young Lions* and the short story "The Girls in Their Summer Dresses," and more. He was huge . . . and a wonderful guy. The best company.

28 This is one of Bob's first collaborators, George W. George. George's father was Rube Goldberg. Prior to marrying Judy, George was married and had two daughters, and they lived in the same building as Bob's parents when they were living in Los Angeles after the war. About a month after I knew Bob, he took me out to meet George and Judy. It was a Sunday afternoon in Brentwood, just off Sunset Boulevard, and they showed us their little baby: Jennifer George, who grew up to be a successful designer.

3

NASHVILLE

BY GIULIA
D'AGNOLO VALLAN

Altman never really favored country over other types of music, but having promised United Artists that he would explore making a movie about it, he sent Joan Tewkesbury from the *Thieves* set in Mississippi to Nashville to take notes for a screenplay. Upon landing, she found herself stuck for three hours on the highway leading to town: A boat had fallen off a truck, causing a huge traffic jam.

From that mix of standstill and confusion originated the opening scene of Altman's next film, the peak of six incredibly creative years and probably the title for which he will always be remembered. One may agree or not that *Nashville* is the director's best work, but it is undoubtedly his most epic, his most emblematic of America at a very precise time in its history, and the one that saw the process he had elaborated on for so many years realized in its fullest form.

OPPOSITE Altman directing on the set of *Nashville*, 1975.
LEFT Joan Tewkesbury's script for *Nashville* and script supervisor's notes on page one.

Hal Phillip Walker *makes sense...* **HAL PHILLIP WALKER**

INFLATION: "No problem is more serious in this country than the intolerable rate of inflation that is eating up life savings and has placed food, housing and medical care out of reach for many of our elderly citizens on fixed incomes. The economic and fiscal irresponsibility of government has by example and effect created and encouraged a situation that now threatens our financial security at home and abroad. Given the example of intelligent money management in government and a cooperative private sector the trend can be reversed as surely as it was created."

CONGRESS: "Congress is composed of 535 individuals. 288 are lawyers. I do not believe that lawyers are best qualified to establish policy in matters of education, finance, medical care, agriculture, foreign relations and labor. By accident or design the record has all too often been one of indifference, corruption and inaction. The time has come to replace lawyeristic-legalistic government with the common sense of farmers, teachers, engineers and the businessmen and women all over this country who make government possible."

TAXES: "It cannot possibly make sense for multimillion dollar incomes to go untaxed year after year . . . for churches to remain untaxed on their vast holdings of land and corporate investments."

NATIONAL ANTHEM: "Nobody knows the words. It is impossible to sing. You can't understand it. But Congress in its infinite wisdom gave us the Star Spangled Banner and I suppose all the lawyers voted for it because a lawyer wrote the words and a judge wrote the tune."

SENIORITY: "I know of no other place in the world where seniority is so cherished and where intelligence and ability are so diregarded as in the U.S. Congress."

SECURITY: "Security should be the first and last design of all government. Security of mind, of health, of heart. I can think of no sensible reason why New York must have 12,000 major crimes committed for every 1,000 committed in Tokyo. We must fathom the cause of crimes and set our goals as those of prevention and correction."

THE PRESS: "I applaud the press for their role in investigating and exposing abuses of trust in our Democracy. It is unfortunate that all too often members of our government bombast the press for fulfilling functions in this country that ought to be carried out by responsible legislators."

THE OCEANS: "We are making the same mistakes today in ecology and intelligent planning with regard to the oceans and seas that we made yesterday on land. It is dangerous and naive not to plan now for the proper use of a great source of energy, food and water itself."

MEDICAL CARE: "Our patchwork quilt of government programs has provided a blanket of false security which has left millions of Americans out in the cold. I favor government leadership that will give proper incentive to the private sector where problems of mental and physical health can and will be solved."

ELECTORAL COLLEGE: "Congress and the courts have gone to great lengths to emphasize the one man one vote rule. The electoral college is a flagrant violation of this rule."

NEW ROOTS FOR THE NATION

VOTE for REPLACEMENT

REPLACEMENT PARTY PRESIDENT

OPPOSITE Photos from the set of *Nashville.*

TOP Campaign button and flyer for the presidential campaign of *Nashville*'s Hal Phillip Walker (played by Thomas Hal Phillips). **BOTTOM** *Nashville* screenwriter Joan Tewkesbury.

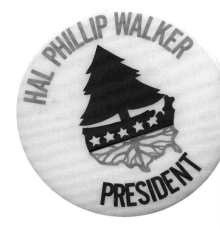

Everything came together for *Nashville,* and to this day all roads in Altman's dense, intricate filmography still take you there. He described the film as "a Russian novel, *War and Peace* with country music."

In interviews, the director said that his desire to make *Nashville* partly originated in the ritual image of young artists getting off the bus in the Tennessee capital (or in Hollywood), armed with a guitar and the desire to make it. Through the screenwriting process, many layers and characters—a total of twenty-four—were added. After Richard Nixon was reelected, in the fall of 1972, Altman also asked Tewkesbury to introduce a political thread. The thirty-seventh president announced his resignation in August 1974, not long after the beginning of production, but his shadow looms large over the movie, and Altman would devote an entire film to him later in his career. Tewkesbury sketched an invisible presidential candidate soon to arrive in Nashville for a rally. Writer, political operative, and occasional actor Thomas Hal Phillips was given a budget to develop the fictional politician's campaign. Also at Altman's request, an assassination was added at the end of the film—the memories of the Kennedys and King assassinations were still fresh. In *Nashville,* however, it was a singer, not the politician, who would die; for Altman, the nexus between entertainment and politics was always a tight one. He would go back to this theme again, most memorably by focusing an entire TV series on it, *Tanner '88.*

By the time he got to Nashville, the director had built a big, varied family of actors and technicians. The collaborative method he had always believed in could be applied most freely and most creatively on this film. Pretty much the whole cast was in the Tennessee capital through the entire shoot. Each of the actors was encouraged to contribute personal experiences and ideas to his or

NASHVILLE

KURT VONNEGUT JR.

A SHADOW PLAY OF WHAT WE HAVE BECOME

AND WHERE WE MIGHT LOOK FOR WISDOM

This is not a movie review. It is talk about a movie.

And I used to think that our machines would kill all of us by and by. I now suspect that we may be rescued or at least refreshed by one of them, which is the motion picture camera. Most of what has been done with that device so far has been as silly as a penny arcade. But now Robert Altman has used the camera to produce a ribbon of acetate that, when illuminated from behind, projects onto a flat surface in a darkened room anywhere a shadow play of what we have truly become and where we might look for greater wisdom.

The name of the film is *Nashville*.

I have often hoped that the arts could be wonderfully useful in times of trouble. I have seen few examples of that.

Nashville, however, fulfills my dream. It is a spiritual inventory of America, splendidly frank and honest.

The movie shows us a system of yearnings and rewards and punishments and physical objects that we have tacked together over the years. It uses the world of country music as a model. *Grand Ole Opry* assumes more importance than the sun itself.

If, as our bicentennial celebration approaches, we ponder such a system rather than blank hokum like the Liberty Bell, we may yet become a nation.

Mr. Altman implies that our understanding of our curious civilization must come from ourselves. He has an actress portray a British documentary filmmaker on a visit to Nashville, fresh from Israel and darkest Africa. She confidently misinterprets all she sees. She has European brilliance and sophisti-cation, which, when applied to the city of Nashville, render her asinine. She says of a country music star's mansion built of logs, "It's pure Bergman." And then she adds, "But of course these are the wrong people for Bergman."**

And I must say that, when the movie was over, not only did I want to cry but I was thunderstruck by how discontinuous with the rest of the world our culture is. It is pure and recent invention, inspired by our random opportunities to gain money or power or fame. Even the past is faked. And those who partake of that culture, especially the weak or simpleminded, feel compelled to invent personalities as novel and arbitrary and commercial as the inventions with which they hope to harmonize.

They lose touch with, among other things, the planet and their fellow men.

While such a culture may not produce insanity, it surely provides a nourishing atmosphere for certain sorts of lunatics, who, after the fashion of

KURT VONNEGUT JR. was the author of such satirical American literary novels as *Cat's Cradle* (1963), *Slaughterhouse-Five* (1969), and *Breakfast of Champions* (1973).

guerrillas, are undetectable when mingling with the general population. And, like guerrillas, those lunatics may have keenly simplified notions of the meanings of all the lives around them—and, on the basis of those notions, they may have fatal enterprises in mind.

Murder can easily become the most reasonable thing in the world.

===

When I was a student of anthropology, it was made clear to me that one culture was roughly as rewarding as another, and that all cultures seemed riddled with absurdities when viewed by outsiders seeking easy laughs or reasons for condemnation. This left me in poor condition to criticize any culture, including my own. And I criticize my own now only because it has become so dangerous. It has somehow become uninterested in our survival. We are somehow rendered terribly unsafe by things we have agreed to believe.

The movie itself opens with a recording session of a patriotic ballad whose refrain argues, with "Battle Hymn of the Republic" drumming behind it, "We must be doing something right to last two hundred years."

And everything goes wrong at the end of the movie. There is maximum ugliness and insanity and meaninglessness. And no great human being or idea or miracle appears to heal the horrified witnesses, a crowd revealed to be child-like in bewilderment and hope. We are not beasts, says Altman. The American people are made by the camera to appear innocent and beautiful.

And leaderless.

And idealess.

And all that can be given to them for comfort by our culture is an enchantingly catchy and heartbreakingly inane ditty played over the public-address system. Everyone is invited to sing along.

Its refrain is this one: "It don't worry me."

===

This movie is going to be a terrific hit, and so is its music. We will all be hearing and singing "It Don't Worry Me" for a little while. The song is one of our sweetest new inventions.

Meanwhile, I think, it is perhaps time for us to invent some deeper things. That an American made this movie is surely evidence that we are capable of depth. And it should be noted that two of the most profound performances in it were turned in by Henry Gibson and Lily Tomlin, who were used to provoke the most empty sort of laughter on television's *Laugh-In* not long ago.

We have perhaps dishonored ourselves too long with silly songs and empty laughter.

And we have surely dishonored ourselves with the manner in which we distribute admiration and power and wealth. For we commonly give those things, as do the people in this movie, to clever persons whose contribution to

OPPOSITE In Vonnegut's words, ". . . everything goes wrong at the end of the movie. There is a maximum ugliness and insanity and meaningless."

human dignity or to the survival of the society is negative, negligible, or nil.

The common people have noticed this, and, in order to weather within a harsh and unforgiving economy, they are necessarily becoming more and more skillful imitators of materially successful persons whose contribution to human dignity or survival of the society is negative, negligible, or nil.

===

Surely what we should invent during our bicentennial celebration, along with Mickey Mouse history, is a scheme for making our economy kinder than it is and saner than it is, in order that our people need not be so panicky about power and wealth, and in order that we more easily distinguish between our saints and our dangerous lunatics.

Having said that, I find that this Yiddishism has popped into my mind: "So what else is new?"

Well—it seems to me that our political and economic leaders are now so devoid of ideas, or an understanding of the American people as they really are, that strength and responsibility are passing over to American artists, especially filmmakers. They are magically observant, and they are far better than the rest of us at show-and-tell.

That much is new.

her character. Lily Tomlin brought some of her family's Southern background to housewife and gospel singer Linnea Reese; singer Ronee Blakley drew from her own journals and childhood memories in the Pacific Northwest to write the long monologue during which country star Barbara Jean unravels in front of her adoring audience; Barbara Baxley wrote the Kennedy Boys speech for her character, Lady Pearl; and Keith Carradine, as country singer and serial seducer Tom Frank, brought Altman a song he had written, "I'm Easy." Geraldine Chaplin, as a self-proclaimed BBC reporter, would flutter among them like a butterfly, ostensibly at work on a documentary.

Actually, Altman asked all his main actors (with or without musical experience) to write their songs. Besides "I'm Easy," among the most memorable ones are Henry Gibson's "Keep A-Goin'" and "It Don't Worry Me," also by Carradine and which Barbara Harris sings at the end. The twenty-five-year-old musical director, Richard Baskin, would help them with the notes. Country music purists and the local musical establishment complained that the music was not "accurate," but *Nashville* was never really a film about country and western. Or, one can argue, even a film about music.

The other great character of the film is, of course, the city. Altman and his cast camped there through most of the hot Southern summer. Even within the constraints of the TV years, Altman always preferred location shoots—by now they had become almost a rule. He used the city of Nashville and its residents as much as possible, creating events to assemble from the local population enough free extras for the required crowd scenes—for Barbara Jean's comeback concert and the grand finale—at the Parthenon.

ABC, not United Artists, ended up backing the film, which was subsequently released by Paramount. As epic as its ambition was, with a budget of about $2 million, *Nashville* was the antithesis of a big Hollywood production—Altman would often remark that it had been made "documentary style." That certainly fits the description of the process of this particular film, but it also suggests that, perhaps, beneath the sophisticated technical artifice and linguistic innovations of Altman's work and his deep passion for actors, beats the heart of a documentarian.

With its reds, whites, and blues deliberately heightened through an extra saturation process, Altman's grand, fragmented, contradictory postcard of America circa 1975 is the image of a country running on empty, one that has lost its center. "It don't worry me," sings the unknown Albuquerque, as she instinctively grabs the mic and the stage only seconds after Laura Jean has been killed—a closing image that perfectly captures both the mindlessness and the beauty of Altman's intricate picture, and, one feels, his view of the country. Seen almost forty years after the Nixon-Watergate, post-Vietnam mindset, *Nashville*'s mythical quality and the flawed humanities of its characters may come across as more defining than its political edge.

Nashville was embraced by critics and audiences alike. Pauline Kael stirred great controversy when she enthusiastically reviewed an unfinished

TOP (LEFT TO RIGHT) Ronee Blakley (as Barbara Jean); Lily Tomlin (as Linnea Reese)—Blakley and Tomlin were both nominated for Best Supporting Actress Oscars for the film; Henry Gibson (as Haven Hamilton).
RIGHT Musical charts for two of the songs from *Nashville*. "I'm Easy" won the film's sole Academy Award, for Best Original Song.

OPPOSITE
CLOCKWISE FROM TOP Keith Carradine (as Tom Frank); Karen Black (as Connie White); artwork created by J. William Myers for the film's opening sequence—a TV ad for a fictitious *Nashville* record album—eventually ended up as the official soundtrack cover.

version of the film, after having attended a private screening organized by Altman. Andrew Sarris and Molly Haskell gave it a great review in the form of a conversation in the *Village Voice*. The European critical establishment wholeheartedly embraced *Nashville* as well, seeing in the film its own ambivalent feelings toward U.S. politics and culture at the time. The National Society of Film Critics named it Best Film, Altman Best Director, Lily Tomlin Best Supporting Actress, and Henry Gibson Best Supporting Actor. The only disappointment came on Oscar night, when the film—which had five nominations—lost Best Picture and Best Director to Milos Forman's *One Flew Over the Cuckoo's Nest*, winning only the Oscar for Best Song, with "I'm Easy." This trend would continue to disappoint for decades, as Academy voters took a long time to embrace Altman as one of their own.

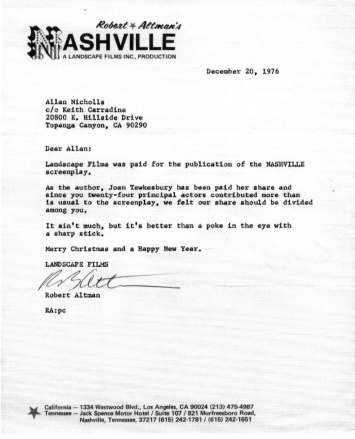

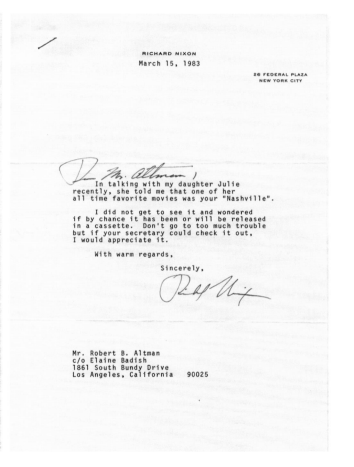

OPPOSITE Photo series of Barbara Harris (as Albuquerque).

TOP Cover of *Film Heritage,* featuring actress Barbara Harris.
BOTTOM Letter from Altman to Allan Nicholls, offering the twenty-four principal actors a share of the income from the published screenplay, in recognition of their "more than usual" contribution.
RIGHT Opposites attract, as shown in this letter to Altman from former president Richard Nixon, requesting a VHS of *Nashville*. He does not seem aware that Altman also directed *M*A*S*H*, which lambasted his politics in Vietnam. But Nixon's presence looms large over *Nashville*. In fact, Altman had asked Joan Tewkesbury to introduce a political thread into the script after Nixon was re-elected. The director did not share Nixon's political views, but in 1984, he would devote an entire film to the thirty-seventh president, *Secret Honor*, in which he made Nixon an almost-sympathetic figure.

COMING: NASHVILLE

PAULINE KAEL

Is there such a thing as an orgy for movie lovers—but an orgy without excess? At Robert Altman's new, almost-three-hour film, *Nashville*, you don't get drunk on images, you're not overpowered—you get elated. I've never before seen a movie I loved in quite this way: I sat there smiling at the screen, in complete happiness. It's a pure emotional high, and you don't come down when the picture is over; you take it with you. In most cases, the studio heads can conjecture what a director's next picture will be like, and they feel safe that way—it's like an insurance policy. They can't with Altman, and after United Artists withdrew its backing from *Nashville*, the picture had to be produced independently, because none of the other major companies would take it on. UA's decision will probably rack up as a classic boner, because this

picture is going to take off into the stratosphere—though it has first got to open. (Paramount has picked up the distribution rights but hasn't yet announced an opening date.) *Nashville* is a radical, evolutionary leap.

Altman has prepared us for it. If this film had been made earlier, it might have been too strange and new, but in the five years since he broke through with *M*A*S*H* he's experimented in so many directions that now, when it all comes together for him, it's not really a shock. From the first, packed frames of a recording studio, with Haven Hamilton (Henry Gibson), in bespangled, embroidered white cowboy clothes, like a short, horseless Roy Rogers, singing, "We must be doing somethin' right to last two hundred years," the picture is unmistakably Altman—as identifiable as a paragraph by Mailer when he's really racing. *Nashville* is simply "the ultimate Altman movie" we've been waiting for.

Fused, the different styles of prankishness of *M*A*S*H* and *Brewster McCloud* and *California Split* become Jovian adolescent humor. Altman has already accustomed us to actors who don't look as if they're acting; he's attuned us to the comic subtleties of a multiple-track sound system that makes the sound more live than it ever was before; and he's evolved an organic style of moviemaking that tells a story without the clanking of plot. Now he dissolves the frame, so that we feel the continuity between what's on the screen and life off-camera.

Nashville isn't organized according to patterns that you're familiar with, yet you don't question the logic. You get it from the rhythms of the scenes. The picture is at once a *Grand Hotel*–style narrative, with twenty-four linked characters; a country-and-western musical; a documentary essay on Nashville and American life; a meditation on the love affair between performers and audiences; and an Altman party. In the opening sequences, when Altman's people—the performers we associate with him because he has used them in ways no one else would think of, and they've been filtered through his sensibility—start arriving, and pile up in a traffic jam on the way from the airport to the city, the movie suggests the circus procession at the nonending of *8½*. But Altman's clowns are far more autonomous; they move and intermingle freely, and the whole movie is their procession. *Nashville* is, above all, a celebration of its own performers. Like Bertolucci, Altman (he includes an homage to *Last Tango in Paris*) gives the actors a chance to come out—to use more of themselves in their characters. The script is by Joan Tewkes-

bury, but the actors have been encouraged to work up material for their roles, and not only do they do their own singing but most of them wrote their own songs—and wrote them in character. The songs distill the singers' lives, as the mimes and theatrical performances did for the actors in *Children of Paradise*. The impulse behind all Altman's innovations has been to work on more levels than the conventional film does, and now—despite the temporary sound mix and the not-quite-final edit of the print he ran recently, informally, for a few dozen people in New York, before even the Paramount executives had seen the picture—it's apparent that he needed the technical innovations in order to achieve this union of ideas and feelings.

Nashville coalesces lightly and easily, as if it had just been tossed off. We float while watching, because Altman never lets us see the sweat. Altman's art, like Fred Astaire's, is the great American art of making the impossible look easy.

Altman does for Nashville what he was trying to do for Houston in *Brewster McCloud*, but he wasn't ready to fly then, and the script didn't have enough layers—he needs ideas that mutate, and characters who turn corners. Joan Tewkesbury has provided him with a great subject. Could there be a city with wilder metaphoric overtones than Nashville, the Hollywood of the C&W recording industry, the center of fundamentalist music and pop success?

The country sound is twang with longing in it; the ballads are about poor people with no hope. It's the simplistic music of the conquered South; the songs tell you that although you've failed and you've lived a terrible, degrading life, there's a place to come home to, and that's where you belong. Even the saddest song is meant to be reassuring to its audience: The insights never go beyond common poverty, job troubles, and heartaches, and the music never rises to a level that would require the audience to reinterpret its experience. Country stars are symbolic ordinary figures. In this, they're more like political demagogues than artists. The singer bears the burden of what he has become, and he keeps saying, "I may be driving an expensive car, but that doesn't mean I'm happier than you are." Neither he nor the politician dares to come right out and confess to the audience that what he's got is what he set out for from the beginning. Instead, he says, "It's only an accident that puts me here and you there—don't we talk the same language?" Listening to him, people can easily feel that he owes them, and everybody who can sing a little or who has written a tune tries to move in close to the performers as a way of getting up there into the fame business.

Nashville is about the insanity of a fundamentalist culture in which practically the whole population has been turned into groupies. The story spans the five days during which a political manager, played by Michael Murphy, lines up the talent for a Nashville rally to be used as a TV show promoting the presidential candidacy of Hal Phillip Walker. Walker's slogan is "New Roots for the Nation"—a great slogan for the South, since country music is about a longing for roots that don't exist. Because country singing isn't complex, either musically or lyrically, Altman has been able to create a whole constellation of country stars out of actors. Some of them had actually cut records, but they're not primarily country singers, and their songs are never just numbers. The songs are the story being told, and even the way the singers stand—fluffing out a prom-queen dress,

like Karen Black, or coolly staring down the audience, like the almond-eyed, slightly withdrawn Cristina Raines—is part of it. During the movie, we begin to realize that all that the people are is what we see. Nothing is held back from us; nothing is hidden.

When Altman—who is the most atmospheric of directors—discusses what his movies are about, he makes them sound stupid, and he's immediately attacked in the press by people who take his statements literally. (If pinned to the wall by publicity men, how would Joyce have explained the "Nighttown" sequence of *Ulysses*?) The complex outline of *Nashville* gives him the space he needs to work in, and he tells the story by suggestions, echoes, recurrences. It may be he's making a joke about how literally his explanations have been taken when in this picture the phony sentiments that turn up in the lyrics recur in other forms, where they ring true. Haven Hamilton, the bantam king of Nashville, with a red toupee for a crown, sings a maudlin piece of doggerel, with a heavy, churchy beat, about a married man's breaking up with his girlfriend ("For the sake of the children, we must say goodbye"). Later, it's almost a reprise when we see Lily Tomlin, as the gospel-singing wife of Haven's lawyer, Ned Beatty, leave Keith Carradine (the hot young singer in a trio) for exactly that reason. Throughout, there are valid observations made to seem fake by a slimy inflection. Geraldine Chaplin, as Opal, who says she's from the BBC, is doing a documentary on Nashville; she talks in flights of poetic gush, but nothing she says is as fatuous as she makes it sound. What's funny

about Opal is that her affectations are all wasted, since the hillbillies she's trying to impress don't know what she's talking about. Opal is always on the fringe of the action; her opposite is the figure that the plot threads converge on—Barbara Jean (Ronee Blakley), whose ballads are her only means of expressing her yearnings. Barbara Jean is the one tragic character: Her art comes from her belief in imaginary roots.

The movies often try to do portraits of artists, but their artistry must be asserted for them. When we see an actor playing a painter and then see the paintings, we don't feel the relation. And even when the portrait is of a performing artist, the story is almost always of how the artist achieves recognition rather than of what it is that has made him an artist. Here, with Ronee Blakley's Barbara Jean, we perceive what goes into the art, and we experience what the unbalance of life and art can do to a person. When she was a child, Barbara Jean memorized the words on a record and earned fifty cents as a prize, and she's been singing ever since; the artist has developed, but the woman hasn't. She has driven herself to the point of having no identity except as a performer. She's in and out of hospitals, and her manager husband (Allen Garfield) treats her as a child, yet she's a true folk artist; the Nashville audience knows she's the real thing and responds to the purity of her gift. She expresses the loneliness that is the central emotion in country music. But she isn't *using* the emotion, as the other singers do: It pours right out of her—softly. Arriving at the airport, coming home after a stretch of treatment—for burns, we're told—she's radiant, yet so breakable that it's hard to believe she has the strength to perform. A few days later, when she stands on the stage of the Opry Belle and sings "Dues," with the words "It hurts so bad, it gets me down," her fragility is so touching and her swaying movements are so seductively musical that, perhaps for the first time on the screen, one gets the sense of an artist's being consumed by her gift. This is Ronee Blakley's first movie, and she puts most movie hysteria to shame; she achieves her effects so simply that I wasn't surprised when someone near me started to cry during one of her songs. She has a long sequence on the stage of the Opry Belle when Barbara Jean's mind starts to wander and, instead of singing, she tells out-of-place, goofy stories about her childhood. They're the same sort of stories that have gone into her songs, but without the transformation they're just tatters that she clings to—and they're all she's got. Ronee Blakley, who wrote this scene, as well as the music and lyrics of all her songs, is a peachy, dimpled brunette, in the manner of the movie stars of an earlier era; as Barbara Jean, she's like the prettiest girl in high school, the one the people in town say is just perfect-looking, like Linda Darnell. But she's more delicate; she's willowy and regal, tipping to one side like the Japanese ladies carved in ivory. At one point, she sings with the mic in one hand, the other hand tracing the movements of the music in the air, and it's an absolutely ecstatic moment.

Nashville isn't in its final shape yet, and all I can hope to do is suggest something of its achievement. Altman could make a film of this magnitude for under $2 million because he works with actors whose range he understands. He sets them free to give their own pulse to their characters; inspired themselves, they inspire him. And so we get motifs that bounce off each other—tough-broad Barbara Baxley's drunken fix on the murdered Kennedys, Shelley Duvall's total absorption in celebrity, a high school band of majorettes twirling rifles, and Robert Doqui's anger at a black singer for not being black enough. All the allu-

sions tell the story of the great American popularity contest. Godard was trying to achieve a synthesis of documentary and fiction and personal essay in the early sixties, but Godard's Calvinist temperament was too cerebral. Altman, from a Catholic background, has what Joyce had: a love of the supreme juices of everyday life. He can put unhappy characters on the screen (Keenan Wynn plays a man who loses the wife he's devoted to) and you don't wish you didn't have watch them; you accept their unhappiness as a piece of the day, as you do in *Ulysses*. You don't recoil from the moody narcissism of Keith Carradine's character: There he is in his bedroom, listening to his own tapes, with one bed partner after another—with Geraldine Chaplin, whom he'll barely remember the next day, and with Lily Tomlin, whom he'll remember forever. You don't recoil, as you do in movies like *Blow-Up* or *Petulia*, because Altman wants you to be part of the life he shows you and to feel the exhilaration of being alive. When you get caught up in his way of seeing, you no longer anticipate what's coming, because Altman doesn't deliver what years of moviegoing have led you to expect. You get something else. Even when you feel in your bones what has to happen—as you do toward the climax of *Nashville*, when the characters assemble for the rally at the Parthenon and Barbara Jean, on the stage, smiles ravishingly at her public—he delivers it in a way you didn't expect. Who watching the pious Haven Hamilton sing the evangelical "Keep A-Goin'," his eyes flashing with a paranoid gleam as he keeps the audience under surveillance, would guess that the song represented his true spirit, and that when injured he would think of the audience before himself? Who would expect that Barbara Harris, playing a runaway wife—a bombed-out groupie hovering around the action—would finally get her chance onstage, and that her sexy, sweetly shell-shocked look would, at last, fit in perfectly? For the viewer, *Nashville* is a constant discovery of overlapping connections. The picture says, This is what America is, and I'm part of it.

Nashville arrives at a time when America is congratulating itself for having got rid of the bad guys who were pulling the wool over people's eyes. The movie says that it isn't only the politicians who live the big lie—the big lie is something we're all capable of trying for. The candidate, Hal Phillip Walker, never appears on the screen; he doesn't need to—the screen is full of candidates. The name of Walker's party doesn't have to stand for anything: that's why it's the Replacement Party.

Nashville isn't full of resolutions, because Altman doesn't set up conflicts; the conflicts, as in Lily Tomlin's character, are barely visible. Her deepest tensions play out in the quietest scenes in the movie; she's a counterbalance to the people squabbling about whatever comes into their heads. There's no single reason why anybody does anything in this movie, and most of the characters' concerns are mundane. Altman uses a *Grand Hotel* mingling of characters without giving false importance to their unions and collisions, and the rally itself is barely pivotal. A lot happens in the five days, but a lot happens in any five days. There are no real denouements, but there are no loose ends either: Altman doesn't need to wrap it all up, because the people here are too busy being alive to be locked in place. Frauds who are halfway honest, they're true to their own characters. Even the stupidest among them, the luscious bimbo Sueleen (Gwen Welles), a tone-deaf waitress in the airport coffee shop, who wiggles and teases as she sings to the customers, and even the most ridiculous—Geraldine Chaplin's Opal—are so completely what they are that they're irresistible. At an outdoor party at Haven Hamilton's log cabin retreat, the chattering Opal remarks, "Pure, unadulterated Bergman," but then, looking around, she adds, "Of course, the people are all wrong for Bergman, aren't they?" *Nashville* is the funniest epic vision of America ever to reach the screen.

The *New Yorker*, March 3, 1975

NASHVILLE

Still of the opening traffic-jam scene, based on a traffic jam that writer Joan Tewksbury encountered when she flew into Nashville on her first research visit.

THIS SPREAD Photo (left) and contact sheet (right) of Ronee Blakley on set. Standing next to Blakely is music supervisor Richard Baskin.

The *Nashville* cast.

LILY TOMLIN

GIULIA D'AGNOLO VALLAN

Nashville **was your first film with Altman.**

It was my first film—period. I imagine there were probably two factors; one was we had the same agent, Sam Cohn. Sam was inclined to populate films in a kind of family way. He probably would influence Bob in some fashion. But also, it's because in 1971 I had optioned a book called *Maiden* by Cynthia Buchanan. I was still on *Laugh-In* and primarily seen as this quirky character comedienne. Ernestine, the phone operator, was more popular and better known than I was. In those days it was very unusual for actors to cross from television into the movies. But I never thought of that as any kind of hindrance to me. So I optioned *Maiden* to make a movie in which I would play the lead character. My partner, Jane Wagner, wrote the screenplay. Bob was looking for a property for Joan Tewkesbury to direct—she had written *Nashville*. Sam

loved *Maiden*, gave it to Bob, and Bob wanted to do it and produce it. Joan was going to direct it in the fall. Louise Fletcher, who was supposed to be Linnea Reese, must have fallen out. Bob said to me: "Come down to *Nashville*, we'll do this movie together, we'll get to know each other, and then we'll do *Maiden*."

I went down to Nashville. In the meantime, Columbia had bought *Maiden* and reimbursed me for everything. Bob had just done *California Split* with them. But the studio wanted him to cut five or six minutes. The executives came down to Nashville to discuss it. Bob punched one of them in the nose, and he fell into the pool....*Maiden* never got done, but somehow I had a role in *Nashville*.

How much of Linnea Reese was already on the page when you got the script?

I don't recall. Bob is always very loose.

We were there for two months in Nashville but very often not on set. Each one of us had very little screen time. We had a lot of days off. And, to prepare for Linnea, I spent a lot of time interviewing the mothers of the deaf children. I also interviewed a lot of middle-aged club women from Nashville about how they would feel about someone like Linnea, whose children were deaf and who sang in a black choir. I heard some pretty harsh, jarring things, but also some compassionate comments that gave me insight into what Linnea had to cope with.

One answer I got was from people who could understand her because she may have identified her children's disability with that disenfranchisement of the black community. They had a similar kind of underscore of rejection. I thought that was good. But others saw her in a very racist light. One called her a name that was really disgusting.

→19   →19A   →20   →20A   S   M   K   F

→24   →24A   →25   →25A   →26

→29   →29A   →30   →30A   →31

My family is Southern anyway, from Kentucky. So I'm very well acquainted with Southern culture. The movie was shot pretty well in sequence. There was a certain amount of improvisation. Julie Christie came down to visit—and of course Bob put her in the movie. Same with Elliott Gould. Bob had also gotten every leading person in the city on the film. One night as we were watching the dailies, I said to him, "I hope we get out of town before they see this movie!" Southerners can have very thin skin, especially at that time.

Had you sung gospel before?

I was raised in a Baptist church by Southern parents. Even though I'm not a religious person now, I grew up in a black neighborhood, so I'm very familiar with gospel music and I love it. I knew I was able to use my background for *Nashville*—it was in my DNA. I related to all that for *Nashville*. And I studied sign language every day for three months. I had a USC student come to my house at eight o'clock every damn morning, knocking on that door to practice sign language. I enjoyed trying to learn it. It is a very beautiful experience, moving really. I memorized passages and things that I could use.

I had spent so much time with the kids, with their mother—particularly Jimmy's—that I knew Jimmy had that great swimming story, and I told his mother to have him tell it during the scene in the dining room with Ned [Beatty]. That kind of thing happened. Because Robert was so open to it, we had such freedom to experiment.

"Family" is a word that has been often used when describing the relationship between Altman and his closest collaborators. How would you describe life on the set of *Nashville*?

There was no set per se, of course. It was all over the place. There were so many actors milling around, townspeople. I used to call Bob the benign patriarch, because he was absolutely in charge

but in no way did you feel intimidated. You knew he was expecting something special from you, but he was never autocratic or imposing. He was just this comforting, solid, anchored presence. He was so unflappable and generous.

It's as if you could go on the playground and you could take the biggest chances. You could jump on the monkey bars, go too high on some apparatus that kids play on. You knew he wouldn't let you fall. You would never fall on your head! And there would be no drive-bys on that playground—nobody was going to drive by and shoot you. The innocence of your child felt safe. You just go on the playground to play.

I've heard an actress say to Bob, "What do you want in this scene?" Bob would say, "I don't know. Why don't you surprise me?" He never put a value on anything. It wasn't like he would say, "Oh, God, you were great," at the end of a scene. Because the next actress listening may be thinking, "He didn't say I was great." There is a certain childlike element here, where actors have to be open and available and want to feel like they are all uniformly loved.

Did Altman want you for weeks there because he was shooting in sequence or because he wanted to encourage some kind of a communal life?

I think he wanted for us to be a community—Karen Black came in for a week, but the rest of us were there for two months, in Nashville in the heat. Half the people lived in a motel and then the rest in this singles complex that had just been built. It didn't have any grass. It was all muddy; no planting had been done. All the furniture was like heavy Mediterranean furniture, and acrylic carpets. I had asthma and could not stand the smell of them. So at some point I went and took a room in a hotel. Bob called and said, "You get back in that complex." I had some money because I had been on *Laugh-In* and I had done lots of concerts. So I could afford to move into the hotel. But he told me I had to get back with the others into

that singles complex. And I did! I bought a bike and I went riding around all the time. It was a great summer.

Still, I'd start bitching to Bob about "How come we have to be here two months and Karen Black is only here for a week?" He said, "You're not supposed to like her." No matter what would happen, Bob would always find the rationale that would just make you stop dead.

Richard Nixon resigned during the shoot. And *Nashville* is a film that seems to reflect the confusion of the time.

Our country had gone through a really hard time. The assassinations—Bobby Kennedy and Martin Luther King—even though they were not that close in time to the movie, in terms of history we are talking about a very short time.

I felt that it was a very big part of the character and plot of the movie. That's kind of Altman's genius. He has all these disparate elements and sticks them together, and then suddenly they are all really springing from the same place. He was going to do a sequel to *Nashville*, and Linnea was going to be running for governor. It never got made. I regret that.

There were so many things about Bob. Everybody partied every night after shooting. Lots of people drinking and smoking pot. He had such capacity and appetite for everything. I would think, he's never going to be able to get to the set tomorrow. Of course, he would be there at five thirty in the morning, riding the crane already. It made him seem superhuman. Actually, Bob was so human; he was so available and unpretentious. That's what kind of tore my heart out. He just was so who he was. He was so *that* man.

Did he ever explain to you why he thought of you for the specific character?

No. When we did *Nashville*, there were twenty-four, twenty-five characters in it. I felt I could have played any four or five of these people. Then, as they started coming in, I began to see them in the context of the cast. I must be more right for this role of Linnea than I realized. One of his real gifts was casting. But he could also be serendipitous about it. The kids that were cast as my children—he only saw two kids, and those were the kids he hired!

Tell me a little bit about Doreen in *Short Cuts*.

Seymour Cassel was originally going to be my husband. I like him as a type. I thought I could relate to him. But I guess he had another obligation. So Bob said, "How do you feel about Tom Waits?" I said, "I love Tom. I'm mad for him." Now I can't even imagine anybody else. Although Seymour could have been that guy, too, Tom is just so eccentric. I just relate to him. I was very excited when I learned he was going to be my partner. I feel like Tom and I have some similar sensibilities. We didn't have to talk about much of anything. You know actors always do little things just between them. We had a little tattoo on our hands. He had half the heart and I had the other half, and we'd rub our hands together. I would kind of bump his hand, and we'd say to each other, "Until the wheels come off."

Every couple shot their main parts one week at a time. We were the first couple, and after those first dailies, Tom and I were so taken with ourselves, we told Bob we thought Doreen and Earl should have their own movie. The first night after shooting, Tom called me on the phone at home and pretended he's Earl driving around in the limo. The poet that he is, it was so great! I would just play along, as Doreen, and then I hung up and I thought, "Why didn't I have something to record that?" Then he called me the next night. I was just stunned. He did it for three nights in a row, and I never did get anything on tape.

In *The Player*, you have a very small scene. You were living nearby when they called you.

I lived in Los Feliz, and they were shooting nearby at Raleigh. I think Scotty [coproducer Scott Bushnell] called me and said, "Bob wants to know if you could come over tomorrow and shoot a scene with Scott Glenn." I said, "Yeah, OK. What is the scene about?" She said, "It's the dailies that they're going to show to the suits at the studio. You're both in a seedy hotel with the neon sign outside." I have a lot of old vintage clothes. I went in the costume room and found an old robe. We just went over and improvised it.

I read that both you and Meryl Streep worked out extensive backgrounds for the Johnson sisters in *A Prairie Home Companion*.

We talked a lot about stuff. I don't know if we wrote anything, but we had a whole backstory, absolutely.

I always had the first line in those dressing room scenes, and I always wanted to surprise Meryl; she loves to play, and she likes to be surprised. And she wants to be right in the moment. So I would always do something at the top of the scene that I knew Bob could cut. You'd never know what he'd keep.... I did that "forever spring" where you exercise your mouth, and Bob kept it in the scene. Once I put weights on my legs, and Meryl didn't know. When the scene started, I stood up and began doing leg lifts in Meryl's direction. The next take after that, Bob said, "OK, let's go again, but let's drop the weight." And he kind of chuckled. That's the only time that I can recall he put the lid on something. But he never made you feel like you were wasting his time. You never felt you shamed yourself or embarrassed yourself.

On *Prairie*, I studied singing every day for three months, because Meryl is a really good singer and I had to hold the harmony. I thought, "I'll never hold a harmony unless I just absolutely drill it into my soul." I studied and studied. But at some point I called Bob and said, "Bob, I don't think Rhonda is going to be a very good singer." To which he replied, "Well, if she can't sing, she can't sing." That's all there was to it. And

we played all that music live; we never dubbed anything!

On his sets you were always miked at all times, right?

Everybody was. You never knew what was being recorded. Like in *Nashville*, when we're kind of all out there, at that party in the yard. I had just visited my mother in Kentucky, and my aunt Eva had just been put in the hospital. She was my mother's sister. She had bumped her head getting out of the car—big hematoma. It was a very good Southern story. I was just recounting that while we were shooting, trying to keep up my end of the scene. And of course it got into the movie.

And there was a story I was trying to get into *Prairie*, when Meryl and I are singing onstage and she starts talking about what hard times we had: "Mama would be scrubbing the floor, and we'd just cheer her up by singing." And I'd say, "But we had a lot of good times." I had this whole family story that I adored and thought would be perfect for the scene. I'd say, "Remember when Mama would try to give us something to do, and she would boil an ear of corn and put it down on the floor and we'd all root around and eat it like pigs?" It is a story from my own family. My dad's mother died young, and there were many kids. His older sister had to take care of three or four little kids that were still left. That was one of her games. She would boil an ear of corn, put it on the floor of the kitchen, and they'd have to try to eat it with their arms behind, you know, like they were pigs. I heard Bob chuckle when I told that story. I was just sure it would get in the movie. But then it wasn't on film; the camera was floating somewhere else at that instant. It was only on audio. So that one didn't make it.

Do you have a favorite Altman scene?

In *Short Cuts*, I love when my daughter (Lili Taylor) comes in with those fish in a plastic bag and Doreen looks at them. She just says, "I haven't seen those in a long time." Sitting there smoking, watching Phil Donahue on TV. I don't know why I like it. It just has a reality to it.... That documentary sense is always in his heart somewhere, I think.

Anything that he left on the cutting-room floor that you were upset about?

Not that I would ever remember. But I recalled once being horrified at the dailies, on *Nashville*. It was the scene in the Exit Inn where I'm sitting in the back and the camera is floating between all those women and Keith Carradine. I thought my eyes had to really be seen to convey what I was feeling. When the dailies came up, I could see my eyes were a lot in shadow. I left the screening almost in tears. I thought this scene was the most important scene I had in the movie. It wasn't necessarily the case, but I felt that way. Don't forget, it's my first movie! Scotty called me over at the old apartment where I lived. Scotty had a lisp. She had kind of like a sympathetic ease when she'd call you and say, "What happened?" They were worried about me because I was visibly upset when I left the room. I felt I had failed the team. And I wanted to get home before I started crying. Scotty called and tried to commiserate: "The scene is really good; everybody thinks the scene is really good." She was trying to make me feel better. And she was right. It turned out to be a really good scene.

I was supposed to be in *Prêt-à-Porter*, and I backed out. That's just not good. I backed out because I was working on an animated television special for Edith Ann that wasn't finished, and I couldn't leave L.A. It was really tough. Even more because I was supposed to be in *Kansas City*, too, and somehow it never materialized. I felt like I was a bad relative who wasn't going to get invited to the family reunions for a while. I think with Bob that kind of loyalty was expected....

But, thankfully, I did get invited back. There was no one like him.

He was singular. There is no simple explanation. It's just him. Somewhere he had that ability—that fire, that ease and that ability. He was working on his next movie when he died.

I was told Meryl and I were both going to be in it. Meryl had lunch with him in New York just days before he died, and they were talking about the movie, *Hands on a Hard Body*. When Bob died, I felt overcome with loss that I would never see him again. Never work with him again. And none of us would ever see the movie he was planning.

NASH VILLE

BY
KATHRYN REED
ALTMAN

Nashville
1974

Bob shot *Nashville* during the summer in that Tennessee city. It was the hottest, most humid environment I have ever been in. He thought it was clever—and it was—for us to live in this really interesting log cabin 1–3 that this guy had bought and refurbished to the point that it was livable. It had a swimming pool that was like a big hole in a rock. Everything was very rustic and in keeping with the period. Bob actually used it in the film as the home of Henry Gibson's character, so they shot there a couple days, but the rest of the time we lived there. There was no air-conditioning, just fans, and it was so damned hot.

We were kind of on the outskirts of town. Everybody else lived in condominiums and apartments right in town. The production offices were in town at the Jack Spencer Motor Inn. We had several places in there for the production office, editing, and so forth. And we'd watch dailies there every night.

But our log cabin was in a residential neighborhood, because Bob's very insightful idea was to have barbecues every Sunday, the day off, and everybody would come. It was a big job, mostly mine, though I had help from Bob Eggenweiler and Tommy Thompson and others. It was a huge cast, with twenty-four main characters, and because Bob had that reputation already that actors loved him, they all got paid the same amount of money. But there were so many of them, and they all had different needs. Some of them were well-established actors like Keenan Wynn, Geraldine Chaplin, and Barbara Harris, and then there were a lot of newcomers. So his idea was that he would cook and be behind the barbecue, and they'd come to him and they would talk—so that

SUMMER IN "NASHVILLE"
LOG CABIN

he could really relate to each one of them separately. They felt comfortable enough in that environment. He didn't have time to sit in the office and see people. It was a good idea and it *obviously* worked, if you saw the movie.

These were really the first summer vacation jobs for Bobby, fourteen, and Stevie, sixteen, and Bob kind of said, "Choose your departments." Stevie went to observe and become part of the sound department, and Bobby went to the camera department. In the camera department were a couple of brothers, the Walsh brothers, who had grown up in the camera world. Their father was a cameraman. They really took Bobby under their wing, and that was a real summer of learning; he just locked right into that department and stayed there. Stevie, because he's a natural-born artist, later went into props and then ultimately production design.

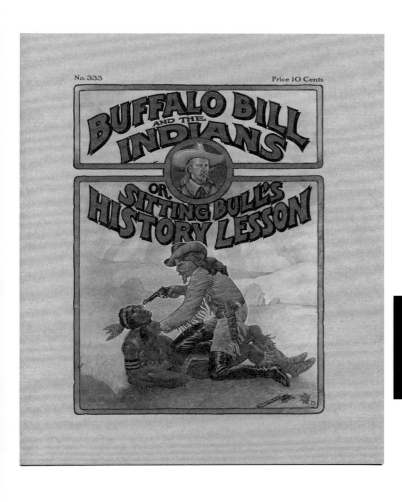

BUFFALO BILL AND THE INDIANS OR SITTING BULL'S HISTORY LESSON

4

THE

SEVENTIES

BY GIULIA
D'AGNOLO VALLAN   (PART 2)

Robert Altman's and Steven Spielberg's paths had indirectly crossed on *California Split*, and it would happen again in June 1975, as *Nashville* opened on the eleventh of the month and *Jaws* reached theaters nine days later. Altman's sprawling American mural, independently financed and conceived like a documentary, could not be more different from Spielberg's tightly structured Universal monster movie. With its unprecedented nine-hundred-theater release, Spielberg's great white shark proved to be a juggernaut at the box office, the first film ever to top the $100 million mark. It also set in motion the process that would once again change the type of films that the Hollywood studios were willing to make.

OPPOSITE Altman and Paul Newman (as William "Buffalo Bill" Cody) on the set of *Buffalo Bill and the Indians*, 1975.
LEFT Cover of promotional booklet and printed script for *Buffalo Bill and the Indians*, 1976.

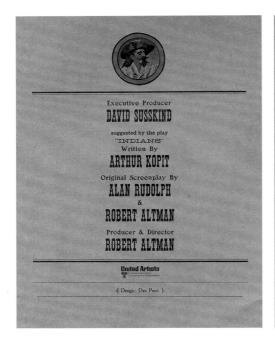

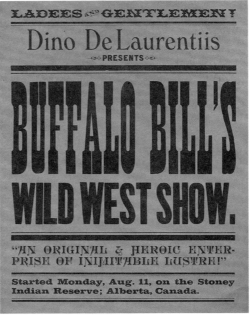

But things were great for Altman in 1975. *Nashville*'s critical and financial success made him a much-sought-after director, and his Lion's Gate was as active as ever. Following Francis Ford Coppola's example at American Zoetrope and that of other directors who were forming small, independent units such as the Directors Company (also founded by Coppola, together with Peter Bogdanovich and William Friedkin), Altman offered his name and his company to foster and shelter the creative freedom of other emerging directors. Within the next four years, he would produce Robert Benton's *The Late Show*, Robert M. Young's *Rich Kids*, and most notably *Welcome to L.A.* and *Remember My Name*, by his longtime collaborator and friend Alan Rudolph, who, from

his days as second assistant director on *The Long Goodbye*, had worked his way up to screenwriter of what was going to be Altman's next movie.

Among a wide variety of projects he was interested in making, Altman had his eye on two important adaptations: Kurt Vonnegut Jr.'s *Breakfast of Champions* and E. L. Doctorow's *Ragtime*, a book whose multiple story lines and blend of historical and fictional characters seemed designed for an Altman movie. The truth is that, for all that has been written and said about his open disregard for literal faithfulness to their work, writers—novelists, playwrights, screenwriters—were a key source of inspiration for the director's creative process all through his career.

Like *Ragtime*, the next film also turned out to be a blend of history and fiction, loosely inspired by Arthur Kopit's play *Indians*. With a script signed by both Altman and Rudolph, *Buffalo Bill and the Indians, or Sitting Bull's History Lesson* was financed by the powerful Italian producer Dino De Laurentiis, who must have loved the combination offered by a hot new American auteur (he would later promote David Lynch's career) and two great Hollywood stars, Paul Newman and Burt Lancaster. Happy for once to be offered a chance to play against type, Newman was cast as the pompous, drunken, cheating, and possibly sexually impotent William F. Cody, aka Buffalo Bill, a man who could not even live up to the myth he had manufactured of himself. Lancaster was Ned Buntline, the dime novelist who first made Buffalo Bill's fame and fortune and then, disillusioned, took it apart.

With its $6 million budget, *Buffalo Bill and the Indians* was Altman's most expensive movie to date. Shot in Calgary against a backdrop of beautiful snowcapped mountains, with lovely production design and elaborate western costumes, it brought together again Altman's well-oiled technical crew and many of his by-then regular actors and collaborators.

Beyond De Laurentiis's request that Altman deliver "a lot of action scenes," it is not known exactly what he expected from the film. It certainly was not Altman's Wild West, tightly enclosed in a circus ring (reds, yellow, and blacks were highlighted in the photography by Paul Lohmann; long lenses were used even on wide shots, to flatten the images for a more cartoonish look). Sitting Bull and the story of the Indians were the focus of Kopit's play. Altman's interest lay more in Buffalo Bill and the opportunity that the western folk hero gave him to riff about some of his recurring themes: America's fascination with fame, its bogusness, the marriage of politics and entertainment, empty leaders. "Truth is whatever gets the loudest applause," says Buffalo Bill in his rambling monologue toward the end of the film. It could have been Altman himself talking.

ROBERT ALTMAN MEMORIAL TRIBUTE

E. L. DOCTOROW

I met Robert Altman in 1975. As the director of *Nashville*, he was Sam Cohn's and Dino De Laurentiis's choice to direct the film of *Ragtime*. I didn't need to be persuaded. Bob was innovative and by nature irreverent, just the man for the job. Smooth talking with that clear, Midwestern twang, that Kansas City intonation. (Pasta was "passta.") And he had been around. He'd fought his way up from TV, paid his dues, as we used to say. Clearly he was the driven sort of self-governed obsessive who was incapable of making "product." So I agreed to write the *Ragtime* screenplay for him.

Of course, I was aware of his working methods, I knew that he tended to be—how shall I put this?—somewhat casual in his attention to a script. He was improvisational: He offered his actors an unprecedented freedom, calling upon them, very often to their own discomfort, to ad lib their scenes, deriving their lines from the roles in which they had immersed themselves rather than in obedience to memorized sentences. Always he wanted what was more real. A corollary of all this was his belief that he could outthink any writer he worked with. Knowing this, I wrote a humongous, 410-page *Ragtime* screenplay, on the theory that whatever Robert Altman did to get out of my book, he'd still be in it.

I was astonished when he told me he loved every scene and declared he would film the whole 410 pages. He would make two three-hour theatrical films and shoot another four hours of film to be added for a ten-hour serialized TV presentation. He had this prophetic vision of an extended, outsize movie. This was before the concept of the miniseries had been articulated by anyone. And while it is true that Bob's relations with De Laurentiis deteriorated during the filming of *Buffalo Bill and the Indians*, I think it was his decision to do *Ragtime* in epic scale that tipped the balance and terrified the producer—who, unsympathetic to visionaries generally, and possibly thinking he was dealing with a madman, removed Bob from the film.

Sam and I went to see De Laurentiis and told him he had made a terrible mistake. But *Buffalo Bill and the Indians* had not gone according to Dino's expectations. He felt betrayed, and he was unforgiving. So that was that, and what was eventually made was neither Bob's film nor a film that was based on a screenplay of mine.

Prior to the big break, my wife, Helen, and I went up to the Stoney reservation in western Canada, where Bob was filming his *Buffalo Bill*. We went there to

---

E. L. DOCTOROW is the celebrated author of such historical fiction works as *Ragtime* (1975) and *Billy Bathgate* (1989). He had a cameo appearance as President Grover Cleveland's adviser in Altman's *Buffalo Bill and the Indians* (1976).

PORTRAIT OF THREE ITALIANS IN A LINA WERTMULLER MOVIE

January 25, 1976

confer about the *Ragtime* film and make plans. But being Bob, he quickly sent us to costume and makeup, and for a week we were cameo players in *Buffalo Bill*. I thought I did pretty well, and that the Academy should start a new category for the Oscars: Best Supporting Author.

Bob liked to have people around him, and people liked to be around him. It was rare that I didn't see him at the center of his solar system. He brought in everyone, cast and crew, to watch the dailies. It was all very communal. At a certain point, one smoky evening, I asked Robert Altman if he had ever read my first novel, *Welcome to Hard Times*. I had been waiting to ask him that because, long before I met him, I had seen *McCabe & Mrs. Miller*, and I had felt that this director, whoever he was, had to have read my book in order to have done what he had done with this movie. But, of course, I wasn't sure and knew myself to be vulnerable to the occupational paranoia of writers. Alt-

man said, "Not only did I read *Welcome to Hard Times*, I stole everything I could from it!" At that moment my fondness for him was made fast.

For some reason I always thought that given our mutual disappointment regarding *Ragtime*, we would get together one day for another project, but we never did. I find it hard to believe that anything, even death, could stop Bob Altman from making movies. Over the years I never looked at any of his films without being intrigued, even with the lesser, more self-indulgent ones. They all have his mark, that fervent love of the medium....So that if you walked in on one of his movies without knowing what it was, you'd know immediately, from the demand made on the audience, whose it was. His personality, his being, is in every frame of every film he ever made. When Helen and I went to that *Buffalo Bill* shoot in Canada, Bob greeted us on the set. He was animated, in high spirits. "Welcome to my world!" he said,

his arms outstretched, a big smile on his face. "Welcome to my world." And so it was, and so it will be.

ABOVE Left to right: Kurt Vonnegut Jr., Robert Altman, and E. L. Doctorow in a photo taken by Jill Krementz, titled by Vonnegut. After *Nashville*, Altman tried to bring to the screen Vonnegut's *Breakfast of Champions* and Doctorow's *Ragtime*. Both films ended up being made by other directors. The two novelists regretted not having had the chance to see their work through Altman's eyes. In fact, contrary to the popular myth that writers dreaded him, they were both very eager to accept the challenge.

127

Buffalo Bill is a very playful film. Its visual richness proved that Altman could handle scale and a bigger budget. The film won the Golden Bear at the Berlin Film Festival in 1976, but De Laurentiis did not like it. In fact, his relationship with Altman had deteriorated so much that he fired the director from *Ragtime*. It probably did not help the Doctorow-scripted project that Altman wanted to make the film in two three-hour parts. It ended up being directed by Milos Forman, in a version much less adventurous than Altman and Doctorow had hoped for. *Breakfast of Champions* fell through as well (although Alan Rudolph would get to make it in 1999).

Buffalo Bill's mixed critical reception and underperformance at the box office did not seem to compromise Altman's standing with the studios, at least with Twentieth Century Fox, run at that time by Alan Ladd Jr. "Laddie" liked Altman's originality and would finance his next five movies over a four-year span.

The first, *3 Women*, is one of Altman's most beautiful-looking and personal films. Sprouting from an actual dream and from a painting of three women that the director had made in the sixties, it taps into that same liquid, mysterious quality that had set *Images* apart from the rest of his work. Like *Images,* it shows Altman's interest in Ingmar Bergman's oeuvre, although its setting is deeply American: a mineral spa and an Old West–themed shooting range in the midst of the Palm Springs desert, whose pinks, purples, and yellows

TOP LEFT A brochure for Coffee's Hotel, the primary location used for *3 Women*.
TOP RIGHT Sissy Spacek and Alan Rudolph on the set of *3 Women*, 1976.
BOTTOM LEFT Altman, assistant director Tommy Thompson, Shelley Duvall (as Millie Lammoreaux), and Sissy Spacek (as Pinky Rose) on the set of *3 Women*.

OPPOSITE
Artwork for *3 Women* created from Millie's diaries, written by Shelley Duvall and illustrated with photos by Jean Pagliuso. Designed by Dan Perri.

Robert Altman's
3 Women

Shelley Duvall

Sissy Spacek

Janice Rule

Sept 19 Thursday

i have a new roomate. Of all people its pinky, the new girl at work. she's a strange person but its better than waiting around for some fat nurse to answer the notice.

on the way home i took her to Dodge City for a beer. all the guys were riding dirt bikes out in back so we didn't stay long. Edgar pulled one of his tricks on pinky. she fell for it til the end. she sure doesn't have much to her name, but she does have a sewing machine and maybe she'll make me a new dress.

jan haglund

design/Dan Perri

we got bombed last night and i turned into a "pinching bug". it was so much fun i laughed till I cried. I chased Edgar a half a block before I caught him and when I did, boy did I pinch

Sept 12

i have the strangest dreams. some of them are wierd like my mother coming into my room with all those red tomatoes but in this one Willie came into my room with all her paintbrushes and little jars of color. i must have seen her that way a million times but this time she asked me to paint. i don't even like her stuff. she's wocked all right but i know she's harmless.

i have a new roomate. Of all people its pinky, the new girl at work. she's a strange person but its better than waiting around for some

129

THREE WOMEN

The following treatment should be considered as a structural outline for
the film, Three Women. It can be considered accurate in terms of casting,
budgeting and scheduling. All the scenes that will be shot are indicated here
and the "story" will closely follow this treatment. The dialogue written here,
may or may not be the dialogue used in the film and is intended only to indicate
a direction to be taken. In other words, I urge you not to judge the 'literary'
quality of the finished film by the way it appears on these pages. It is my
intention to write continually as the film progresses in order to take full
advantage of the input of the actors and other creative persons involved with
the production. What will be missing in this treatment will be the color,
mood and tone of the film. Suspense and mystery will always be the main feeling.
The audience should be frightened by the developments of the action and this
shall be stressed at all times.

CAST

Millie Lammoreaux . . . . Shelly Duval
Pinky Rose . . . . Sissy Spacek
Willie . . . . Janice Rule

OPPOSITE
TOP LEFT Treatment for
Altman's *3 Women*.
TOP RIGHT The lives of
Millie and Pinky, played
by Shelley Duvall and
Sissy Spacek, intersect
in *3 Women*.
BOTTOM Artist Bodhi Wind
created the murals used in
3 Women.

TOP Cast portrait for
A Wedding.
BOTTOM *Film Comment* cover
featuring *A Wedding*, 1978.

would end up dominating the entire palette of the film, down to the set design and costumes. As the title says, it is a story about three women: Millie (Shelley Duvall) and Pinky (Sissy Spacek, whom Altman had noticed in Alan Rudolph's *Welcome to L.A.*) are attendants at the Desert Hot Springs spa, where they help older patients in and out of mineral baths. The first is self-absorbed and self-assured to the point of delusion. The second, meek and inexperienced, appears smitten by her friend's poise. Willie (Janice Rule) paints eerie creatures on the bottom of a swimming pool, and she is pregnant. The main male character of the film is her husband, Edgar (Robert Fortier). According to Altman, amid this strange triangle of female shifting identities, the macho, boozing, womanizing Edgar is sort of a "last man on earth."

Altman, who had in mind a vague plot about identity theft, started the film with little more than a thirty-page outline. The actual details of most scenes, he would recount later, were eventually worked out right on the set at the time of shooting. Continuing her collaboration with Altman and the tradition that his actors contribute as much as possible to their characters, Shelley Duvall wrote all of Millie's diary entries, letters, and cooking recipes.

Duvall won the Best Actress Award at the 1977 Cannes Film Festival, in May, and Spacek was awarded Best Supporting Actress by the New York Film Critics Circle in the fall.

Altman followed with another "personal" movie. Legend has it that *A Wedding* was born of a total whim, a facetious answer the director shot back at a reporter when asked on the *Buffalo Bill* set about his next project: "I will film a wedding." He would later recall, however, that the subconscious origin of the movie most likely lay in a specific Altman family photograph, an ensemble picture portrait taken at his Aunt Pauline's marriage. The director, who must have been about five years old, was the ring bearer.

Shot in an Illinois mansion with a huge, typically Altmanesque cast made up of his regulars, TV stars untested on the big screen, movie stars from Europe (Vittorio Gassman) and even the Hollywood silent era (Lillian Gish), *A Wedding* is the incarnation of Altman's concept of filmmaking as a "family" process (both behind and in front of the camera) at its most literal.

He doubled the number of characters he had in *Nashville*, going from twenty-four to forty-eight. Some of them, he said, had been inspired by relatives of his. But aside from the individual characterizations, the social milieu of the film, as well as the specifically Midwestern new-old money marriage and clashes, suggests Altman's own upbringing.

131

With the exception of *Countdown*, science fiction had never been high on the list of Altman's interests. Although *Quintet* is set in some kind of post-nuclear ice age future, he has instead described it as a Western, a samurai adventure, and, most of all, a fairy tale. He also acknowledged that the mood of the film may have been affected by the fact that both his parents had died within a few years before the making of what remains his bleakest, most hermetic work.

Altman had asked his agent at the time, Sam Cohn, to approach British-born Canadian writer Lionel Chetwynd (*The Apprenticeship of Duddy Kravitz*) to work on an original idea that came to him as a dream as well as a merchandising concept. The notion centered on a Monopoly-like board game in which five players plus a "puppeteer" try to kill one another. The backdrop is a planet so hopeless, frozen, and desolate that betting one's life for no apparent reason is all that is left to the survivors. Chetwynd wrote the basis for the script, which would eventually be credited to Altman, Patricia Resnick, and Altman's childhood friend Frank Barhydt Jr. (son of his old Calvin boss). Lion's Gate patented the board game, called Quintet, which the director himself had designed in detail, down to the rough, stylized tokens that identify the players. The abandoned Expo 67 complex in Montreal provided the ideal location for the otherworldly, sepulchral premise. The photography emphasized white on whites. Scott Bushnell's costumes had a vaguely medieval touch.

Besides Paul Newman, who comes to town at the beginning of the film and leaves it at the end like a lone Western gunfighter, Altman cast European stars Vittorio Gassman, Fernando Rey, Brigitte Fossey, and Bergman regular Bibi Andersson—all speaking in English but maintaining their own accents.

As in *A Wedding*, the diversity and richness of the cast reflected not only Altman's genius at this particular part of the filmmaking process, but also his great clout in international art-house circles. It also spoke of his canniness as a producer. It is common today that A-list stars cut their fees in order to work on smaller independent projects, thereby helping those films get made. In the early to mid-seventies, Altman would be one of the first independent filmmakers who understood that process and used it freely to his advantage.

Casting was definitely at the center of *A Perfect Couple*, one of Altman's more inherently sentimental films, one of his least seen, and his second musical. Marta Heflin and Paul Dooley, whose work Altman had loved in *A Wedding*,

132

play the couple of the title, Sheila Shea and Alex Theodopoulos. They are an improbable match from their very first encounter, arranged through the services of a computer dating agency called Great Expectations. It happens at the Hollywood Bowl and is blessed by torrential rain and a Cadillac malfunctioning in every possible way. Alex and Sheila have in common music and a little awkwardness about them, but little else. He comes from a wealthy, conservative Greek family of classical musicians, while she is a backup singer in a rock-and-roll band and lives in a communal loft with her fellow band members. As in *A Wedding*, one can see some autobiographical projection woven into the film's thread. But the touch is lighter, more tender, the satire (with the exception of the domineering Theodopoulos patriarch) less high-pitched. Altman thereby pays tribute to romantic love and music; he also finds a way to make a little fun of certain sixties clichés, such as the free-spirited artistic commune of Sheila's friends. The band of the film, Keepin' 'Em off the Streets, had its origin virtually within Lion's Gate: It was assembled by longtime Altman collaborator Allan Nicholls.

Broader in humor and more traditionally Altmanesque (multiple characters, big cast, a plot dense with political satire), *HealtH* would be the last of the director's string of films at Twentieth Century Fox. Adlai Stevenson (whose presidential candidacies Altman had actively championed in fifties) and Dwight Eisenhower are represented in the guise of, respectively, Glenda Jackson's and Lauren Bacall's characters, Isabella Garnell and Esther Brill, bitter rivals in the run for the presidency of a national organization of nutrition cultists. With the health food craze in full bloom, Altman and Frank Barhydt Jr. set the whole film during a convention staged against the bright pastel colors of the Don CeSar Hotel in St. Petersburg, Florida. By the time shooting was finished, however, Alan Ladd Jr. had left Fox and the studio was under new management. Following the disappointing critical and box-office response to the director's last three films, *HealtH* was given a tiny and long-delayed release, and it disappeared quickly.

ALTMAN AFTER HOURS

ALAN RUDOLPH

OPPOSITE Contact sheet of on-set photos from *Welcome to L.A.,* 1976, a film directed by Alan Rudolph and produced by Altman. Top left, Keith Carradine (as Carroll Barber) at the piano; at right, Rudolph behind the camera.

Human experience is different for each human. The outside defines the inside, and the reverse. The best of it, for me, seems to have a proper dose of wisdom and everlasting abracadabra. For instance, taking flight on Robert Altman's magic film carpet in the 1970s personally ranks up there. High.

While living out his version of American filmmaking, Robert Altman was also influencing every aspect of it. Including the bigger picture. That takes some doing. True, and true to himself, on-screen or off, Bob had the dazzle to back his razzle.

Altman's alchemy reshaped film performance, narrative, technique. Film language, vocabulary, grammar meta-

morphosed as Bob made the process his. If he needed a new approach or pioneering equipment, he'd invent it. If there were money, he'd spend it. If not, he'd outsmart it. And he was shrewdly smart. He knew the luster of gold wasn't exclusive to the gold mine. Bob could see through facades and hear into fuzzy fringes.

Altman created top-quality original work in great volume for a very long time. In fact, all the time he had. When his inspiration reached the screen, it was multilayered. At the source it was basic. Bob had one mission in life. All else sprang from it. Feed the ferocious lion at the gate. Serve the authentic artist-beast that is Robert Altman. Paint your next canvas as the most essential

since the last one. Take no prisoners, no regrets, no sugar-coating, no saccharine. But plenty of voyagers and a bounty of fun. Entertain and shock them with your dreams, your suspicions. Your jokes for the human comedy. Revel as they giggle and give in. Then do it all over again. One continuous reverie. That's the goal, your job. Keep a-goin'.

Bob knew who he was, what he had, and what he had to do. His life was his obligation. He basically told me as much one night after dailies during the first week of shooting *Welcome to L.A.* in 1975. This was Altman's initial venture into producing someone else's work. I had been his assistant director on *The Long Goodbye, California Split,* and *Nashville,* then screenwriter on *Buffalo Bill and the Indians, or Sitting Bull's History Lesson.* Life changers all. But this was a singular thrill. My own film. And Robert Altman was the producer. America's most important film artist had confidence in

---

ALAN RUDOLPH is a filmmaker who, early in his career, worked as an assistant director on Altman's *The Long Goodbye* (1973), *California Split* (1974), and *Nashville* (1975). He also wrote the screenplay for *Buffalo Bill and the Indians* (1976). Rudolph went on to be a successful director of independent films such as *Mrs. Parker and the Vicious Circle* (1994) and *Afterglow* (1997). His most recent film was *The Secret Lives of Dentists* (2002).

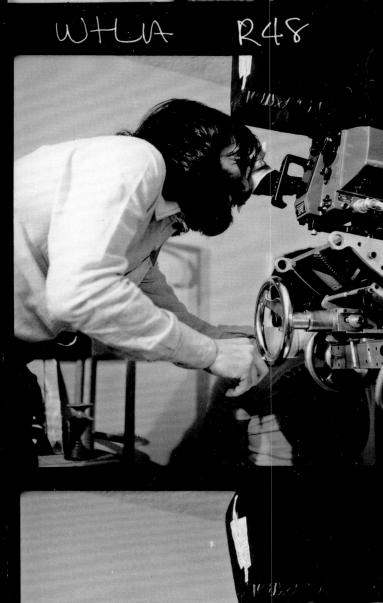

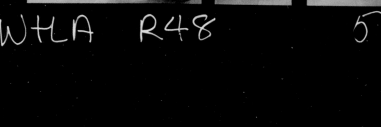

my confidence. My only instructions were to keep the budget very low and "don't make a chase movie."

Bob's unique shine was powerfully bright and provocative, the most stimulating irreverence and clever humor. He could have sold his tongue or smile. His magnetism and poise were real, his interest genuine, his grace the wicked kind, elusive yet correct. He lifted those around him, suffered neither fools nor suited bosses. Battles were legion and legendary. Money and Pain. Yet Robert Altman could not be defeated. Would not. He won the war in life and on film, essentially the same thing for him. His creations were exactly his, and as they always would be.

Being around Bob was a steady, heady buzz. Spellbinding, elevating, irresponsible. Ideas lit up like news from the labyrinth. If an inspiration was yours and added another piece to his puzzle, Bob declared it "the best thing I ever heard in my entire life." And for that moment it felt so.

Every now and again, provoked or betrayed, slow to burn until scorching,

Robert Altman could also display intimidating displeasure.

In 1971, before American independent film was a brand, I was first assistant director on studio shooting sets, envisioning my own European-style films, something I thought wasn't being done in Hollywood. Times were turbulent, movies were petrified, cash was scarce as always. I began writing for myself.

Then I received a call from Robert Altman's Lion's Gate Films, a name he later sold to help finance his next sand castle. They wanted to arrange a meeting as soon as possible for an assistant director. I politely explained I no longer worked in that function. I could have said I was scaling Everest or starting a jail term. "Bob wants to meet you," was the only response. Then a secretive, "You won't regret it." That part intrigued me. That and my mother's maiden name is Altman—no relation.

Back then, in Westwood, California, Robert Altman's creative playground and production office was a Tudor-style building surrounding a hidden courtyard. I first saw Altman seated behind

an imposing desk, beneath mobiles of *M*A*S*H* helicopters, playing solitaire with tarot cards. He was large, experienced, full of mystery. His eyes flashed a hint of X-ray vision as he looked up to stare. I'd already worked with some stars, a few successful studio-system directors, quasi-rebel or two. But I had never encountered anyone with Bob's daunting and aware presence. His playful ease, lack of airs. Seen nothing approaching his smart individualist operation, beyond the scope of my dreams. This was a personal filmmaking universe, and Robert Altman was its big bang. He had mashed the planet and wanted more.

I was offered *The Long Goodbye* as second assistant director, years and steps back for me. My aspirations weren't of much interest to Altman. I was told jobs and titles blurred here. I asked for the weekend to consider, something to which Bob was clearly unaccustomed. He instructed me to see *McCabe & Mrs. Miller*, opening the same day. I did so that evening, Friday. Then again Saturday afternoon. And Saturday night. Twice more Sunday. I watched the film five times but had never seen anything like it. Monday morning I was slumped inside my car waiting for Lion's Gate to open. With Robert Altman seeing the light, I was ready to dig the tunnel.

A few years later, between setups on the *Nashville* set, casually munching a sandwich, Bob mentioned the possibility of me directing something in the future. Then he walked away. Altman's hole cards were always hidden; his greatest gift was himself, how he reacted to human behavior. He didn't teach. He simply was. And you learned. Bob trusted his instincts and the gamble of it all to carry him where he needed to go with a minimum of stress.

I felt I could pull whatever-it-was off without disappointing Bob. He galvanized my self-assurance. I knew that Bob was eager to pay for staff and overhead on someone else's dime. So smiles all around. Until the first week of shooting— the only time in our relationship that Altman was angry with me to my face. And he was rather fucking steamed.

It's a rare thing and big deal

ABOVE Photo from the set of *The Long Goodbye* in Los Angeles, 1972. From left: dolly grip Harry Rez, Altman's son Matthew, cinematographer Vilmos Zsigmond, and Altman.

to have another person, let alone an acknowledged ace, zoom into your life and do the old "insight-out." Yet this could happen to almost anybody Altman engaged, certainly any persona working with him. Casually, in simple language—a relaxed word or thought from Bob could zing straight to the axiom of any matter, sending you back to your starting point of view with new illumination.

Each night after dailies during the first week of *Welcome to L.A.*, I entered the lion's den across the courtyard from the converted-garage screening room. In his office, both glazed, Robert Altman would evaluate my film to me. As usual there was immense reward in what Bob said, inspiration, support. But immediately it seemed we were viewing this expedition through different portholes.

Fellini once told Altman that raw dailies made the best films. For his own films' nightly viewings, Bob would reward a simpatico audience with egalitarian festivity. Food, drink, everyone rooting for everyone else, comments welcome. Regardless of what else was around, the most potent smoke always came from the heat on screen. Each take was alive and real, no two alike. Yesterday's magic served to intensify today's riches and tomorrow's opportunities. You couldn't wait to get back to the set. Bob made actors feel there were no mistakes for them to make. He read a character's mind, not the script. Robert Altman's films are among the best ever made. They will keep film history honest for a very long time. They are also reminders of the daily thrill it was to make them.

By the end of the first week of *Welcome*, it was evident that Altman the producer was different than the other Altman. He viewed rushes alone in the afternoon while we were still shooting and then waited in his office as we watched that night.

One thing was evident from the outset. Though proudly, mightily influenced by Robert Altman, my signature was definitely not his. Nor could it be. Nor was it trying. Which was the point.

By the end of our dailies, Bob would appear to laud everyone as only

he could. He was genuinely pleased with the work we were doing, especially the actors. Everyone's spirits were elevated as people lingered in the courtyard for just one more. Later that late night, Bob told me what he didn't like. The physical work was fine, but why was something interpreted this way and not that? Why this moment, or that approach? After seeing just one day's worth of film, the first day, I was defensive about preferences and defining choices large and small. Choices I really liked. The rookie versus the titleholder. There was no bullying, but it was unexpected, rattling. Yet oddly reassuring: knowing I felt so positively from the start. Might that have been Bob's purpose? Day two, same routine. Lurking inside praise was contrarian penalty. And I was accused of shooting scenes not in the script. From Robert Altman. I savored the praise part.

By day three, the set was safe haven for my mental picture. But Altman would phone wherever we were with criticism that just couldn't wait. The most vital filmmaker I would ever meet, a true American master, my boss and friend, was constantly furious. Once while we were rolling on an extended single-shot scene through an empty house, I darted from behind the camera to grab a ringing telephone and save the continuing take. As actors disappeared down a hallway, Bob was on the other end of the phone to chew my ass for something he just saw in dailies: a lack of scuff marks on shoe soles propped on a salesman's desk (my choice to indicate the guy never went anywhere). I endured Bob's rant until I heard the final line of dialogue from the scene ongoing without me around the corner. "Cut. Print."

I had to avoid my producer. Yet I always wanted to hear from him. A heavy shadow from any angle. Friday's dailies were really good, best of the week. Afterward, from the courtyard, through night mist, I saw Bob laughing inside his office, silhouetted in the doorway, smoke curling from his cupped palm, in spirited conversation. This was a great image for every possible reason. I was the luckiest clown in filmland.

Bob wanted to know why we hadn't spoken in a day. So I told him. I reminded him that not only was he my producer, but also he was who he was. Everything he said had huge impact on the work and on me. And much of what he'd been saying was hard to take. Things he would never tolerate for himself. Or that I could change had I wanted. Sensibilities. The only way I could withstand the force of it was by limiting contact with him.

Bob stayed silent for a pull of eternity, that penetrating stare. I could feel the lava bubbling, anticipated flares. Instead, calmly, warmly, Altman-ly, "You're right," he said. "I've been an asshole, because those are the only kind of producers I know." Then he added something I still ponder: "And because I have an imperial obligation to myself." From that moment forward, Robert Altman became the most supportive producer imaginable.

Bob and I were comrades over four decades, someone I loved and treasured. He produced five of my films, a brilliant collaborator, present if needed, away if not. In fact, the less Altman was bothered, the happier he was. Immeasurable value in my life came from either side of the lens during our friendship, which is still very much alive. Separate venues have not added distance. Altman's signal remains strong, his ink indelible.

Great artists never change. They lead the way. The torch gets passed, the message out, the influence permanent. They are essential to the rest of us for their truthful answers to difficult questions. And for their mysterious selves.

For his expansive, courageous, stimulating, humane existence, to the stars and back, Robert Altman will always be his art.

BUFFALO BILL AND THE INDIANS, OR SITTING BULL'S HISTORY LESSON

Photo of Paul Newman on horseback battling the Indians on the set.

OPPOSITE ABOVE Photos of Wild West show banners.
OPPOSITE BELOW Photo of the cast of Buffalo Bill and the Indians, including Paul Newman (as Buffalo Bill), Harvey Keitel (as The Relative),
Kevin McCarthy (as The Publicist), Pat McCormick (as President Grover Cleveland), and Frank Kaquitts (as Sitting Bull).
The Native American extras came from the Stoney Indian Reserve, and the cowboy extra came from the Calgary Stampede rodeo.

3 WOMEN

THIS SPREAD Personalities blend together in the most beautiful, mysterious, and chilling of Altman's "women" films. A vampire story without the fangs, it was inspired by a dream. With Sissy Spacek as Pinky Rose and Shelley Duvall as Millie Lammoreuax.

Still of Shelley Duvall as Millie Lammoreaux.
OPPOSITE Contact sheet of photos of Spacek and Duvall drinking a beer on the set.

→12   →12A   →13   →13A   →14

KODAK SAFETY FILM 5063   KODAK SAFETY FILM 50

063   →17   →17A   →18   →18A KODAK SAFETY   →19

KODAK SAFETY FILM 5063

ETY FILM 5063   →22   →22A   →23   →23A   →24

KODAK SAFETY FILM 5063   KOD

28   29

Robert Fortier (as Edgar Hart) and Sissy Spacek (as Pinky Rose).
OPPOSITE Altman on the set of *3 Women* at the Desert Hot Springs spa.

Vittorio Gassman (as father of the groom Luigi Corelli) and Amy Stryker (as bride Muffin Brenner) on the set. OPPOSITE Altman and Geraldine Chaplin (as wedding planner Rita Billingsley).

PROD. "A WEDDING" #C17
CAM. C. ROSHER DIR. R. ALTMAN
DAY ☐ DATE 6-17-77
SCENE   TAKE
4 NT

OPPOSITE TOP Carol Burnett (as mother of the bride Tulip Brenner).
OPPOSITE BELOW Amy Stryker (as Muffin Brenner).
THIS PAGE Altman, Amy Stryker, and Paul Dooley (as Snooks Brenner).

QUINTET

Quintet was shot on location in Canada during the winter.
OPPOSITE TOP Still of Paul Newman (as Essex).
OPPOSITE BOTTOM Altman and Paul Newman.

Stills of the band Keepin' 'Em off the Streets. The band was created by the film's cowriter, Allan F. Nicholls. OPPOSITE: Marta Heflin (as Sheila Shea) and Paul Dooley (as Alex Theodopoulos).

1980

HEALTH

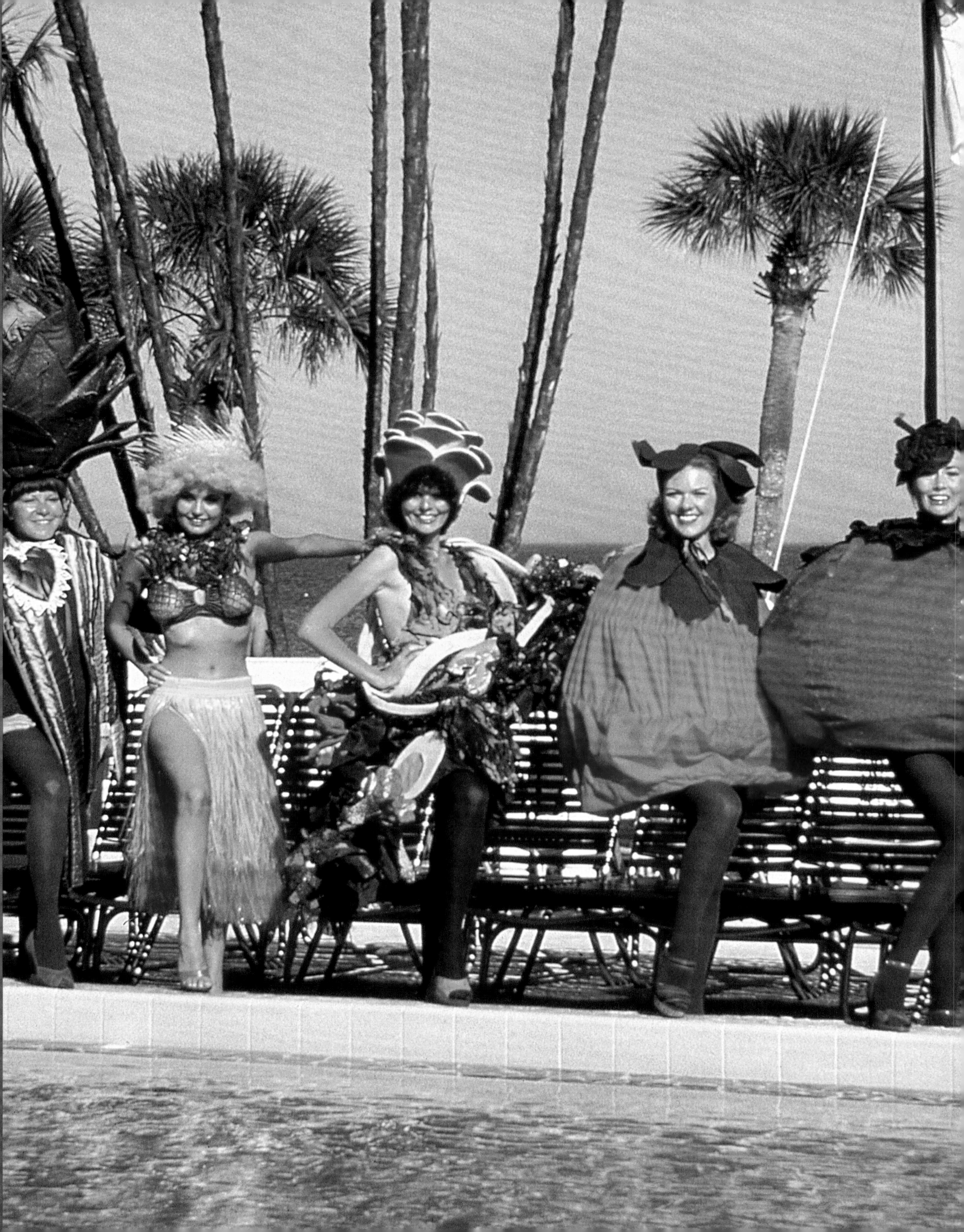

OPPOSITE Scene from *HealtH*.
ABOVE Lauren Bacall (as Esther Brill) and Glenda Jackson (as Isabella Garnell) being interviewed by Dick Cavett.
THIS PAGE Campaign stickers from the political satire *HealtH*.

3 Women
1975

1 Bob conceived of *3 Women* while I was in the hospital. I had to stay there quite a while, about two or three weeks, because they couldn't figure out what was wrong with me. They finally found an ulcer that was very, very deep. I guess I had buried my stress very, very deep. It was touch-and-go there for a while—a scary time. While I was there, Bob came to visit me on his way to a meeting. He told me about a dream he had had. He had gone to bed the night before, and then Matthew got into bed with him. He was aware of Matthew in the bed because there was sand in the sheets from Matthew coming up from the beach. Bob dreamed a lot and dreams were very important to him; he always wanted to discuss them in great detail, and he always asked me about mine. He was *fascinated* with dreams and twins and things. So he had this dream, and he woke up and wrote it down so he wouldn't forget it, and then he went back to sleep. When he woke up in the morning, he realized that he had dreamed the *whole* thing: He had *not* woken up in the middle of the night; he had *not* written anything down. He doesn't even have a pad and pencil by his bed—never had. Never wrote down dreams, ever. So he dreamed that he had dreamed. A dream upon a dream. And he was on his way to Fox to pitch this idea that he had never written down to Alan Ladd Jr., who was always very supportive of Bob. So Bob signed that deal right then to do three films with "Laddie" for Fox. He ended up doing *3 Women*, *A Wedding*, and *Quintet*. The first was one of the two things that Bob actually wrote from scratch, the other being *Images*. I always think of *3 Women* as the daughter of *Images*. They're both so spooky.

Buffalo Bill
1975

2–4 We shot *Buffalo Bill* on the Stoney Indian Reservation outside Calgary, where we lived. Calgary was a really hot town, because in the summertime they have the famous rodeo there. We were in a hotel. It was like a Ramada Inn or something, except really tall. We were on the thirty-fifth floor, and there were just three suites. One was for us, one was for Paul Newman, and the other was for visiting dignitaries such as one of the producers, Dino De Laurentiis; Dick Cavett; Burt Lancaster; and David Susskind, another producer, and his wife, Joyce.

So we shot on this reservation, and a lot of the crew lived there. The Indians were wonderful to us. It was a very interesting location, as they all were.

Paul Newman was just full of practical jokes. That was his big thing. Apparently, he and Redford had established it on *Butch Cassidy and the Sundance Kid*. And Bob knew that. We had just met. Paul was very easy; he and Bob had a wonderful rapport. He always kidded Bob about the white wine we drank. Paul was a connoisseur of wine. His wife, Joanne Woodward, was very interested in ballet, and a big supporter of the New York City Ballet, and he'd talk about her and the ballet a lot. Then he would talk about famous wines and cheeses. He was really just the guy next door from Cleveland. Yet he kept tossing around these two names all the time, and I was too embarrassed to ask what they were. One was "Montrachet" and the other was "Baryshnikov." I didn't know whether they were wines or cheeses or what. I learned later, of course, that Baryshnikov was Mikhail Baryshnikov, the famous ballet dancer, and that Montrachet was a white wine—and also a cheese.

We used to drink a white wine called Soave Bolla, which I guess was a really cheap wine then. And Paul used to tease Bob about drinking "goat piss." So they started these jokes. Paul loved popcorn, which he later went on to make with Newman's Own. So the first day Bob filled

Paul's trailer to the brim with popcorn, like you open the door and popcorn comes out. That was Bob's joke. And then Paul pulled a joke on Bob that Bob never thought was very funny and never got over for most of his lifetime. The Indians or wardrobe or the mayor or someone had given Bob a beautiful pair of leather Indian-motif gloves with big cuffs, all beaded and with fringe yet practical to wear, sort of. And Paul *fried* them, I guess with Crisco or lard, and presented them to Bob at lunch—and Bob *really* didn't think that was funny. He tried to, but boy, he must have mentioned it about once or twice a year after that. That *really* got him.

It's like when they presented the Palme d'Or [for *M*A*S*H*] on the stage of the Palais des Festivals in Cannes. (There's a new one now, but it was the old one, with a lovely, old-fashioned theater.) Ingo Preminger, the producer, reached out, held it, and then walked off the stage with it. We never saw it again. It's supposed to go to the director, for the mise-en-scène, but Ingo just kept walking and kept the Palme d'Or. Bob never got over that one either. He'd laugh as he told the story—"And Ingo just walked right off!"—but I knew it was killing him. Same way with those gloves. But they had a nice rapport. Paul was a lovely guy.

The wrap party was at a restaurant with sprawling grounds a little bit out of town, and I remember John Considine, who was a member of the cast. They dressed him all up as a girl. And the whole thing was set up as a nightclub, with acts going on all evening. In the middle of it, John came over, dressed as a girl, and sat right on Paul's lap! Then a little later, with everyone there among the buffets and the waiters all dressed in cowboy attire, Paul made an announcement that he had a present for Robert Altman, and they brought in this present and put it on Bob's lap: It was a baby goat! Paul said, "Here's your wine supply for the rest of your life!"

Father and son fishing
1975

5 When Bob was a father, he was *all* father and completely dedicated to the family. He loved family life. He was enthusiastic about every holiday and birthday. He was a real family guy. He loved his kids, and he got huge kicks out of them. But when he was working, it was *all* work. He was kind and considerate of family, but work was really number one, which we all respected and honored.

1976

Oscar Night
"Nashville"

16

6–15 Here we are leaving for the Oscars. This is the courtyard of our first offices on Westwood Boulevard, called Lion's Gate. It's still there, that building. It's an English Tudor building. It was originally built with the concept that you lived over your wares, over your shop, so they're all two-story offices with circular iron staircases. We had one, then another, and another, breaking through as they became available. We just rented there through the years. It was a great place. It was unusual. Nobody else's offices had fireplaces and brick and iron and hardwood floors and great big rugs. It was extremely innovative and homey, and it made the actors who came there feel very comfortable. He never had a door to his office; it was always wide open from one room to the other. Bob was in his prime then, really hot.

Nashville had nominations for Best Director, Best Picture, Best Supporting Actress for both Lily Tomlin **13–15** and Ronee Blakley **7**, and Best Original Song—and we were beaten out by *One Flew Over the Cuckoo's Nest* on every level except for Best Song. That was the song Keith Carradine **10** (right) wrote, "I'm Easy." Everybody thought we were going to win, but who knew that Milos Forman would just wipe us out?

16–19 This would be our third Cannes Film Festival. We went for *3 Women,* which was in competition for the Palme d'Or, and we chartered a boat again.

The first time we had stayed at the new port, and this time we stayed in the old port on one side of the cove of Cannes, which is really picturesque and terrific. We could walk from our boat up the cobblestoned streets and stop at the various shops and restaurants. You know, it's usually balmy there in May, and the streets are jam-crammed at night. It's extremely festive. This time we took this boat called the *Pakeha*, with a crew from New Zealand. It was a wonderful boat, and we did lots of entertaining on it. We had friends in and out.

16 This is the press conference. Each film that is in competition has a day, and it starts with a screening in the morning followed by the press conference. The director and actors and so forth are on the panel up on the stage. I love the press conferences, especially in Cannes, because everyone is shouting questions in many languages and they are all translated into English. The same translator had been there every year we were there. I just loved him.

It was fascinating to sit there, with the picture being such an enigma anyway, and to have these people from all over the world ask questions, and then for Bob to answer them. It was fun, and you can tell Bob was having fun in this picture. I remember being very impressed, specifically at our first festival and consequently at all the rest, that Bob was always pushing his next project. People would start talking to Bob about his film, and then he'd immediately start talking about his next one.

17 Jean Pagliuso was one of the photographers on *3 Women* and *Thieves Like Us,* and she did some work on *Buffalo Bill*. She was around all through the seventies. She took some great pictures, of which this is one.

18 And here is Bob with an extremely young Francis Ford Coppola.

At that festival, Shelley Duvall was named Best Actress for *3 Women*. She had been in *Brewster McCloud*, *McCabe & Mrs. Miller*, *Thieves Like Us*, and *Nashville*. Then Bob wanted her to be in *A Wedding*. **19** She was still going with Paul Simon, which started here at Cannes, and he was kind of running the show. He apparently didn't want her to do it. And she didn't. But she went on to be the world's greatest Olive Oyl.

Bob got very distraught over how things were being handled or something; I wasn't really sure what. Whatever it was, he got pissed off and somehow kind of disappeared once we got into the theater for the awards. He couldn't get out without going by all the press, so we figured out later—though he never really admitted it—that he must have walked across the rooftops to get back down to the street and then to the boat. He was on the boat when we got back. He'd been in some kind of a real snit. I was hugely embarrassed, worried to death, and couldn't figure it out at the time. And I was there with Jean Pagliuso, Shelley Duvall, Lauren Hutton, Sissy Spacek, and all these other people we had been socializing with. Turns out that he was upset that Shelley and Sissy didn't both win the award, that it wasn't a tie.

A Wedding
1977

20–24 The location for *A Wedding* really stands out in my mind. It was summertime. It was one of Carol Burnett's first feature films. All the kids were around. Bob's dad, who had just remarried after having been a widower since 1974, visited. It was very special.

The location was in this very exclusive suburb of Chicago called Lake Forest. Matthew and Bobby and I flew from Los Angeles to Chicago with Carol, and she was very, very hot then. Her television show was popular, had been for years and still was—she was huge. I was so impressed with how she handled herself at the airport in terms of learning everyone's name from the skycaps on up. I remember talking to her about it, how she had developed that skill. She felt it was important. She is really a lovely, wonderful human being, whether she'd ever been a performer or a big star or not.

The cast and crew all stayed in Waukegan, Illinois, a town just north of Lake Forest. When I was growing up, the Jack Benny radio show was the big show of the week. And he was from Waukegan, Illinois! He used to talk about it, so I grew up hearing about Waukegan.

We stayed at this Ramada Inn. We also had some condos near there for families. Geraldine Chaplin's then-partner, the prominent Spanish director Carlos Saura, came over, and they had a little son, Shane, so they had a place. And it was Paul Dooley's first picture with Bob, and he was with his girlfriend, Margery Bond, whom Bob gave a little part to. Both places had big parking lots, and roller-skating was all the rage. And we all just roller-skated all the time—Geraldine, Lauren Hutton, Jean Pagliuso, everybody. A lot of good times. Bobby had his

eighteenth birthday party there. We celebrated it after dailies one night.

We kicked off the picture when everybody was arriving with a big Fourth of July party in a park that we took over. It was just a great time. And Bob had really locked in on how to handle his characters, his actors, in regard to the environment. It was terrific.

20 This is Bob being funny in the Episcopal church, where the opening shot of the picture was.

21 And this is the bride that he chose. When she came for her interview with him she had braces, but she said she'd be happy to have them removed—and he said, "Don't!"

22 Jean Pagliuso took this picture of Bob and Leonard Cohen when he visited the set. Bob had Margaret Ladd singing Leonard Cohen's "Bird on the Wire" as the closing song, and I found that way more interesting. We are great fans of Leonard. Bob scored *McCabe & Mrs. Miller* with songs from his first album, from 1968, simply called *Songs of Leonard Cohen*.

A Wedding, San Sebastian
1978

23 In 1978 we were invited to the San Sebastián Film Festival, in Spain, for Bob's film *A Wedding*. We had had the premiere in Chicago, since the picture was shot in Lake Forest. Then the PR tour took us to a lot of places—really a lot of great experiences, particularly the San Sebastián Film Festival. San Sebastián is practically right across the border from Biarritz, in France, and it's also within driving distance of the Spanish town of Bilbao, where the famous museum designed by Frank Gehry is now—I wish it had been there then! So we took this trip, and we took our two sons, Matthew and Bobby, who would have been approximately twelve and eighteen at the time. Geraldine Chaplin joined us there with Carlos Saura. This picture brings back so many memories of us as a family. Bob was sort of midway through his successful career. It was a very happy and exciting time. Afterward we went on to France and Italy to do even more promotion for *A Wedding*.

24

25

26

Joan, B. C., and Barbara Altman
1978

24 Bob was the oldest of three children. He had two sisters: Joan was just a few years younger; she married the director Richard Sarafian and became Joan Sarafian. After maybe three or four more years, Bob's baby sister, Barbara, was born; she is now Barbara Hodes, has four children, and lives in Kansas City. Joan had five children. So Bob's and my six children have nine cousins. B. C. [Bernard Clement Altman] was a wonderful father. I don't know that he was such a wonderful father day to day, but certainly overall—very much like his son, I might add. Joan was in the middle, and she and Bob were a bit competitive, but Barbara idolized her older brother.

Lion's Gate offices
1978

25 June 1, 1978
Closing Lion's Gate on Westwood Boulevard; this was the last night. Alan Rudolph was there. Maysie Hoy (an assistant editor then) and Ned Dowd (later an assistant director) were there. I took the plastic wine glasses and stacked them up so high. Tony Lombardo (who had edited *A Wedding*) took this picture. I love it. Then we knocked them all down.

26 June 2, 1978
The opening of Lion's Gate on Bundy Drive. We had just left the original Lion's Gate on Westwood Boulevard, where we had rented since 1963, and moved to this building, which we bought at Bundy and Olympic. At the same time, in 1978, we took a pied-à-terre, as we called it, in New York, and started slowly moving offices there, ultimately selling the office on Bundy, in 1981, and never again having offices, except during production, in California.

Quintet
1978

For Expo 67 in Montreal, they enlarged Île Sainte-Hélène in the St. Lawrence River and had the World's Fair there. It was a phenomenon. I don't think any World's Fair has been that well known since. The fairgrounds had been sitting there deteriorating on this island since 1967, and then it was 1978 and they were getting ready to demolish it. It was in complete disrepair. Every year the snow piled up on it and eroded it more and more. Well, it was just *exactly* what Bob wanted! There were old exposed escalators and big glass panels. And that's what egged him on. He kind of wrote *Quintet* as he went along. Craig Richard Nelson was in it. He and Bob were the ones who dreamed up the idea of the game, and all the game companies—Mattel and Parker Brothers—came up there. Of

27

28

29

30

well known big pink hotel. This was when retirement centers were just becoming prevalent. I remember hearing about "snow-birds" who go from Minnesota or North Dakota and all those other cold places down to Florida. Glenda Jackson said, "St. Petersburg is like God's waiting room." That was the first time I heard that line, and it broke me up.

The film was about a big health convention, so the set was a lot of fun. Walter Cronkite came down to visit because his son, Chip, was on the crew. Lauren Bacall played Esther Brill, who was based on one of the first health-food gurus, Adelle Davis. But Esther Brill, the character, tends to fall asleep because she is old and out of it, and every time she falls asleep her arm goes up. It becomes a real joke.

We lived in this fabulous condominium right on the Gulf of Mexico. We were all in the condos—Carol Burnett and Glenda Jackson were there. And Dick Cavett arrived. He was taking tap-dancing lessons on his own time and then teaching us all, so we were always having little tap-dancing classes in the kitchen. And when production asked Carol Burnett and Glenda Jackson what they would like to have in their rooms, Carol said that she would like an ironing board, because she grew up ironing and loved it. Glenda wanted a Hoover. I had Matthew in a little school that he didn't like. He ran away, and I had to go back and get him and put him back in. I had such a hell of a time educating him in every city.

HealtH
1979

30 *HealtH* was an interesting experience, loaded with stars like Dick Cavett, Lauren Bacall, Carol Burnett, Glenda Jackson, Donald Moffat, and Jim Garner. It was one of Alfre Woodard's first films. We shot it at this famous hotel in St. Petersburg, Florida, that's still there: the Don CeSar, called "the Pink Lady." It's a very

course, they thought it was going to be a big movie with all these stars.

We had a screening in New York, and Bob invited Leonard Bernstein to see it because he wanted him to score it. I was in the lobby, and it was halfway through the screening, and Leonard came storming through the double doors from the screening room to the lobby. He had his camel hair coat over his shoulders, and he was so handsome, and he had a son and a couple of other people with him—and he was yelling, "Is he crazy? What is he thinking?" It seemed that John Williams came up there, too, at some point, but Bob and John had a falling-out. Tom Pierson ended up doing the music.

27, **28** This shows the disrepair that the fairgrounds were in. They did very little in the way of set decoration.

This **29** was the first thing that Wolf Kroeger (left) did for Bob as art director. Wolf went on to *Popeye* as production designer. That's Leon Ericksen (right), the very brilliant production designer.

5

THE

EIGHTIES

BY GIULIA
D'AGNOLO VALLAN

Even by Altman's idiosyncratic standards, the creative partnership that united the director with Hollywood producer Robert Evans and East Coast playwright–cartoonist Jules Feiffer is a strange one. After years as head of production at Paramount (*The Godfather* was made under his tenure), Evans had set up his own independent company at the studio. There, he wanted to follow up *Chinatown*'s success with a musical. *Annie* (on Broadway in 1977) was his original choice, but the rights were too expensive. He must have been looking into old studio properties when he encountered Popeye, the 1929 E. C. Segar comic strip character that Dave and Max Fleischer had turned into popular cartoon shorts for Paramount in 1933. Evans hired Feiffer, who was known for his *Village Voice* comic strip, as well as *Little Murders* and *Carnal Knowledge*, both originally plays that had been made into movies. Dustin Hoffman and Lily Tomlin were to star. Then Hoffman fell through, and, not unlike *M*A*S*H*, *Popeye* became one of those "hot" scripts that nobody wanted to touch—with the exception of Robert Altman.

LEFT Altman in front of the Sweethaven set, built on the island of Malta, for *Popeye*, 1980.

Ro

TOP TO BOTTOM, LEFT TO RIGHT Shelley Duvall (as Olive Oyl); Donovan Scott (as Castor Oyl); Shelley Duvall, Wesley Ivan Hurt (Altman's real-life grandson, who played Swee'pea), and Robin Williams (as Popeye); Robin Williams and Ray Walston (as Popeye's father Poopdeck Pappy); Paul Dooley (as Wimpy); Paul Smith (as Bluto) in *Popeye*.

OPPOSITE
TOP LEFT Stickers featuring Olive Oyl, Wimpy, Swee'pea, Popeye, and Bluto.
TOP RIGHT The town of Sweethaven set from *Popeye*, Malta, 1979.
BOTTOM LEFT An issue of the *Falconette Gazette*, periodically published by the publicity department for the cast and crew.

Sharing Feiffer's passion for Segar's vision, the director was also keen on Evans's suggestion to cast an untested TV actor as Popeye the Sailor: Robin Williams, of *Mork & Mindy* fame. His Olive Oyl would be an actress—the director told her over the phone—"born to play the part": Shelley Duvall. Altman regulars Paul Dooley (Wimpy) and Robert Fortier (as the town drunk, just as in *McCabe*) were also part of the group. Altman's grandchild, Wesley Ivan Hurt, was cast as tiny Swee'pea.

Besides his kinship with Feiffer's and Segar's satirical souls, Altman loved the idea of another musical. *Popeye*'s scale was considerably bigger than anything he had done before. In interviews he recalled how Evans had told him to go along with Paramount's projected $13 million budget, even if he thought it was not enough; nobody would stop the picture in the middle once he had start spending more, especially since production was set far away, on the Mediterranean island of Malta. *Popeye*'s final tab ended up between $20 and $25 million.

Altman's choice for musical director was pop singer-songwriter Harry Nilsson (whose career in film included the soundtrack of Otto Preminger's *Skidoo*). He liked the immediacy of his songs, as well as an animated TV movie Nilsson had done about a kid with a round head in a land of pointy-headed people. Despite that unconventional move and Altman's determination not to use professional singers and dancers, *Popeye* is by far his most traditional musical, well in the vein of Hollywood fairy-tale musicals such as *The Wizard of Oz*. In that lies its charm. It is also, uncharacteristically for Altman, a real family film, and, over the years, would prove extremely popular with children.

As he had done in *McCabe*, Altman built a whole town from scratch: Sweethaven. Besides most of his Lion's Gate collaborators and his stars, he brought from the United States a group of physical entertainers, including clowns and jugglers. Among them was Bill Irwin, whose film career started with *Popeye*. From Italy came director of photography Giuseppe Rotunno (who had worked for Fellini and Visconti) with his camera crew. Quonset huts were used to house the individual departments (among them, wardrobe, special effects, a dance training hall, a recording area). Altman also gave considerable thought to how to re-create, on a big screen, the look and feel of a comic strip. The actors were dressed in bright primary colors and set against a monochrome background in order to accentuate the impression of cartoon

AN INTERVIEW WITH
JULES FEIFFER
GIULIA D'AGNOLO VALLAN

When producer Bob Evans asked you to write *Popeye*, you said, "If you want to do E. C. Segar's *Popeye*, I'm the only person that can write it." What did you mean?

The Segar strip was a work of genius, and Segar didn't do it for that long. He invented *Popeye* in 1929, which coincidentally was the year of my birth, and he died about ten years later, of cancer, I think. During those years, he created this fantastically original funny slapstick. It was easily on the level of what W. C. Fields and the Marx Brothers were doing. It was totally unique and original as opposed to Max Fleischer's animated cartoons, which were loud and raucous. They were only about Popeye and spinach and beating up Bluto. One form, the newspaper strip, was

humor at its highest possible and most inventive level, and the other was very commercial, tacky, and one that audiences loved—but I didn't.

Sweethaven has a tax collector. Olive is supposed marry a man she doesn't even want to marry. Not your typical idyllic town.

I invented all that. The town of Sweethaven didn't exist. I thought the story needed a town. The reason Sweethaven is known is not because of me but because of Harry Nilsson's song. It was Bob's idea to get Harry. I had been out of every pop culture scene since the 1940s, so I didn't know who Harry Nilsson was. I barely knew who Elvis Presley was. After a kind of suspicious coming together, we became

a love story. We had a wonderful time working with each other and enjoyed each other. I would sit with Harry and talk about what I saw as the score, and he would throw out suggestions, and then he would go away and write something entirely different, which was better.

How did you and Altman end up working together on *Popeye*?

I had written a script, which had been turned down by a number of people, except for Jerry Lewis. I thought I would rather die than have Jerry Lewis do it. I was one of the few people who couldn't stand Jerry Lewis on film, although I liked his television show with Dean Martin. I met him a couple of times in person and found him impossible. Altman was the only other director that loved the script.

He and I were friends for some years before all this. We used to see each other at Elaine's. He knew who I was, and

---

JULES FEIFFER is a Pulitzer Prize– and Oscar-winning cartoonist, playwright, and screenwriter. In addition to writing the screenplay for Altman's *Popeye* (1980), Feiffer wrote Mike Nichols's *Carnal Knowledge* (1971).

I knew who he was. We both admired each other's work, and then we sat down and it turned out we both admired each other's drinking. We were very convivial—and it was very easy to be convivial with Bob. And with Kathryn there, and whatever group—he never came in with less than three or four people. He had a troop.

Carnal Knowledge, which you wrote, came out in 1971, and M*A*S*H came out in 1970. Did you have a sense then that people like you and Altman were changing Hollywood?

When we were shooting *Carnal Knowledge* in Vancouver, Bob was up the hill shooting *McCabe & Mrs. Miller*. When I had a break I'd drive up there, and they were building this town as they were shooting the film, which is pure Altman. That's when I met Warren Beatty for the first time, and then later at a party I introduced him to Jack Nicholson. It was great fun. Those were the two films that were contemporaries at the time. Very different from each other, but I thought *McCabe* was a wonderful movie.

About *Popeye*, Bob said he didn't want to change a word in the script, and I had a thought balloon in my head saying, "What bullshit." I didn't think he deliberately lied or anything. What Bob told me was to get me working. It's hard to know what Bob really thought or what Bob really meant or what Bob really believed—and I'm not sure that Bob even knew. Bob worked by the seat of his pants. He was kind of an Abstract Expressionist of film. Whatever he said had nothing to do with what he was going to shoot, because he would figure that out when he got up that morning. When it worked, it was extraordinary. When it didn't, it was often remarkable.

But he was no gift to a scriptwriter.

Don't get me wrong; I knew all of this when we went into it. I said from the beginning I would be lucky if I got 50 percent of my script on-screen.

You said you eventually got 60 percent in.

We had a falling-out, and I left Malta at one point. If I had stuck around, I would have gotten even more in. Actually, I expected more fights between us, because he just thought words were noise to frame the images that he wanted to put on-screen and the gags he wanted to put on. Some of them were good gags. He got wonderful people. Whoever heard of Bill Irwin before Bob found him or Linda Hunt before Bob found her? He made a star out of Paul Dooley. He had a terrific casting sense. But Robin Williams was Bob Evans's idea.

I think our views on satire were different. Bob was older than I was, but he was much more of a kid. He was much more of an anarchist and an adolescent. He enjoyed making trouble. He enjoyed putting people's noses out of joint. He enjoyed getting producers upset. If you were in a position of authority, you were already the enemy. But when he was in a position of authority, he couldn't stand anybody disagreeing with him. It was a mixed bag. He had this enormous charm, and a great sweetness and likability. It was impossible, even if you were mad at him, to dislike him, because underneath all that ego was essentially a very good heart. It was wonderful to see how he was with Kathryn and the kids.

What's the thing that you were most upset that didn't make it into Popeye?

Popeye was Robin's first starring role. He didn't really know what he was doing. He was improvising, something he wouldn't do later on, once he got experience. He was just doing Robin Williams in Popeye makeup. Altman and others around thought that was hilarious. It became very quickly the Robin Williams improvisational show, and the characters were thrown out the window.

Take the scene where Popeye meets Olive Oyl; their relationship was supposed to be developing in that scene. I imagined it and tried to write it as a latter-day Hepburn–Tracy: two opposites. That all got trashed in the shooting and in the editing. It stopped the scene being about them meeting and getting to know

each other and their rivalry, and became a scene with Robin shooting one-liners at Shelley. There was no character. When I complained to Bob, he really didn't see the point. But he saw that I was upset, and he did something directors just don't do: He allowed me to go into the cutting room with producer Tommy Thompson. He was a loyalist and against any of the changes I wanted. But I made him cut until we got the shape of the scene as it was supposed to be. Bob looked at it and nodded his head and said, "Good, let's keep it." That, I thought, was an extraordinary gift he gave me as a scriptwriter.

But it didn't go like that all the time....Harry and I worked on the "I Yam What I Yam" number as Popeye's declaration of self. We both saw it as Robin's version of Gene Kelly's "Singin' in the Rain."

At the time it was shot, I had to leave the set to attend a funeral. I was away for a few days. When I flew back, he was all excited about that scene and said it was terrific. To me it looked like everybody was in the scene—except for Robin Williams. He seemed like an extra in what was supposed to be his biggest musical number.

I went in to Bob, and we had a big fight. I said, "I'm just going home. There's no point in being here." We both were so angry at each other that night....But he called me and he said, "I want you to stay. You're the only one here who would tell me the truth, whether I believe you or not." I stuck around for another couple of weeks, but I knew it was not going to be Segar's *Popeye* anymore; it was going to be Altman's. In fact, the final result was kind of half and half, and better than I expected.

Altman was tough, and he knew what he wanted. He basically saw filmmaking as a one-man show, and you know who that one man was. Because he was a genius, he could get away with so much of it and make so much of it work. But he had a hard time bringing other people into the shaping of his films.

Paramount had introduced a new sound system in *Popeye*. It was supposed to be this super-incredible, realistic sound. We screened the film in L.A. for the first time. As it opened, you could hear the waves in the ocean and the thunder so well; it was incredible. Everything sounded incredible—until people started speaking, and then you couldn't understand a word.

After about a half hour, I had enough of that, and I walked into the lobby. A third of the audience was already there. Visually it looked great, but nobody could hear it. I started drinking heavily and said, "This is a disaster." As the movie ended, Bob and his troop came out, and they were beaming. They thought it was a triumph. I went back to my hotel—I was staying at the Beverly Hills—and called Bob Evans. He also was bubbling over with excitement. He said, "I've got Jimmy Caan here. Jimmy thinks it's great." And put Jimmy on the phone. I've never met James Caan. "Julie," he said, "Great film! Great masterpiece. Wonderful. Great job, everybody." I said, "Jimmy, could you understand what was being said?" "I couldn't hear a fucking word." I said, "Will you tell that to Bob?" He said, "Bob, I couldn't understand a fucking word." Evans grabbed the phone: "What am I going to do?" I said, "Just get rid of this awful sound system that Paramount imposed." Whatever they did, they made it more audible.

I flew back the next day to New York with Altman, who had not taken seriously at all anything I said. Halfway through the trip he came to me and said, "I was sitting next to a lady who was at the film last night, and I guess we have to do something about the sound because she couldn't understand it." A complete stranger had credibility that I lacked, because I was the writer. *[Laughs.]*

You mentioned Gene Kelly before. Despite the improvisational technique, *Popeye* has a classical quality to it—in its look, the colors, the size. It's very much in the tradition of Hollywood fairy-tale musicals.

One of the things that Bob does in all his films, and did remarkably in this one, is take some characters and create a com-

pletely credible universe around them, where you believe they exist still as comic-strip characters but somehow in a non-animated cartoon sense. Robin was great, but Shelley Duvall was even better. One morning she came down in makeup to sit next to me at breakfast. I thought, "How nice, Olive Oyl sitting next to me." I didn't see Shelley, I thought Olive Oyl, which she was. And the same thing with Paul Dooley's Wimpy and Robin's Popeye and Paul L. Smith's Bluto. All the characters had a wonderful reality to them, as well as a cartoon oversize quality.

The town had the same mix of real and yet so cartoony. The designer—Wolf Kroeger—had built a real, complete town there. At nights when I was feeling depressed because of what happened in the script—and because the woman I had been living with for nine years had just busted up with me prior to my leaving for Malta—I would take a glass of Scotch up to the top of the set and just walk around, as if this were my town, and loved it.

Bob was wonderful at putting together these combinations. He had a real vision, and when the vision worked, it was remarkable. When it didn't work, it still had a more interesting look than just about anybody else's working in film. As mad as I got at him, I still couldn't help getting over it and getting over it fast, because I so respected, admired, and really loved him. He was just a pain in the ass to deal with.

The film was perceived as a financial failure, when in fact it was a success. Why?

It's interesting. Michael Eisner and Barry Diller were running Paramount at the time. It was easy to hate Altman if you were studio brass, and they hated Evans as well. Maybe they wanted to break his contract. So even before the movie opened they started circulating rumors, calling it Evans's Gate—after the big disaster *Heaven's Gate*. When the movie came out to lukewarm reviews, it was considered a financial failure. It wasn't until about a year and a half, two years later that somebody brought up to me

the figures. It was one of the top-grossing pictures that Paramount had that year. But they never publicized it. They didn't want anybody to know.

I guess because it wasn't their typical Hollywood film. It wasn't anything they could claim as their own. It was Bob Evans's, whom they hated, and Robert Altman's, whom they hated even more.

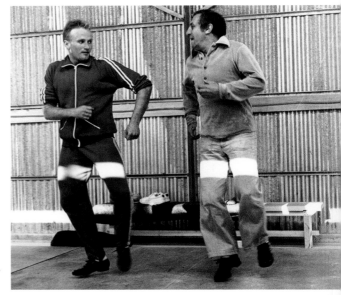

two-dimensionality, a world of complete fantasy. It was a highly stylized, unreal look that influenced later comic-book adaptations such as *Dick Tracy* and even real-life and cartoon blends like *Who Framed Roger Rabbit*.

The shoot in Malta lasted six very long months. Back in Hollywood, by the end of the seventies, the enthusiasm for independent-minded, adventurous directors had started cooling off. Altman's recent commercial and critical disappointments had hurt his standing, and even though Evans protected him from Paramount's direct intervention and did not interfere much himself, reports from the *Popeye* set back to the United States spoke of a production out of control, marred by self-indulgence, delays, and drug abuse. In fact, no matter how chaotic that set might have been, Altman's hard-won technical and cinematic skills—learned at Calvin, during the TV years, and in more than a decade of shifting between genres and studios—are clearly exhibited in *Popeye*'s scale, technical prowess, and exquisite production values.

But in a studio culture that was rapidly becoming more and more corporate, even Bob Evans started to feel a little too independent for Barry Diller and Michael Eisner's Paramount. The studio never really embraced *Popeye*. Perhaps they had unrealistic box office expectations; perhaps they did not like the people involved; perhaps they just did not understand the picture. It was released at the end of 1980, and with more than $50 million in domestic ticket sales, it did quite well. Still, Paramount never admitted it was a success.

Robert Altman's biggest picture to date, and one of his most financially profitable, marked the end of his Hollywood phase. He would go back there to work again on occasion, but as much more of an outsider than he had ever been, or felt before.

The breakup was also a physical one. In 1981 the director sold his beloved production company, Lion's Gate, and relocated his family and his operations to New York. "The films the major companies want to make now, they are films I don't want to make," Altman told Patrick Watson in an interview for the CBS Cable series *Signature* that year. "I can't make them. I can't make *Superman* and *Raiders of the Lost Ark*. And I don't want to. . . . There is a magic number they use: one hundred million dollars. . . . I just can't do that. I mean, I am tired of car crashes and spiders. It's just a time when we are not in tune with the people who put up the money and the people who make the films. It's just time to split, that's all. And by splitting I mean separate."

In 1981 he also accepted an invitation from Bill Bushnell's Los Angeles Actors' Theatre to direct two plays by Frank South, the monologue *Rattlesnake in a Cooler* and *Precious Blood*—Altman's first return to the stage since the Resident Theatre in Kansas City, where he had cut his teeth working with actors in the fifties.

The following year marked Altman's debut on Broadway, at the Martin Beck Theatre, with Ed Graczyk's play *Come Back to the 5 & Dime, Jimmy Dean, Jimmy Dean,* starring Sandy Dennis, Karen Black, almost-newcomer Kathy Bates, and, in the role that would eventually launch her film career, pop singer

TOP LEFT Cans of spinach, the food that gave Popeye his strength.
TOP RIGHT Robin Williams rehearsing for his role as Popeye.
ABOVE Altman watching rehearsals for *Popeye*.

OPPOSITE
TOP Broadway cast of the play *Come Back to the 5 & Dime, Jimmy Dean, Jimmy Dean*, 1982, which Altman later turned into a film.
BOTTOM Cher, who played Sissy in both the play and the film of *Come Back to the 5 & Dime, Jimmy Dean, Jimmy Dean*, with Altman on the set, 1982.

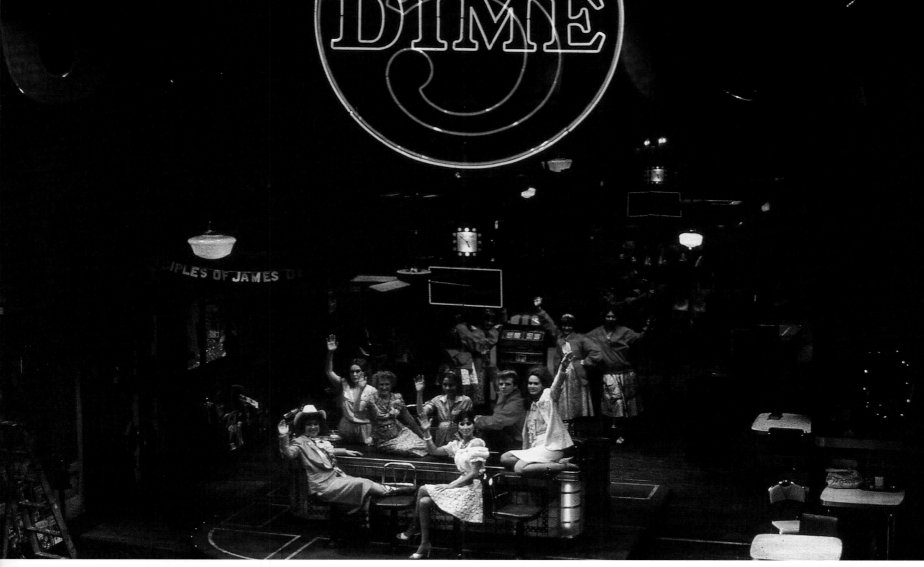

Cher. Set at a James Dean fan club reunion in a Texas dime store, Graczyk's piece offered Altman the chance to go back to some old themes (fame; ethereal, damaged women; reflecting surfaces; Bergmanesque moods)—and, unexpectedly, to make another movie. Downsizing to Super 16 mm with a budget below $1 million, Altman filmed the play in a Manhattan studio immediately after it ended its run. He formed a new production company, christened Sandcastle 5. Financing was in part provided by Viacom, acquiring the rights to present the film on its Showtime cable channel. With this small project, born out of his unshakable resilience and a physical desire to keep making films, Altman won several critics back to his side. Old champion Pauline Kael, who had not been kind to his post-*Nashville* period, loved *Come Back* and recognized in it the director's curiosity and his ability to work with, even elevate, any material. "When Altman gives a project everything he's got, his skills are such that he can make poetry out of fake poetry and magic out of fake magic," she wrote in the *New Yorker*.

Altman's ever-moving camera and his instinct for multiple points of view turned out to be great assets for turning theater into cinema. He seemed a natural at it, his adaptations never really displaying the two-dimensional, flat feel that filmed plays often have. They come across more like explorations of the text. Simple expedients such as mirrors or TV screens provided extra depth and visual texture. In this most minimalist phase of his long career, he mostly worked directly from the playwright's page, pretty much forgoing a script altogether. The on-set collaboration of two of his sons became more and more important. Bobby had been a focus puller and then second assistant camera since *Nashville*. He would become his father's most trusted camera operator and eventually his cinematographer for *Tanner on Tanner*. Stephen had started as a prop master on *A Wedding*; at this stage he was just about to graduate to art director, then to production designer on several of his father's last pictures.

After *Come Back to the 5 & Dime* came David Rabe's war drama *Streamers* (1983) and Donald Freed and Arnold M. Stone's harrowing one-man play *Secret Honor* (1984), with Philip Baker Hall playing a drunken, post-Watergate Richard Nixon in stream-of-consciousness mode.

To a certain extent, Altman was using this quasi-new medium to go back to places he had been before: James Dean, war, and American politics. If *Streamers* (which won an ensemble prize for Best Actor at the 1983 Venice Film Festival) gave him a chance to revisit his dislike for war while hinting at the ongoing U.S. military involvement in Central America, *Secret Honor* reflects Altman's complex view of the political process. His Nixon is almost a sympathetic figure, a tragicomic Hamlet. Few critics saw in the enraged, sputtering, lost, "betrayed' president Altman's projection of his own exile—from Hollywood, as well as from the United States of Ronald Reagan. During his tenure as a visiting lecturer at the University of Michigan in Ann Arbor, the director had turned the production of the film into a course; the crew was mostly made up of graduate students. He was thrilled by the experience. George Burt, one of the university's professors, composed the music, which was played by the student orchestra.

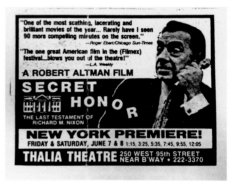

In between movies he also took a stint as opera director, staging Stravinsky's *The Rake's Progress* at the University of Michigan. He returned to opera in 1992, cowriting the libretto and directing the world premiere of William Bolcom's *McTeague* for the Lyric Opera of Chicago.

The oddest episode of Altman's struggling, introspective, formally austere, East Coast eighties brought him back to Hollywood, and to MGM, where the director whose first feature had been a dark riff on the late fifties teenage movie craze went to make . . . a teenage movie. Altman seems the unlikeliest director to engage in a comedy à la *Fast Times at Ridgemont High* or *Valley Girl*, Amy Heckerling's and Martha Coolidge's very successful high school romps. That was a genre—and a generation—he really did not care for. But perhaps, he thought, *O.C. and Stiggs* was something he could work with. It

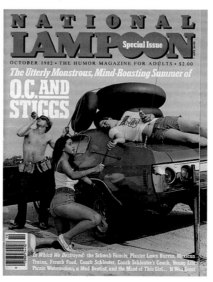

was, after all, the product of minds that shared with his a taste for iconoclastic satire. *M*A*S*H* and *National Lampoon*, both introduced to the world in 1970, emanated a similar anarchic streak. Furthermore, Doug Kenney, Henry Beard, and Robert Hoffman's wonderfully subversive, elitist magazine had been born out of a distaste for the same sixties "peacenik" counterculture that Altman had always been suspicious of. In 1978 the first *National Lampoon* movie, *Animal House*, had become the highest-grossing comedy to date. In search of another property to bring to the screen, *Lampoon* opted in 1983 for "The Ugly, Monstrous, Mind-Roasting Summer of O.C. and Stiggs," the last of a series of articles about the mischief of two highly unruly teenagers. Altman took the whole thing as a satire of teenage films and amped up the destruction. The folks at *Lampoon* and MGM did not get the joke. The film was buried until 1987, when it opened and disappeared, barely seen at all.

The most film-like of Altman's theater adaptations was financed by Israeli producers Menahem Golan and Yoram Globus. Known for the *Death Wish* pictures and for having launched Chuck Norris's career, their Cannon Films was also supporting the work of maverick filmmakers disillusioned by Hollywood: John Cassavetes, Francis Ford Coppola, Norman Mailer, Andrei Konchalovsky. Sam Shepard, a fan of Altman's theater adaptations, called him about doing a film version of *Fool for Love*. The director liked the idea and convinced the playwright to undertake the lead role. Kim Basinger became the incestuous sister, in a performance that brought to mind Marilyn Monroe's in *The Misfits*.

By the film's general release, in the spring of 1986, Altman was no longer living in the United States—he had decided it was time to move even farther away from Hollywood. For a long time Paris had been a destination for all sorts of American artists, especially ones who did not feel loved enough at home. The director's status in Europe was still riding high in the mid-eighties (as with so many of his films, *Fool for Love* was invited to screen in Cannes). So in 1985 he had decided to move to the French capital, with his mind set on making a movie about fashion. Ironically, though, the first feature film he made while living there would be a New York–based comedy: *Beyond Therapy*, a crowded satire on modern psychiatry with Jeff Goldblum and Julie Hagerty. Although Altmanesque in its ingredients, it was perceived as lacking the sharpness and the invention of the director's best comedies.

While in Europe, Altman had also continued to adapt plays for TV: *The Laundromat*, by Marsha Norman, for HBO in 1985; two by Harold Pinter,

The Room and The Dumb Waiter, filmed in Montreal for ABC and aired in 1987 (later screened at the Montreal Film Festival under the umbrella title *Basements*); and Herman Wouk's *The Caine Mutiny Court-Martial*.

Then the opportunity of another big shift of gears presented itself.

The cable channel HBO had asked *Doonesbury* creator Garry Trudeau to write a comedy series about a presidential candidate. It was Trudeau—whose comic strip often sports *M*A*S*H*-like absurdist humor—who suggested Altman. Together the writer and the director came up with the notion of mixing reality and fakery by inserting a fictional candidate in the midst of the actual 1988 race for the White House. Altman's documentarian aspiration, his passion for satire, and his disillusionment with the political process could all be engaged at the same time. In *Nashville* he had shown us politics flirting with show business. In *Tanner '88* television has engulfed the whole thing. It is all that is left of politics.

Set during the Democratic primaries, the eleven-episode series follows the campaign of liberal Michigan congressman Jack Tanner (Michael Murphy, with a touch of Kennedy) to the party's convention in Atlanta. Cynthia Nixon is Tanner's idealistic daughter, Alex; Pamela Reed, his tough main adviser, T. J. Cavanaugh. With its small pool of stars and a tiny crew, Altman followed the steps of the actual campaign, showing up at events held by real candidates and having his actors interact with them. Bob Dole, Gary Hart, Pat Robertson, and Bruce Babbitt appeared on the show, becoming part of Altman's artifice. Trudeau was writing new episodes as the campaign evolved, Altman mixed what was on the page with what he was capturing on the ground, and HBO would quickly broadcast the results. Jack Tanner's candidacy became so real that Gloria Steinem, Ralph Nader, and Studs Terkel announced that if Tanner were to be elected, they would be part of his cabinet. Altman could not have hoped for a better incarnation of his democratic philosophy of cinema. He always considered *Tanner '88* one of his most important and exciting experiences, and the series won an Emmy Award for his direction.

In truth, one cannot overestimate how groundbreaking the show was. In *Tanner* are both the seeds and an implicit criticism of the contemporary

TOP LEFT Altman relaxing with the sports pages between takes of *Tanner '88*, the TV series, written by *Doonesbury*'s Garry Trudeau, that follows a fictional presidential campaign. Altman enjoyed betting on sports.

TOP RIGHT Cynthia Nixon, Senator Bob Dole campaigning in New Hampshire for the Republican nomination for President, and Michael Murphy in *Tanner '88*.

BOTTOM RIGHT Garry Trudeau, Robert Altman, and Vermont Senator Patrick Leahy, 1988.

OPPOSITE Altman directing a scene during production of *Vincent & Theo*, 1990.

craze for reality television. By thrusting his cameras at the heart of a presidential campaign, Altman also anticipated the audience/electorate's growing fascination with the political process as spectacle, reflected in such series as *The West Wing*, *Veep*, and *House of Cards*.

Altman's last work out of the French "exile" period is a film about art—and about an artist who saw his work rejected his entire life. A pool of European television companies had asked Altman to direct a four-hour miniseries of Julian Mitchell's script about Vincent van Gogh and his art-dealer brother, Theo. He accepted on the condition that he could also cut a theatrical version of the piece. *Vincent & Theo* was made for very little money, with British actors Tim Roth and Paul Rhys. A group of French art students, supervised by Stephen Altman, painted reproductions of Van Gogh's work. They do not have to be perfect, the director told them; we will never photograph them straight on. Opting for a more oblique take than other Van Gogh biopics, such as Vincente Minnelli's romantic and tragic *Lust for Life*, Altman's film depicts the relationship between the brothers, Theo's attempts to protect Vincent, and his fruitless efforts to sell his brother's paintings. Well received by European as well as American critics, *Vincent & Theo* is also a film about how art relates to an artist's life, portraying Van Gogh's painting as an almost compulsive gesture. Looking at Altman's struggle through the eighties, it does not seem too far-fetched to suggest that he may have felt the same way about making movies.

SOME THOUGHTS ABOUT TANNER '88
MICHAEL MURPHY

In the fall of 1987, Bob assembled a bunch of guys on a decommissioned military base in Port Townsend, Washington. For one reason or another, he had undertaken to make *The Caine Mutiny Court-Martial* for television, and as my fellow "sailors" and I tried on our newly tailored dress blue uniforms, I had a fleeting memory of my long-ago boot camp days, which turned out to be somewhat prophetic. The production was very insular in that Port Townsend is an *island* unto itself—situated on the Olympic Peninsula—and the cast of the *Caine* is 100 percent male. In addition, because we were essentially re-creating a play (and Bob wanted to shoot long takes), some fairly serious homework was going to be required of us. So it looked as though we were going to be living rather quietly for a bunch of actors on location,

spending our days shooting in an old gym on the base and most of our nights learning lines.

In retrospect, I think that if ever the possibility existed for that old, destructive nemesis tension to make an appearance on one of Bob's sets, this could well have been the one. I mean, there's nothing quite like reeling off big, important speeches from a famous Broadway courtroom drama in long, single takes, with hardly any rehearsal. It's the stuff of the actor's paranoid nightmare. Bob, however, was throwing this party, and his personality quickly set the all-important atmosphere in which we would eat, sleep, and work for the next few weeks. As per usual in an Altman movie, his performers could do no wrong, and we immediately began to feel confident, protected, and happy to be there. We started in, and the play came to life and began to hum along with barely a hiccup. Suddenly it was the 1940s again,

and World War II was upon us.

One afternoon we had broken for lunch, and Bob and I sat across from one another in the base chow hall. Out of nowhere, he fixed me with what I had long before come to recognize as the Altman "look." (He had very piercing blue eyes that could stop you in your tracks at a sizable distance.) "What?" I asked. "Well," he said, "I think we're gonna run you for president." And that's how one of the truly great adventures of my life began.

The people at HBO had approached Garry Trudeau to do "something on the 1988 election." Garry initially turned them down, but the network guys persisted. Finally, sure that he was asking the impossible, he said he would do it, "if you can get Robert Altman to do it, too." Well, what turned out to be an examination of America's political foibles, written by Trudeau no less, was more than Bob could resist, and he quickly signed on. So that afternoon, over lunch in an old mess

hall, I was cast as Jack Tanner, with this little Altmanesque qualifier: "And listen, Murphy, don't think this was my idea. Trudeau's the one who wanted you." Vintage Bob.

We reconnoitered back in New York, and Bob quickly cast Cynthia Nixon, Pamela Reed, Danny Jenkins, Matt Malloy, Ilana Levine, Jim Fyfe, and Kevin J. O'Connor to compose a kind of core group that he would expand as the story progressed. Then we set off across the country.

From our first days in New Hampshire to Jack's eventual demise at the Democratic convention in Atlanta, my cohorts and I chased the nomination.

Along the way, we shared situations so unique that, regardless of where our subsequent paths have taken us, I know for certain that all of us surely look back on *Tanner* as a once-in-a-lifetime experience. And this, of course, had everything to do with Robert Altman.

Throughout the entire show, a kind of controlled chaos ruled. We were shooting on videotape, as Bob wanted a very real, very immediate look, and it seemed as though *everybody* had a camcorder and was shooting something. Many of the actors playing press people, for example, had cameras, and half the time you never knew when, or by whom, you were being photographed.

Encouraged by Bob, the show quickly took on a life of its own. Because we were shooting in "real time," our characters reacted to whatever was going on in the other campaigns at any given moment. Garry, meanwhile, worked like a dog in New York, faxing us not only scripts and revisions, but reams of scenes and ideas that could be used to tie some of this free-floating stuff together. It was by far the best collaboration I've ever seen between a writer and a director. They liked, admired, and trusted one another, and Garry—perhaps knowing what he was in for from the get-go—fully embraced Bob's style, not only complementing it but adding to it immeasurably.

One evening in New Hampshire, some of us were gathered in Bob's hotel room, having a drink or two and watching what we had shot that day. In the midst of this little party, Allan Nicholls, our assistant director, popped in and said, "Jack Kemp's in the lobby giving a speech. Wanna see it?" Without missing a beat, Bob looked over at me and said, "Go get your suit on." I did, and we went down to the lobby. Once there, a couple of our guys quietly slipped in with the TV journalists, and I was stealthily photographed watching Kemp give his press conference. When he finished, I introduced myself as Jack Tanner and told him that I was now in the race. He looked a little puzzled but went along with the game, and we got some very interesting footage. Unfortunately, none of Kemp's stuff made the final cut, but it was then and there that Bob decided to integrate us as fully as possible into the various campaigns. This resulted in my eventually taking a stroll down along the Potomac with Governor Bruce Babbitt, during which he stated that he "could be interested in supporting" me now that he had dropped out of the presidential race. I was also the first candidate to welcome Gary Hart back into the campaign after his unfortunate boat ride on the *Monkey Business*. These opportunities presented themselves on an almost daily basis, as we campaigned everywhere from Nashville's malls and music venues to the factories of New Hampshire and Michigan.

Once this ball got rolling, most of the politicians and newspeople were happy to be on the show; if not, we would occasionally bushwhack them. One morning in Concord, for example, we heard that the TV evangelist Pat Robertson, who was also a Republican candidate, was in town. I climbed into my suit, and we caught up with him on the steps of the city hall for a little impromptu face-to-face. He wasn't quite sure what was going on, but he could see that a pretty big crowd had gathered and that a lot of cameras were in evidence, recording our every move. He jumped right in. We were passing a few pleasantries back and forth when suddenly Kevin O'Connor piped up with, "What's with this 'Christian hardball' you're always talking about?" Robertson, not exactly sure who Kevin was—an actor, a member of the press, a cranky New Hampshire voter?—quickly searched his brain for an appropriate answer. He came up with a quip about his having been an athlete (a "pretty good boxer") in his youth and how this somehow applied to his political campaign. As I stood there, I could practically watch the wheels turning in his head. A few minutes later, as we parted company, I heard someone in his entourage murmur, "What the hell was *that*?"

Before long I was being interviewed on network news and on the morning shows, often as Jack Tanner. At the Democratic convention, for example, I appeared on *Good Morning America* with the very smart, spontaneous Charles Gibson. We went on the air, and the first thing out of Charlie's mouth was, "Well, Congressman, it's getting late in the game, why do you think your message isn't getting out?" We chatted about the treachery of politics for a while—and I don't recall him ever letting the audience in on the joke! It seems that life was somehow imitating art, which was somehow imitating life.

And speaking of networks, during the 1980s, HBO was primarily a movie channel, and it is my recollection that *Tanner '88* was their first venture into series television. At any rate, it must have been as much of a wild ride from their perspective as it was from ours. They gave Bob and Garry total freedom to just run with the show, but things moved and changed so quickly on the campaign trail that we usually made our airdates by the skin of our teeth, and I often wondered if the guys at HBO had a chance to watch the show before they put it on the air. Indeed, there were stories floating around to that effect. I can't begin to imagine the possibility of that sort of thing happening today.

As the years went by, Bob publicly stated on more than one occasion that *Tanner '88* was "the most creative thing I've ever done." Well, he was prone to the occasional *pronouncement*, and this one may have been stretching things a bit. I mean, it was indeed a groundbreaking show and more, but Bob lived a long, full life and spent most of it making exceptionally creative movies. And this I know for a fact: Robert Altman absolutely *loved* every single movie and every single television show he ever made. Without exception. How can this be? We all have our favorite accomplishments, right? I don't know, but my guess would be that perhaps it was because he was an artist who loved his work completely and without reservation. It was truly his life, and though the movie gods smiled on him, he also paid some heavy dues.

If you know Bob's work, you know that he was eternally fascinated with the big, messy saga that is America and her people. Who we are; where we've been and why; where we're headed. To this end, *Tanner* was just about perfect for Bob. To be able to dig into a real presidential campaign just as it was unfolding, to have the chance to create the machinery and run his own candidate in that campaign, to record and reflect what was going on and *what was at stake* in the 1988 election, made Bob a very happy man indeed. The pace was furious, the budget lean, but the work was so much fun and so satisfying that, through it all, the Altman grin—sometimes conspiratorial, sometimes just plain joyful—never seemed to leave his face. What a time it was for all of us.

Cape Elizabeth, Maine
July 2013

POPEYE

The cast and crew on the Malta set.

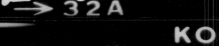

OPPOSITE Robin Williams and Paul L. Smith (as Bluto) rehearsing their fight scene.
TOP Still of the Walfleur sisters.
BOTTOM Shelley Duvall (as Olive Oyl) with Julie Janney, Patty Katz, Diane Shaffer, and Nathalie Blossom
(a.k.a. The Steinettes) as the Walfleur sisters. Altman had also used the musical quartet in 1980's *HealtH*

1982

COME BACK TO THE 5 & DIME, JIMMY DEAN, JIMMY DEAN

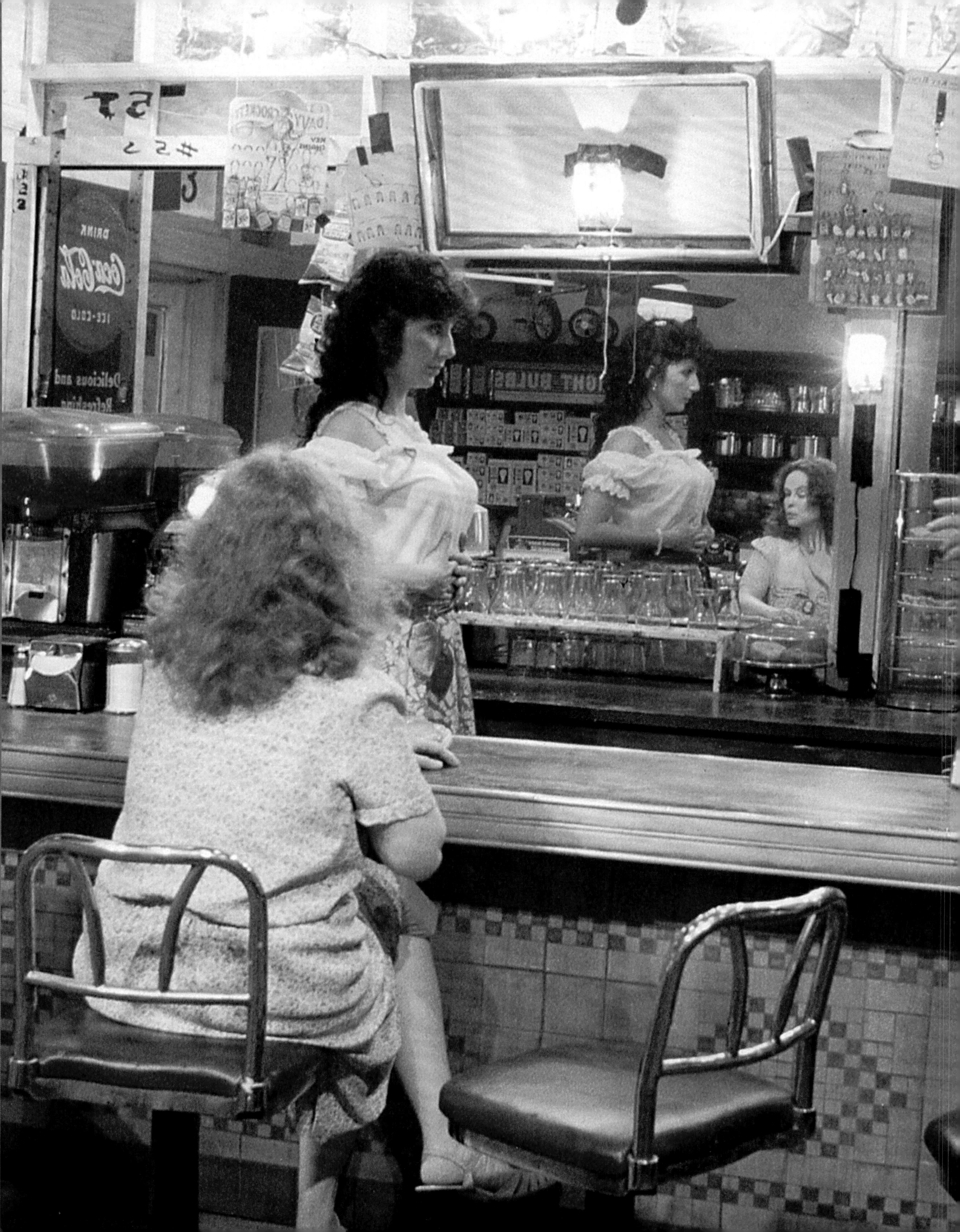

OPPOSITE Altman on the set with Cher (as Sissy) and Sandy Dennis (as Mona).
TOP Karen Black (as Joanne) and Kathy Bates (as Stella Mae).
BOTTOM Sandy Dennis, Cher, and Mark Patton (as Joe)

STREAMERS

TOP Altman on the set of *Streamers*. David Rabe's play was one of the hits of the 1976–77 Broadway theater season. It was Altman's second experiment in filmed theater.
BOTTOM Credit sequence from *Streamers*.
OPPOSITE TOP Mitchell Lichtenstein (as Richie).
OPPOSITE BOTTOM George Dzundza (Cokes) at left; Guy Boyd (Rooney) at right.

SECRET HONOR

Philip Baker Hall (as President Richard Nixon).
OPPOSITE Altman directing Philip Baker Hall.

→10 →10A →11 →

KODAK SAFETY FILM 5063 KODAK SAFETY

→16 →16A →17

M 5063 KODAK SAFETY FILM 5063

O.C. AND STIGGS

KODAK CM 400 5079

7   7A   8   8A   KODAK

12   12A   13   13A

KODAK CM 400 5079

OPPOSITE Daniel Jenkins and Neill Barry
(as O.C. and Stiggs).
THIS PAGE Altman on the set.

FOOL FOR LOVE

OPPOSITE TOP Kim Basinger (as May), with Sam Shepard on the left and Robert Altman on the right.
OPPOSITE BOTTOM Kim Basinger.
THIS PAGE Sam Shepard as Eddie in *Fool for Love*. Shepard did not initially want the part. He preferred Ed Harris, who played the role in the original stage productions in San Francisco and New York.

BEYOND THERAPY

TANNER '88

TOP Altman with then-Massachusetts Senator John Kerry.
MIDDLE Congresswoman Geraldine Ferraro (far left) with Pamela Reed (far right), who played campaign manager T.J. Cavanaugh, with Ilana Levine (center).
BOTTOM Larry King and Michael Murphy.
RIGHT Michael Murphy on the set.

VINCENT & THEO

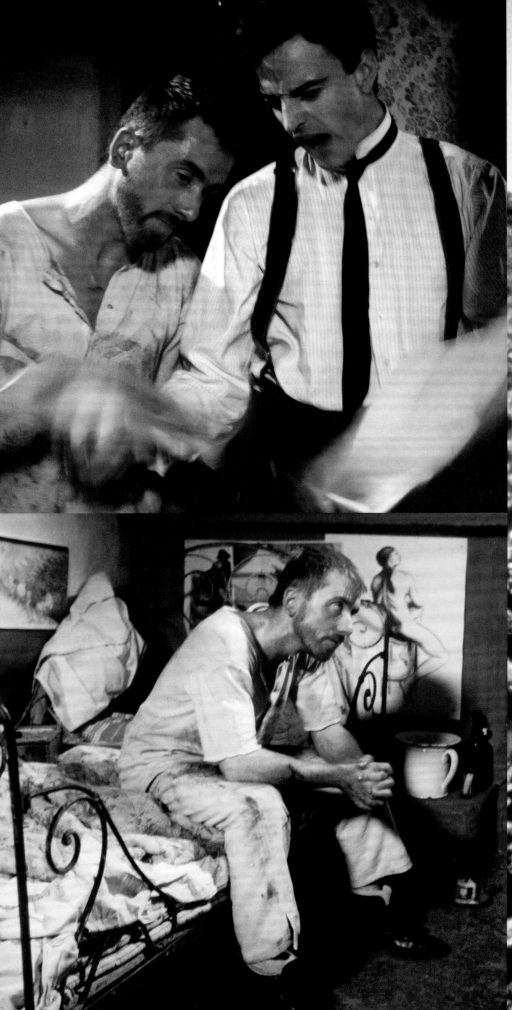

TOP Tim Roth as Vincent Van Gogh and Paul Rhys as his brother Theo.
BOTTOM Tim Roth.
RIGHT Altman in a field of sunflowers.

BY
KATHRYN REED
ALTMAN

Popeye
1979–80

1–7 *Popeye* was the longest location shoot we had during Bob's whole career. We went to Malta in the fall of 1979 and were there until about June 1980. We had Thanksgiving and Christmas there, but the actual shoot didn't start until January or February. Christmas was kind of fun, because we had to really pull it together and give funny presents.

Most of the cast and crew for *Popeye* were housed in a resort hotel, all done in Arabic or Danish architecture, called the Mellieha Holiday Centre. This hotel was built as a resort for lower-income, lower-middle-class holidays. The English would go to either Spain or Malta for their vacations, and a lot of Danish and Swedish people came to Malta, too, because it was inexpensive and they were offered package deals—but it was just pathetic. The sand was gravel. There were no waves.

We had a lot of wives there, a lot of families, and a lot of things happened. Somebody had a baby. Somebody had a terrible fall: Doug Dillard (Clem the banjo player in the film). He lived in a building that had an atrium entry, so you could stand at the bottom and look up at the different floors; he was leaning over from above with a drink in his hand, talking to somebody down in the atrium, and he fell. Van Dyke Parks (Hoagy the piano player, and the arranger and conductor of the songs) and his wife, Sally, had a baby there.

Visitors came and went. Everybody had visitors there. Malta had declared its independence from Britain some years back but only recently cut its last ties, so it was a starving little country having a hell of a time making it work. The reason we went there to begin with is because some prior production had built this tank, this big pool. It just kind of melded into the Mediterranean. They got a big income renting that out, and lots of films were shot there. It was perfect for us.

6 Of course, Bob chose his grandson, Wesley Ivan Hurt, to play Swee'pea. When Bob's daughter, Christine, had brought her infant son to visit us in Malibu, he had this little kind of crooked smile, and Bob thought that was the perfect spot for the baby's pipe to go. And it was. I think Bob laughingly said—and I'm sure he must've done it—that he tied the baby's feet together near the end of the picture so that he couldn't walk or stand up, because he had to crawl in that little nightshirt with a drawstring at the bottom. He just scooted along.

We had a lot of parties, a lot of good times, a lot of traumas. There were many breakups and makeups, a lot of friends and relatives. There was always some gossip going around. Stevie Altman lived about ten minutes away, in an apartment building where the ground floor held retail stores and the top were apartments. He'd cook these Mexican dinners, and he'd have everybody over for big parties. One night we were at one of those parties and were all driving these little cars. The cars were small because the streets are very narrow, and everything is kind of small there. It was maybe a Hillman Minx. We were pretty loaded when we got in the car. It was probably two in the morning or something; the street was completely quiet and empty. We got in the car, and there weren't any curbs—well, there were

really low curbs; sidewalks hardly existed. And Bob went into the wrong gear and drove right into a furniture store—right in, just shattered the glass! There we were, right in the furniture store, the two of us. Oh God, it was hysterical! And we looked at each other, and he had this panicked look on his face, and I said, "Let's get out of here!" He went into reverse, drove out, and drove home. And he went in to work the next day and didn't say a word. And someone said, "You know where Stevie lives? Somebody ran into that furniture store." And he never copped to it—until *waaaay* later.

The location was phenomenal—the set was a complete replica that had never really existed outside the funny papers. It was all from Segar's drawings—the man who created *Popeye*—and then the cartoons on television. Wolf Kroeger, the production designer, was able to replicate that entire little town of Sweethaven, and it still stands today. They charge admission now, and it's another little moneymaker for Malta.

4, **5** The special effects department did fireworks for Bob's birthday. Another great night.

Christmas in Aspen
1982

8–**9** We took a house in Aspen, where Konni and Signe lived at the time, for three weeks over Christmas. Stevie and his girlfriend, Lisa, were with us, and Matthew and Bobby. Everybody skied except Helen and me. We were scared, so we cross-country skied.

9 Steven Spielberg was there too. Just as Bob turned to go into the restaurant back there, his ski slipped sideways

and he fell and wrecked his ankle. He had to stay off his feet, so he couldn't go with us to Ashcroft. We were so disappointed. **8** This picture was taken the day before, just before he slipped. He was at the very top of Aspen Mountain.

Bob bought everything. Any time he went on a fishing trip or a boating trip, he would just go buy out the whole sporting goods store. He had every parka, and mittens and gloves and goggles. That's just the way he grew up.

University of Michigan/opera
1982

We spent a lot of time, from 1982 on, at the University of Michigan. Paul Boylan, who was the dean of the

The University of Michigan School of Music presents
STRAVINSKY'S
the Rake's Progress
Power Center for the Performing Arts   November 4,5,6,7
Gustav Meier *Music Director*   Robert Altman *Stage Director*

10

School of Music, approached Bob to direct an opera with the students. The opera was *The Rake's Progress*, Stravinsky's only opera. And somehow or other, as the deal evolved and Bob had nothing going at that time in terms of film, he accepted it. It entailed us living there for about three months, and Bob taught and directed the opera. He was there for all the performances. He used Wolf Kroeger, who had done *Quintet* and *Popeye*, to build the set.

They gave us a lovely home in a gated community that had lakes and ducks, beautiful groves and grass. We had a very nice time there. We were involved in all the activities, and having never gone to college, I was fascinated by it all.

I remember once I snuck into his class. I felt like Betty Co-ed. I snuck in and took a seat in the back. Nobody knew who I was, of course. I didn't know before what he did in these classes. I would ask him, but he would never give me a straight answer. So I found out for myself: The students would watch a film and then go into the classroom, and it was like a Q&A. He was just sitting on the edge of the desk answering their questions, like he was sitting in the living room with them. It was the strangest thing. They loved it, of course. The opera was a big success, and he loved doing it.

In 1986 Bob was invited to the capital of all operas: Lille, in France. It has a world-famous, beautiful opera house. **10** They invited Bob to direct a performance of *The Rake's Progress*. He refused to do it without having half the cast be University of Michigan students. So they brought students over and also peppered it with professionals. We were living in Paris at the time, which is just a train ride from Lille, while in preproduction for *Beyond Therapy*.

In May, while we were living in our apartment in Paris and also staying at a hotel in Lille for the opera, we went to the Cannes Film Festival for *Fool for Love*.

Altman family : Amérique insolite !

CANNES 86
39e Festival international du film

Dans ce 39e Festival du film où, pour cause de psychose, la cinématographie américaine compte plus de films en sélection officielle que d'interprètes « corps présents » pour les soutenir, Robert Altman — dont le film « Fool for Love » est attendu comme l'événement de la journée — se distingue de ses frileux confrères : il est là depuis hier. Et même un peu là : il est venu en famille. Avec Katherine, sa femme, et ses deux fils aînés, Steve et Bobby. Donc c'était d'ailleurs la place : le premier, parce qu'il est le chef décorateur du film ; le second, parce qu'il y a cumulé les fonctions d'assistant metteur en scène et de photographe de plateau... Notre photo : Altman family au balcon du Carlton.

(Photo Alain Brun-Jacob)

► En dernière page, les articles de René CENNI et Maurice HULE

The French love American film-makers and movie stars, and they make a big deal out of their visits to the Cannes Film Festival. It happened to be during a European terrorist scare, so the attendance at the festival was quite small. **11** Our photos ended up on the front page of *Le Figaro*, the big Paris newspaper, stating, "Altman is not afraid of the terrorists." It was Stevie, Bobby, Bob, and me on the balcony of the Carlton Hotel. We went back to Lille and finished the opera, then back to Paris and finished the film.

The opera wasn't Bob's only professional connection to the University of Michigan. In 1984 he had the opportunity to do some very lucrative commercials for Miller High Life Beer, and he chose to shoot them there, which the university appreciated. And when he did that one-man film, *Secret Honor*, he shot it in 1984 at the Martha Cook Residence Hall **12** on campus. So we had quite a lot of affiliation with the school—our grandson Wesley Ivan Hurt graduated from there. And now it has the Altman archives.

================================ *Streamers* ================================ 1983

13 *Streamers* was one of the projects that Bob pulled out of a hat. *Streamers* had been a very successful play on Broadway that had a long run. It was written by David Rabe and featured an all-male cast. I don't know how the deal came about, but Bob chose to make the film. I guess it was brought to him by the two guys who had backed it—and they were absolute crooks, but we didn't realize it at the time. I think one of them is dead, and the other one should be if he isn't. They were just horrible guys. They put up some money, and we moved to Dallas.

It was a very short shoot and a very low budget, but it was fun. We had a great time with a very interesting cast: Matthew Modine (I think this was his very first picture, and he had a big part in it), David Alan Grier; Michael Wright: Mitchell Lichtenstein, Roy Lichtenstein's son. A lot of interesting people. But it was a nightmare near the end because the two guys disappeared and did not come up with the money to finish it.

Finally, some lovely man named Nick Mileti from Cleveland came up with the money, saved the picture, and ended up getting a producer's credit. And the film went on to do quite well, actually. It closed the New York Film Festival in 1983. Bob couldn't go, so I went onstage on the arms of David Rabe and Nick Mileti. That was the first time I'd done anything to represent him such as that. It was quite an event.

In 1984 we were doing a promotional tour for *Streamers* in Europe. We stayed at the Connaught in London. Then we went to a special event in northwestern France, in a place called Quimper. They gave us a lavish party. It was in the stables of some castle, and it was all candlelit with crystal glasses and big, long tables loaded with every kind of food and beautiful arrangements of flowers. The wine flowed, like you can imagine, and we had to get a plane the next morning. We ended up just getting about four hours' sleep. We could barely make it. Denise Breton, our PR person for all the European activities throughout Bob's entire career, could barely get us there. Anyway, we made it. We got back to Paris around ten in the morning and got right into bed at the Hotel La Trémoille. They had asked us previously, "When you come through Paris, what would Mrs. Altman like to do?" I had said, "Well, I'd like to see a fashion show." I'd never seen one. The fashion show was in the Tuileries Garden. It was Sonia Rykiel prêt-à-porter, or ready-to-wear. I had a hangover, too, but Bob really did not want to get out of that big, soft, beautiful bed. I got up ahead of him and started getting myself together, and I kept saying, "It's almost time for the fashion show." It was damp and dark outside. And he told this story many times later. He said, "I came so close to not going to that fashion show, but I took one look at her face and I knew, boy, I had to go." So he pulled himself up and out, and we took a cab over to the Tuileries Garden and picked up our tickets.

It was drizzly and cold. We stood in line, and then we went into this enormous tent. There were bleachers on both sides with the runway down the center, ending with the stage at the end. The music was really loud; it sounded great! As I recall, the first thing I heard was Streisand singing something. It was really quite festive, and, thinking back, we were both getting kind of excited about it. All of a sudden the lights went down, and out on the stage came five women in five different versions of the same red knit dress. The music was blasting, and they shot single file down that runway through the center of those bleachers—and all hell broke loose. It was like that for the next hour and a half. We were just out of our minds, off our seats. Bob couldn't wait. The very next day he contacted Sonia Rykiel, and they started right then and there. That was 1984, but they were never able to get *Prêt-à-Porter* made until 1993.

14–17 Bob made all his jobs happen, and sometimes they took us to far and strange places. But he was able to keep all the balls in the air throughout the entire decade of the eighties and also do things that he really enjoyed. At one point we were really flat broke, or damn near. Our big, beautiful house in Malibu was leased, because we thought we had a location coming up. But then the picture fell through. And we had rented our office on Central Park West out to Steve Tesich, a writer who has since died. He was a client and dear friend of our agent, Sam Cohn.

All of a sudden there we were in the middle of a hot New York summer in

Queen Elizabeth 2   Photographed on board 1984   Queen Elizabeth 2   Photographed on board 1984

17

18 *Fool for Love* was Stephen Altman's first job as a production designer, after years of working his way up through the art department. I don't have pictures to show the set, but it was an old motel with cabins and a main building.

Sam Shepard wrote the play *Fool for Love*, and it was a big success off-Broadway. In fact, it is still being performed all over the world. Bob and I saw it. Sam Shepard is a true artist, and he has an artist's temperament: He's hot and cold. So here he was starring in this piece that he wrote, but somebody else was directing. Bob was really dealing with the writer part of the time and the actor part of the time. It was a hard job.

1984 with three youngsters. Matthew was eighteen, Bobby was twenty-four, and our granddaughter, Signe, was fifteen. We had the three kids and had to figure out something to do. I remember I got the boys roller skates, and Bob made a remote control car with Matthew that he ran up and down the halls of the Delmonico, where we were living. Then we had this idea to find an inexpensive place to rent in London and take the kids. That way Bob would be able to meet with possible investors and other people over there about future films. It wasn't for a vacation. He *never* took a vacation for vacation's sake, ever! It was almost always work connected. That was such a typical trait of Bob's. I don't think that's anything you can acquire; I think you have to be born with it, that energy, that inclination to make something happen.

Our friends, Gillian Freeman and Edward Thorpe, who live in London, found an inexpensive place in Earls Court **14** **15**, which is not anything like Kensington or Chelsea, where we lived before and after. It was just a little attached house, and it seemed like a great idea. So we bought coach tickets and flew over.

Bob wanted to meet with people in Paris, and he did. That was a productive trip for him. He was on the wagon at the time—so he was trying to smoke pot instead, because, as he used to say, when the sun went down, he had to do something to change his temperature. He must have gotten a deal going, because when we went back to London, he came home one day and had five tickets in his hand and said, "We're going to go home on the *QE2* **16**. You're going to go on ahead, and I've got to go back to Paris." So we boarded in England, and then the ship made a stop in France, where Bob joined us. It ended up being quite an interesting family experience.

18

Bob and Sam—who was living with Jessica Lange—ended on pretty good terms, though. Later Sam made some derogatory remarks about Bob that were published in a magazine, for which he later apologized.

19

21

21 At some point in early 1985, we were thinking about finding a place in New York. When we were looking for an apartment, Bob came home one night and said he'd seen one that was a little kitschy, with an Egyptian motif in the common areas. It had been built as a temple for the Knights of Pythias in the mid-twenties. It became a lot of other things through the years. Elliott Gould had

taken tap-dancing lessons there at one time, somebody's mother had played mah-jongg there, and then it was a recording studio—Buddy Holly had his last recording session there. And now it was apartments. They maintained the Egyptian motif. The apartment we were looking at had a two-story living room ceiling. We bought it, gutted it, and designed our own apartment.

Architectural Digest
1985

19, 20 In 1990, *Architectural Digest* did this spread on our apartment. Paige Rense, who was the editor of *Architectural Digest* at the time, loved Stephen Shadley, our interior designer. Jaime Ardiles-Arce was the brilliant photographer who made our apartment look like a series of in-depth oil paintings.

In 1986, while Bob was doing the opera in Lille, we met an English filmmaker named Don Boyd who'd gotten hold of the rights to ten classical pieces from the Columbia recording library. He had this idea of finding a director for each piece and putting them together for television. Each director got to choose his piece and would then write a screenplay around it and film it as a short subject to be assembled with the others. The directors were Bob, Bruce Beresford, Bill Bryden, Jean-Luc Godard, Derek Jarman, Franc Roddam, Nicolas Roeg, Ken Russell, Charles Sturridge, and Julien Temple. John Hurt was the narrator.

Bob's piece was called "Les Boréades," excerpts from an opera by

Rameau. He chose that because he figured he could use the wardrobe that he'd used for *The Rake's Progress*, since it was the same period. And he knew where he wanted to shoot it: in this beautiful old church right in the heart of Paris. It's short, about four or five minutes. And it's filled with characters reminiscent of the period—women with their breasts sticking out and overly made up, filling the theater and the stage—all crazy and exciting. Don Boyd got it into the Cannes Film Festival, and we all went. It was fun. 22–25

26–31 In 1987, Bob was asked to do a piece for CBS, and he chose to do *The Caine Mutiny Court-Martial*. It was originally a play by Herman Wouk 26–28, who came to visit the set and give us his seal of approval. We shot it in Port Townsend, near Seattle, which was originally a naval base—and this film is all about naval officers. The picture starred Brad Davis, who had made his name as the lead in *Midnight Express*. Jeff Daniels was also in it. Mike Murphy was the judge. It was one of the first films for both Eric Bogosian and Peter Gallagher.

31 At the wrap party, Brad Davis gave Bob this anchor as a gift. We used to have it hanging outside on our deck in Malibu. Bobby has it now.

32–34 *Tanner '88* was shot in several cities from the winter into the summer of the election year 1988. Episodes were shot in New Hampshire, Nashville, Washington, D.C., Los Angeles, Detroit, and Atlanta. In Atlanta we took our candidate, Jack Tanner, played by Michael Murphy, right into the Democratic convention. We—the Democrats—nominated Dukakis. The Republicans unearthed some really crummy publicity about him, and that knocked his numbers way down. He lost the election to George H. W. Bush. Anyway, Jesse Jackson, who was running for president, was there, and he made a big speech.

Bruce Babbitt, who was the governor of Arizona, had been trying to get nominated. He didn't make it, of course, but he had had his hat in the ring and had done his year in Iowa trying to get his campaign together. But he lost out. He was a very interesting man, and Bob used him in the series. **32**, **33** Here he is: Jack Tanner, as a candidate himself, walking with a fellow candidate along the Potomac River discussing politics.

34 This picture defies everything that I had set out to do when I married Bob. When I met him I had been working as an extra for seven years. That's how we met, and that was all wonderful, but

I said, "I'm never going to do it again." Any time he or his assistant directors would try to get me in a shot, I would never do it. On this one day, on *Tanner '88*, they were shooting in Los Angeles at a hotel on Wilshire Boulevard. Mike Murphy and Ilana Levine, as one of his campaign workers, are in a scene where many people are lined up to meet this candidate, and they needed "bodies," as Bob used to say, to fill the scene. So I walked in there just at this moment to visit—and all of a sudden I heard Bob holler out across the set: "You and Lori"—that's our friend Lori Young—"you and Lori get in the shot and walk through." Well, I could hear it in his voice and I could see it in his expression: I knew this was no time to get coy or cute. So we got ready to do our walk-through, and I looked over and here was my son Matthew, a production assistant, of all people, giving us our cue. It was a weird, weird day, and this photograph just brings back all those memories.

35–41 *Vincent & Theo* was financed to be a four-hour miniseries sponsored by Canal Plus. Then, as he did with *Jimmy Dean*, Bob cut it as a feature as well. It was given a theatrical release, but not widely distributed. At one point we were shooting in a town outside Amsterdam called Bussum. These photographs were taken during pre-production. We were invited on somebvody's boat to celebrate a big holiday: Queen's Day. We rode up and down the canals where, along the sides, everybody brought out all their wares, and foods like pot brownies and cookies. People were selling all kinds of stuff. People were legally smoking dope. Bands were playing. It was so festive.

Then the whole company moved to the South of France to shoot the part when Van Gogh lost his marbles and ended up in the sanitarium in Saint-Rémy-de-Provence.

41 When Bob would drive every morning from our hotel to Tarascon, where the crew stayed, listening to Tommy Flanagan or Tom Waits's "On The Nickel," he'd pass these sunflowers.

6

THE NINETIES

BY GIULIA
D'AGNOLO VALLAN

A proposed sequel to *Nashville* and a Raymond Carver project eventually brought Altman back to the United States. The first, *Nashville 12*, reprising some of the characters in the original film twelve years later, never materialized. In order to get the second financed, the director had to take another job first. It is an irony that did not go unnoticed by Altman that he would owe the biggest of his many so-called comebacks to a film about an industry that, he felt, had wholly rejected him.

LEFT Altman directing Madeleine Stowe (as Sherri Shepard) and Tim Robbins (as Gene Shepard) on the set of *Short Cuts*, 1993.

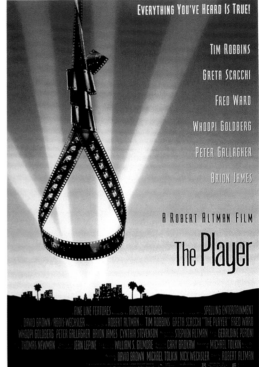

Adapted from Michael Tolkin's 1988 novel of the same title, *The Player* is the story of Griffin Mill, a studio executive who kills a writer he thinks may be stalking him, then lives happily ever after—unpunished, promoted, and married to the dead writer's girlfriend. Beside Tim Robbins in the lead role, with Whoopi Goldberg, Peter Gallagher, Fred Ward, and Greta Scacchi, *The Player* also features a multitude of stars, industry types, and Altman collaborators—in all, about sixty-five of them—playing themselves in cameo roles: Julia Roberts, Burt Reynolds, Malcolm McDowell, Peter Falk, Bruce Willis, Sydney Pollack, Buck Henry, Karen Black, and Tolkin himself, among many others. They were all paid scale. "For them it was almost like signing a petition," recalled the director, who called them personally, one by one.

Produced by Avenue Pictures and released in April 1992 by newcomer specialty division Fine Line Features after a small bidding war among companies, *The Player* was welcomed as a scathing satire of Hollywood (in his review, Roger Ebert spoke of "glorious vengeance" on the director's part; *Variety* described it as "mercilessly satiric" and compared it to Billy Wilder's *Sunset Boulevard* and Minnelli's *The Bad and the Beautiful*). In fact, on many occasions, Altman called *The Player* a "very, very soft indictment."

"Although we did lift up a few rocks, Hollywood is much crueler and uglier and more calculating than you see in the film," he would tell David Thompson in 2005. From the seven-plus minutes of its tour de force opening shot, to the Altmanesque star-studded cast, to the conceit of getting away with murder, to the playful circularity of the ending, *The Player* is uncharacteristically tongue in cheek for Altman. It is probably his most farcical film and, by design, one of his most cunning—with just enough criticism that Hollywood could take and enough movie stars to spin your head around. A voyeur's delight both for insiders and for those of us stuck on the outside.

It worked exactly the way it was supposed to, bringing Altman back to the limelight as well as winning the award for Best Director at the 1992 Cannes Film Festival, where Tim Robbins was named Best Actor. It was also a considerable financial success for Fine Line. More than anything else, it allowed the director to secure financing for the film he really wanted to make.

An intricate mural of various humanities against the backdrop of a city much more sprawling than Nashville, *Short Cuts* put Altman right where he felt most comfortable—among multiple story lines, open-ended narratives,

and a big ensemble cast. Jazzier and moodier than anything the director had ever done before, the film is made up of nine short stories and a poem by Raymond Carver that Altman and Frank Barhydt Jr. took apart in little pieces and then reassembled in a loose, new puzzle, relocating Carver's fiction from the Seattle area to the suburbs of Los Angeles. The film's ten story lines are less interconnected than *Nashville*'s or *A Wedding*'s, its twenty-two characters crossing each other's paths sometimes without even knowing it, by virtue of simply appearing in the same frame. Small accidents, coincidences, and an earthquake are the connecting tissue of the film, technically speaking. What actually holds together this ambitious free-style opera is Carver's and Altman's shared interest in the emotional power hidden behind the most mundane moments in the everyday life of unextraordinary people. Three fishermen, a policeman who betrays his wife, an artist's model, a sex-phone operator, a young woman who plays cello, her jazz-singing mother, a guy who cleans swimming pools, a cranky baker, a waiter, a limo driver ... compared to *Short Cuts*, *Nashville*'s environment seems positively exotic.

Always a very popular director among actors, at this stage of his career Altman had virtually no problem in casting pretty much whomever he wanted to work with. Lily Tomlin, Tom Waits, Julianne Moore, Tim Robbins, Lyle Lovett, Robert Downey Jr., Annie Ross, Chris Penn, Frances McDormand, Jack Lemmon—*Short Cuts* is populated both by old friends and newcomers. To make it easier on the actors' schedules, Altman requested each of them for only one week of work, and he shot the film one couple at a time over a ten-week period. As usual, he asked them to contribute to their characters. In that spirit, after visiting a Los Angeles sex-call center and taking notes, Jennifer Jason Leigh wrote all her character's phone conversations.

GREENER PASTURES
MICHAEL TOLKIN

Is no one going to say that Robert Altman was a great pothead? Let me, then. Robert Altman was a great pothead. In the war on drugs, he won. To look at his work without thinking about marijuana's specific gifts and poisons ... umm ... specific ... What was I saying? Oh. Right. Altman. Robert Altman. I met him; did I tell you that already?

Or as Fernando Pessoa says, "But he must be on fire somewhere. Otherwise, he will not cook the goose of his human inferiority."

Six years before *The Player* (1992), I stopped smoking pot, for the typical reasons, but not the least of them was paranoia. And it was the eighties, the parentheses of aerobics between the cocaine years and the advent of the age of caffeine. After Altman signed on to direct the film, I worried that I would break my abstention, which was private; I wasn't in the program, but it held me well for that time. And Altman's pot didn't come out until we had been in the production offices for a week.

We were in his office, and as the joint was on its way to me, I took it with a little rationalization, something like, "Altman has already told you he hates plot, so anything you can do to get closer to him will help the movie." We were friendly but not familiar, and then, only as friendly as a writer can be with a director who hates plot, and says so. The carpet nap grew warm vines.

The script, which I wrote for David Brown after he read the galleys, had gone to a few directors. In the transition from the book, my novel about guilt had become a story about Holly-

wood, a subject Hollywood had avoided for years. We were asked to change the story to a steel mill. This is true. I did a rewrite for Mark Rydell, but nothing came of that. I sent the script to Chevy Chase and had a meeting with him in the Beverly Hills Hotel. He brought along a rich guy in tassel loafers, whose role other than pal of the star was unclear, but he was an early avatar of the very big money, and they gave me notes on the script and I did a few drafts for them, too. All the drafts were just rearrangements of the same blocks of story, and none of them took a long time, and like most revisions after the story and characters are set and before the reality of budget, they were useless because the thing was never going to be anything other than what it already was. Then Altman switched agencies and went to William Morris, where I was, and they gave him the script, one of the earliest drafts.

MICHAEL TOLKIN is a novelist, screenwriter, and director. He adapted his own 1988 novel, *The Player,* for Altman's 1992 film of the same name. Tolkin's other screenplay credits include *The Rapture* (1991), *Deep Cover* (1992), and *Changing Lanes* (2002).

David Brown, Nick Wechsler, and I had a meeting with him. Altman took a chair while his line producer, a thin, depressed chain-smoker, distractingly hostile, slouched like an embarrassed teenager. She didn't look healthy. Neither did he. One of Altman's eyes was weeping, and he had a boil on his neck. He apologized. He said it would all clear up soon. He was nearing seventy.

He was calmly enthusiastic but not gushing with praise, saying nothing about what he wouldn't change or what he would; it was all very general and friendly and honest, with inevitability like a trade wind. I think he had already cast Tim Robbins.

After Altman left, David Brown, a great man, said that we should ignore Altman's health, that Altman was a brilliant director who hadn't had a hit for a few years and was due for one.

Altman worked with a lot of the same people, and his circus knew how to pitch the tent. The production office was happy, with the usual intrigues and alliances. He had a good cook making our lunch every day.

There are directors whose movies are just delivery systems for their self-confidence, in which self-confidence is really the thing that entertains, because it takes a bold confidence to successfully tell a stupid story, and for sure there are useful energies we suck from awful films that begin with the director's amazing love of himself. The films of such directors are always the same, until they lose their confidence, and then their movies fail in every way—no fun for us, no money for them. Altman never told the same film twice.

To Altman we can apply Jean Giraudoux's insight that only the mediocre are always at their best. But Giraudoux also said that the secret of success is sincerity, which contradicts what Oscar Wilde said about bad poetry being unfailingly sincere. But back to Pessoa: "Not sincerity in the absolute, but some sort of sincerity, is required in art, that it may be art."

Some sort of sincerity: Robert Altman was a misanthrope who loved having people around, to watch their behavior. This made him a great host. He should have adapted Poe. He never made a horror film, and if I've ever been sorry that I didn't know him better, it's for this: Thinking about it this morning, I would have loved to pitch "The Gold Bug" to him, a story about something meaning something to people, the meaning being more important than the thing. This formula is a bit like his movies or marijuana, and the element that divides those who like his movies from those who don't, since his movies don't have the sharp perspectives that always point out the one thing the film wants watched.

I had forgotten how pot works, the way it rearranges the significance of things, the way internal distractions become interesting or threatening paths. It's not a happy drug at all; it's not two flutes of nice champagne and a pretty face and perfume in the air. After I smoked a little pot with him—and other than one morning in the office, he didn't smoke during the day—some of his methods made sense, and if it was pot sense, the sense is not invalid.

As the host, he didn't cast his films; he invited actors to join him. The first call he made for casting the background movie stars for *The Player* was Harry Belafonte. After that, he was able to tell everyone else he wanted that Harry Belafonte was going to be an extra in this protest march against Hollywood. Schwarzenegger refused, which pissed off Altman because he'd given Arnold a nice little part in *The Long Goodbye* (1973). Early in the shoot he lost the center of a few scenes because, as a good host, to make his guests comfortable, he gave them too much to do, and he had to control the impulse to be generous to everyone. He held to his original plan in the party scene where Sydney Pollack confronts Tim Robbins about the rumors, while Jack Lemmon is at the piano and Rod Steiger wanders around looking at the furniture.

It isn't that he trusted actors as much as that he loved to see them work, which is why his lighting is rarely shadowed; he needed to light enough of the set to give the actors room to move, and he mounted the camera on a custom-designed boom so that he could conduct the camera operator to float his attention through the scene.

He told me he wanted the film to be like white jazz, a distinction he didn't define. Watching his work after he said that, I think I understood what he meant: He'd have rhythm and swing, but no deep blues, especially no faked blues, which would violate the rule or necessity of sustained sincerity. Or maybe sincerity is a mistranslation of integrity, or maybe integrity is the better word.

For a screenwriter, jazz as the model offers the scariest of all hazards: improvisation. You can't improvise a plot, and you can improvise your way out of coherence, but screenwriters tend to be too precious about specific lines instead of making sure that the intentions of the scenes are clear enough to withstand whatever happens as the actors and director play. And the improvisations had more to do with exercises for the actors to get deeper into character than they were for dialogue, which I didn't understand while the movie was in production, so I was out of my mind a few times on the set, at one point taking Altman outside to rant at him in a way that was primitive, stupid, and rude, and then, when the film was finished, the meanderings that upset me were gone. But he was never high on the set, and he wasn't stoned in the editing room.

My favorite Altman films are *M*A*S*H* (1970), *McCabe & Mrs. Miller* (1971), *California Split* (1974), *3 Women* (1977), and *Gosford Park* (2001).

225

Short Cuts had its triumphant world premiere at the 1993 Venice Film Festival, where it won the Golden Lion (together with Krzysztof Kieslowski's *Three Colors: Blue*) as well as a special Volpi Cup for Best Acting Ensemble. Fine Line released it in the United States in October, to great reviews. Altman was nominated for the Academy Award for Best Director, but lost to Steven Spielberg for *Schindler's List*.

As he was riding the wave of his two last successes, the American film industry was going through another change, which had begun in the second half of the eighties. Inspired by Altman and his seventies peers, a new generation of independent filmmakers was making waves outside the system. Meeting the taste of an audience starved for content not to be found in blockbuster-oriented studio product, the early films of Jim Jarmusch, Spike Lee, the Coen brothers, and Jonathan Demme did well both critically and at the box office. A small number of independent distributors noticed the trend and started investing in young directors and art-house cinema; among them were Miramax, Ira Deutchman's Cinecom, Fine Line, Orion, and October Films, which was founded in 1991. In 1985, Robert Redford's Sundance Institute took over the ailing U.S. Film Festival, soon renaming it and making it a major launchpad for independent work. A new taste, aesthetic, and demand for non-studio cinema was being created. Robert Altman had been one of the early instigators of this change, and as such he was welcomed into the fold.

Harvey and Bob Weinstein's Miramax enthusiastically provided financing for Altman's long-in-the-making fashion project. He had become interested by the fashion world in 1984, after he and his wife, Kathryn, attended one of Sonia Rykiel's Paris shows. Shortly after that, he hired *San Francisco Examiner* film critic Barbara Shulgasser to write a script. Miramax bought the film based on her draft—which Altman subsequently reinvented entirely. Both by design and by circumstance, *Prêt-à-Porter* comes closest among all his features to having been completely improvised, the closest to the director's ideal of instigating an event and capturing the reality of it as it happens on film. Following the mockumentary model he had intuitively aimed at in *Nashville*, codified in *Tanner '88*, and parodied in *The Player*, Altman brought his entire production right into the middle of the Paris fashion shows. He actually shot five of them. The first cut of the film did not include any of that footage. Then they were slowly added in, multiplying layers of reality.

ROBERT ALTMAN & FRANK BARHYDT

TESS GALLAGHER

OPPOSITE *Short Cuts* contact sheet of Altman setting up a shot and Altman discussing a scene with Julianne Moore and Madeleine Stowe.

Robert Altman sits next to me on the bed with Anne Archer in her cotton nightie squeezed against him, his hand balancing at her waist. She readies herself as "Claire" to cross to the bathroom where she will speak back toward Fred Ward (Stuart) from the *Short Cuts* script.

By then I've read the script in at least two different versions. Before that I'd seen revisions and published versions of the story, "So Much Water So Close to Home" by Raymond Carver, on which this scene had been based. In its final form it had appeared in Ray's last collection *Where I'm Calling From*.

The reverberation of this current connecting Ray's writing with the script by Altman and Barhydt, passing into these flesh and blood characters being fixed on celluloid has begun, in the cramped space of that room, to cause my molecules to chatter and collide. I hope it isn't audible, because the half-threat call of "Rolling!" has already gone out and Walt Lloyd, the cinematographer, is bent to the camera. *Film is rolling*.

There is a vibrant calm at the center of fire. This is the calm I entered in the unbearable heat of the tiny bedroom of Claire and Stuart on location for *Short Cuts* as it was being shot in L.A. in August of 1992.

Someone had cut the power to the motorized, body-thick duct of cool air that had been shushing into the space through a second-story window. At dawn the house had been cloaked in black tarp to shoot these night scenes.

The camera is rolling. It is the quiet of unfinished arguments, of Mafia hats at dawn—the air impending and alert. But what a population looks on! Members of the crew hover unobtrusively in doorways and crannies, crouched and leaning in the stairwell, stilled like children in a game of statues on a postage stamp-sized lawn.

Claire looks back at her husband, Stuart, who's just told her that for three days and nights he'd left a woman's body tied in a river while he fished with his friends. *The camera is rolling*. Claire's expression of bafflement shifts into slow but steady disbelief in the icy flicker of the monitor which shows what the camera is picking up. Her face seems enormous like anything newborn because, I suppose, of that special amplification time takes on when you know its images are being preserved.

The moments I was living had been a long while arriving, it seemed.

TESS GALLAGHER is a celebrated poet, essayist, and short story writer. She is also the widow of Raymond Carver, whose stories comprised the basis for Altman's film *Short Cuts* (1993). Her 1992 collection of love poems to Carver, *Moon Crossing Bridge*, was written and published after his death.

All the way back to a newspaper article which had sparked Ray's story, forward to Frank Barhydt's sister giving him a book by Carver in 1988, the year Ray died, and then to Altman on a plane coming home from Italy, reading Carver stories as aftermath to his own changed direction.

The curious thing, too, was that even with all the import of filming I've just described, there was also a casualness about what movement did take place around the shooting. Casualness and ease. Someone, something, or several someones were in control. Everything was going to happen the best it could and if things went wrong, there would be a way to handle it, even to use slippage to advantage. This agility of spirit Altman brings to his work seemed to free everyone to do their best. I was to appreciate the consistency of that spirit during the numerous visits I would make to the filming locations in August and October.

There is a feeling of brine and high seas about Robert Altman. He's scow and schooner, scrappy and tested. In stature his 6' 2", his love-to-eat heft, uncannily reminded me of Ray. Directing, he's like a genial, no-nonsense captain with a tender, flexible grip on things, even though he seems to be relying on everyone else present to do exactly what needs to be done, largely without him. When he does speak, it's calmly, as if he's teasing things out, yet with an exactitude rooted deep in the heart of the action as it's evolving from the script. But he's most live to what's coming through the actors in that moment of shooting.

This exploding yet controlled time of the camera-rolling which I've tried to describe would have been sheer chaos without the firm scaffolding of this fine script, initially drafted by Frank Barhydt, a lean, down-to-earth man who laughs easily and whose laconic manner is quietly disarming. Having met him first on the page in his work on the script, I knew myself to be in the company of an impressive writer on his own ground. He also understood the way Ray's characters thought because he had down how they talked. I liked it that in person he didn't seem to need to prove anything to anyone. His relationship to Altman goes back through his own father who'd been Altman's boss in some past era. Barhydt has also worked on three previous projects with Altman.

After discussions with Altman, Frank had roughed out the *Short Cuts* script. Then they put Carver's books aside for the next phase. Over the following months, Altman and Barhydt began to eat, sleep, and live Carver's world in its essences, imagining how it could find new life in film and in the things they each had to offer. Frank's Missouri-tanged voice picks up color and velocity remembering how they worked, the way their ideas began to feed into each other out of Carver, so that in the end, it's hard to remember who gave what.

The two would perform variations like jazz musicians on the Carver stories, inventing their own characters to add to his, getting scenes onto colored note cards that let them visualize the wide mosaic on the wall behind them at the initial production office in Malibu. Once, on the phone, Bob and I had talked about how scenes could go more than one way. The scripting of the stories began to reflect this variability of direction. I mentioned to Bob in a follow-up letter that such exploration was deep in the spirit of poetry, all the way back to Aristotle, who says poetry deals with "a kind of thing which might happen, i.e. what is possible."

But behind, under, and inside this script remain the nine short stories and the poem, "Lemonade," of Raymond Carver. His clarity and precision, the elisions of his character's speech, the ways they glance off each other in conversation, bruise, circle, plead, lie, or seek to persuade are unmistakably carried forward from Carver. As Frank is quick to acknowledge, much of Carver's dialogue was just too good not to use. But it couldn't simply carry at other times, either. Film, as Frank puts it, is "wordier." Sometimes an action demands two lines in film where one serves on the page. Sometimes a written thought or attitude will take a series of actions to translate onto film.

Besides the collateral of Carver's wonderful ear for the spoken word as it carries the unspoken, the script also had the charged fabric of Carver's world in which those life verities one depends on might at any instant give way. Altman and Carver probably join at this strange hinge "luck," both of them chancers and creators willing to stake their lives, artistic and otherwise, on the precarious rim of possibility. They've known the dive and swoop of fortune, which takes us a step beyond mere courage to that helpless place we all hit at some point where we realize anything could and does happen, and to us.

What I keep admiring in this film script is the way the stories more than coexist. The failure of so many scripts of Carver stories by others I'd seen prior to the Altman/Barhydt project had been to stay so close to the originals that a robotic pandering to the text resulted. They were like someone ice skating with an osprey's egg on which the bird is still nesting. Nothing new came to the stories and they were damp with poignant silences.

Altman and Barhydt broke the frames on the stories and allowed the characters to affect each other's worlds or not, as if to suggest that we are both more "in this together" *and* alone than we ever suspected. There is a high element of surprise and delight simply in re-meeting the characters *Nashville*-style in unexpected conformations. These interactions move Carver into new territory. Often it seems Altman and Barhydt are using Carver to cue what might have been said and done, but was under the surface in the stories.

The trick in this scripting is, of course, to give enough of the unsaid while somehow communicating Carver's gaps and darkness. The shuttle motion of picking up and dropping stories at intervals is one mechanism the film uses to suspend us in its current, then allow us to reapproach what's going on down river.

In early March of 1991, I'd sent Bob five pages of notes, what I called a "champagne read" of the first script I'd seen. I would later send "hard read" notes. But early on I was simply cheerleading. The caliber of that initial script verified my early joy at Altman's having undertaken to use Ray's stories in a film. I could see that he and Barhydt honored the spirit of Ray's work, knew how to give its Kafkaesque "gay and empty ride," its shadows as well as that Chekhovian side Ray came to in the last seven years. I'd read the scenes with what I called "dead-alive eyes," meaning I'd tried to let Ray, as I'd experienced him in our own collaborations, look through. I'd felt how amazed Ray would have been to meet his stories interwoven on one huge canvas in this extraordinary script.

Early on I'd realized that literary widows can get sickeningly nostalgic with "he would haves." So I ration that assumptive verb tense. Nonetheless, it serves honestly when I think how much Raymond Carver truly *would have* hated missing the glow and sweep of what has gone forward in the evolution of this scripting. It has passed from his stories to Bob and Frank, to the contributions of the crew, the inspiration of the actors, then into the cutting room and now into theaters around the world, embraced and chastened, galvanized and amplified, reinterpreted by the many-headed hydra of collaborative intensity which is filmmaking—admittedly a galaxy away from the solitude in which Ray's writing was accomplished. But Ray was a realist who knew the difference between the action of the hive and of the cleaver. This scripting is amazing for how it orchestrates for both.

Risking trespass, I will say I believe Ray's attitude toward Altman's use of his work would have been one of permission to an artist of equal stature. Ray's capacity for delight is legendary. He surrendered to those things he loved. He was a straight-on admirer of Robert Altman, whose *Nashville* we'd watched more than once on video together and considered one of the most inspired, patently American films yet made.

Ray would have shown a generous curiosity about the new shape his stories would inevitably take. I imagine him exuberant at the dailies, swilling lemonade, laughing with his whole body at his smaller violences of snipped telephone cords becoming larger, more surgically destructive in Stormy Weathers's chainsaw massacre of his wife's living room furniture. He would appreciate the shifting of emphasis in Altman's version of "So Much Water So Close to Home"—how he uncovers something about the differences between the sexes by being more evenhanded with blame in a story which belonged firmly in Carver to the dilemmas of its women.

Altman and Barhydt both have a great sense of the dryly comic, and they've brought to the surface Carver's own willingness to laugh with, not at, his characters. He was nose-to-nose with them, feeling the ruptures in intimacy and coherence which split their lives apart. This was to hint at restraining one of Bob's most potent and incisive artistic tools—irony. I typed up and gave him lines from Rainer Maria Rilke's *Letters to a Young Poet* which, while admitting that irony "cleanly used is also clean," advises that one shouldn't be governed by it ... Seek the depth of things: thither irony never descends...."

While such advice smacks perhaps of the confinements of the literary, it is also true that irony, in the more public mediums of television and film, often becomes the contemporary escape hatch to avoid genuine feeling. Ray's story "A Small, Good Thing" would have set Bob's compass in this regard if I'd said nothing. Because it centers around the death of a child, it required and got Bob's consummate skill in keeping the depth, yet not tipping into sentimentality or drawing away from the emotions. It is the story left most intact by the scripting, and, along with the Jack Lemmon portrait of the adulterous father, it is one of the places the film lets the suffering of the characters open out most—hands and heart on.

Altman's difference from Carver is that he often shifts the cries of the characters into the wider arena of the audience by withholding them on screen. For instance, in a Carver story like "Jerry and Molly and Sam": the adulterous husband silently asks himself "Is there a chance for me?" But in Altman, we see Gene retrieve the family dog he's abandoned, then return home as if he's never betrayed anyone—though he has, and the fact that the audience know it serves as the inner ache he is too compulsive even to acknowledge.

Carver's characters grapple with their fates in the matter-of-fact voices of his narrators, but in film this all has to happen as action, not introspection. The effect of this necessary translation is at times to toughen and speed up what is tender and circuitous in Carver. Altman and Barhydt's intuitive feel for the need to restore tenderness can be felt in moments of vulnerability with characters like Doreen Piggott, the waitress played by Lily Tomlin, when she runs after the child she's hit with her car, pleading with him to let her take him home—realizing aloud to her husband (Tom Waits) later, then to her daughter (Lili Taylor), that her whole life could have changed if the child had been killed. The audience must bridge this near-escape to bear the truth—that the child *does* in fact die. Doreen's ignorance of this caresses the audience's pain register each time she repeats how close she came to killing the child.

With Altman, we can't escape the steepness of the ravine rushing up at us. If Carver fans miss the redemptive interior voices of his baffled Middle-American characters in the film, it's because in the stories these brief glimpses of their hopes being blunted by realities do serve to cushion our fall.

I'm reminded of a remark by Pablo Neruda's friend Roberto Matta: "One has to be in despair about everything, in order to defeat despair." This hard assignment—to feel the pervasiveness of the American malaise—seems crucial to Altman and Barhydt's revisioning of Carver. The film audience, to a large extent, becomes its own interior narrator, a dazed character eventually forced outside the theater who keeps ruminating the half-articulated, glancing-off pain they've just witnessed.

Both stories and film use the whole keyboard of human proclivities, but the film is huge with appetite, and because it combines and interlocks stories, it has a ricochet power which the individual stories alone don't carry. There are the reverberating themes of infidelity, denial, sexual exploitation, the alcoholic merry-go-round, irrevocable loss in the death of a child, anonymous and grotesque death in the neglect of the woman's body in "So Much Water So Close to Home," and the disappearance of certain characters into fantasy.

When, at last, in January of 1993, the film was assembled in its bladder-breaking three-hour-and-ten-minute version in the cutting room in NYC, Altman held a special showing for me. There were celebrities attending, but I wasn't able to spot most of them without cueing from my photographer friend, Marion Ettlinger. (I did recognize and meet Lauren Bacall in the elevator!) All the better to focus on Altman and the film with the lively ghost of Ray beaming in on me.

The fan of images was projected in that small, crowded viewing room. Time again slipped out of itself. The jigsaw tapestry of the lives on the screen began to intersect with my own, to make a kind of earthquake in my solar plexus. I was absorbed, hypnotized by the spectacle. It was as if the film compelled its audience to recognize its own deceits, betrayals, exposures, and abandonments as Altman recreates them from Carver and adds his own. By the end, the beautiful flawed confusion of human lives had worked its spell on me. Yet it was beyond spell, out into that territory which John Updike says demands "great natural health," in which we are asked to sustain life without illusions.

There was a pervasive sadness

and loneliness in the room when the film ended. But also a palpable exhilaration that comes from having been through something large and inexplicable, more achingly comfortless than anyone had guessed they'd have the stamina and will to experience. But we had. We've come through. When the lights went up, we belonged to that world, the fusion of Altman–Carver, made visceral on film— naked, obsessive, rawly innocent, chaotic. It was a poetry of the impure, as if we could suddenly see ourselves worn away by the acid of not knowing what's happening to us as we do what we do, the poetry of food stains and shocks, doubts and stupidities, of loneliness and pirated rooms, injured sex, clingings over hospital beds, splinters of glassy hearts in the freshly vacuumed carpet.

It was natural in aftermath, at the restaurant, to want to talk about hope, that elusive Carver manna heaven is always intending to drop. Had Altman inscribed our brows with William the Silent's "One need not hope to undertake?" Were we cut off as a people from our pain and suffering because we don't know how or what to hope for anymore? Whatever the intricacies of the diagnosis, we felt the images of the film challenging us.

Art as distinct from the purely entertaining isn't obliged to provide the antidote for its revealed poisons. Ray also had to fight this notion from readers and critics—that the artist was supposed to do more than diagnose the condition of its characters—that he or she was also sup-

posed to rise like the Statue of Liberty on the horizon with some sort of redemptive light.

But in Altman's films, as with Ray's stories, the questions are the redemption. What we do with our recognitions, once we gaze into their harsh and tender mirrors, is really on our own ground, outside both the stories and the film. That's the provocative nature of art itself. It says what is, as honestly and truly as it can envision it. On this count both Altman and Carver are relentlessly true. They both reach these truths lyrically. Altman's lyricism works by dislocating the narrative, by jump-starting it, by allowing it to love its lost causes even as it leapfrogs them onto the wet cement of the next enormous instant.

On one of my last nights in L.A. at a meal at the Granita restaurant, Altman and I had been talking about our mutual fascination with doubles, the wild probability of gaining that extra likeness which might extend your life into the secret fruitfulness of the path not taken. "Ray was a Gemini," I told Bob, in my by now habitual reflex of keeping Ray present in our conversations. We also spoke about poetry—Ray's love of it. I said I felt Ray's stories had the hum and leap of poetry inside them. Later, as we left the restaurant, Bob came back from the car to where I was standing with Frank at the curbside to plant a kiss on my mouth so firmly it was brotherly. "Goodnight, Poet," he said, and without a beat I answered: "Goodnight, Other Poet." Thinking double.

LEFT Robert Altman and Tess Gallagher on the set of *Short Cuts*.

OPPOSITE Contact sheet of Tim Robbins (officer Gene Shepard) with Madeleine Stowe (Sherri Shepard).

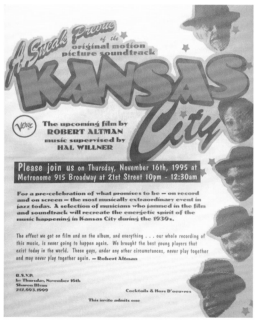

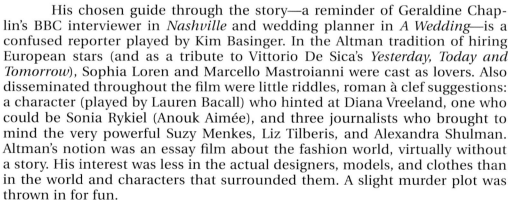

His chosen guide through the story—a reminder of Geraldine Chaplin's BBC interviewer in *Nashville* and wedding planner in *A Wedding*—is a confused reporter played by Kim Basinger. In the Altman tradition of hiring European stars (and as a tribute to Vittorio De Sica's *Yesterday, Today and Tomorrow*), Sophia Loren and Marcello Mastroianni were cast as lovers. Also disseminated throughout the film were little riddles, roman à clef suggestions: a character (played by Lauren Bacall) who hinted at Diana Vreeland, one who could be Sonia Rykiel (Anouk Aimée), and three journalists who brought to mind the very powerful Suzy Menkes, Liz Tilberis, and Alexandra Shulman. Altman's notion was an essay film about the fashion world, virtually without a story. His interest was less in the actual designers, models, and clothes than in the world and characters that surrounded them. A slight murder plot was thrown in for fun.

Hollywood had very much enjoyed witnessing its own spectacle in *The Player*, but the fashion world was not amused by *Prêt-à-Porter*, to say the least. The hype around the project was such that some took umbrage with the film for reasons that had nothing to do with it. Critics were ferocious: Altman's dare of really improvising a picture as it went along did not work. Whether he himself thought the film had succeeded within its own premise—and on occasion he seemed to acknowledged it had not—in the clamor over *Prêt-à-Porter*, the most fascinating aspect of the film was overlooked: how much Altman seemed to have truly enjoyed, explored, and admired its very unlikely subject. One could see he was having fun. That same curiosity and a similar anthropological drive would illuminate more of his later choices of material.

OPPOSITE

TOP LEFT Robert Altman in the middle of some of the Hey Hey Club musicians. From the left: Christian McBride, bass; Mark Whitfield, guitar; Geri Allen, piano; Victor Lews, Drums; Jesse Davis, alto saxophone; Nicholas Payton, trumpet; Joshua Redman, tenor saxophone; James Carter, tenor saxophone; Don Byron, clarinet and baritone saxophone; James Zollar, trumpet.

Like the band "Keepin' 'Em off the Streets" from Altman's *A Perfect Couple*, members of The Hey Hey Club band performed a few live concerts after the release of *Kansas City*. Performances from the film were edited into a music documentary, *Robert Altman's Jazz '34*.

TOP RIGHT An unreleased poster for *Kansas City*.

BOTTOM Promotional materials for *Kansas City*.

ABOVE Polaroids from the set of *Kansas City*.

Before that, though, Altman went home. A mix of what he called "exaggerated memories" of his childhood years and jazz were the basis of *Kansas City*, a tale of corrupt politicians, organized crime, brilliant musicians, and two women set in his hometown in 1934, against the backdrop of a very violent election day and a strange kidnapping. Altman and his Kansas City–born cowriter, Frank Barhydt Jr., blended fiction with historical records of the city as run by Tom Pendergast's powerful Democratic machine and with personal recollections of residents living at that time. Altman said the film also came from stories that his father had told him as a child and the impressions that the adults' world around him left on his young mind, which is interesting because *Kansas City* is probably one of the director's most romantic films, and its dark story, mythical ambience, and characters do feel filtered through a boy's wonder, starting with Jennifer Jason Leigh's Blondie: moll, kidnapper, and number-one fan of Kansas City native Jean Harlow. Also referred to in the film is the woman who introduced Altman to jazz, his childhood maid Glendora Majors.

"I look at *Kansas City* like a musical piece, a fugue, with each character represented by an instrument," Altman told David Thompson. "Harry Belafonte was the trumpet, Dermot Mulroney the trombone, Jennifer Jason Leigh and Miranda Richardson were tenor saxophones doing a duet, and in a way their dialogue was like variations on a theme that did not have too much to do with advancing the plot." Music is central to most of Altman's films, and jazz has often been mentioned as a key to understanding their structure. *Kansas City* is the most explicit tribute to the form. Altman delighted himself in restaging—in a six-minute musical number recorded live on location—the legendary "battle

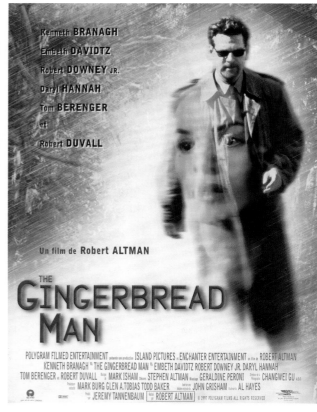

of the saxes" between Lester Young (played by Joshua Redman) and Coleman Hawkins (Craig Handy). The film featured other jazz musicians, such as David Murray, Victor Lewis, and James and Ron Carter. All the arrangements were freely inspired by thirties styles. Their performances became a documentary directed by Altman and narrated by Harry Belafonte, *Jazz '34.*

Altman followed *Kansas City* with three Southern films, all very much anchored to specific cities and/or their local cultures. The first one came from an unlikely source of material, a manuscript by John Grisham called *The Gingerbread Man.* Grisham adaptations were popular in the nineties. Sydney Pollack had made *The Firm* and Francis Ford Coppola *The Rainmaker.* Altman was intrigued by the opportunity of making a thriller, one of the very few genres he had not tried yet. The project had been offered by Polygram to British actor Kenneth Branagh, who liked the idea of working with Altman and agreed that he could rewrite Grisham's script. The story was moved to Savannah and soaked in a hurricane that haunts the whole picture. As usual, Altman played around with some of the genre conventions. He also hired real judges and lawyers (among whom was then-President Bill Clinton's powerful friend Vernon Jordan) to be

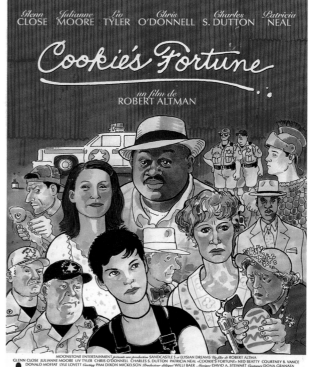

judges and lawyers in the film. The end result is an atmospheric piece, more a noir than a straight-out slick thriller in the vein of the other Grisham films.

Over his long career, Altman had made it almost a habit to give people he found interesting and talented their first shot at writing a script. It had been the case with Joan Tewkesbury and Frank Barhydt Jr., and now it was so with Anne Rapp, a former script supervisor he had known for a few years. She had recently enrolled in a creative writing course at the University of Mississippi, and Altman read some of her short stories. He liked them so much that he put her under contract and turned one of the stories, "All the President's Women," into an episode of a TV series, *Gun*, on which he was executive producer. Their collaboration also generated two features, *Cookie's Fortune* and *Dr. T & the Women*. One was set in the Old South community of Holly Springs, Mississippi, the other in upscale Dallas. Both are behavioral studies (Altman said that Rapp's writing reminded him of Eudora Welty and Flannery O'Connor), with strong regional flavors, a Gothic touch, and women very much at their heart. In both projects Altman surrounded himself with a great variety of actresses: Patricia Neal, Glenn Close, Julianne Moore, and Liv Tyler in *Cookie*; Helen Hunt, Laura Dern, Farrah Fawcett, Kate Hudson, and Shelley Long in *Dr. T*. In the latter, Richard Gere plays the male lead, a gynecologist who has little understanding of women. From dramatic and narrative standpoints, *Dr. T*, *Cookie's Fortune*, and *The Gingerbread Man* are more conventional and linear than Altman's most celebrated films, but this late, regional phase of his career remains unjustly overlooked and underestimated.

THE LONG TAKE OPENING

--OPEN: on a mural in LEVISON's bungalow. Camera
pulls back to reveal a MAIL GUY and his bicycle. He
delivers mail to CELIA and SANDY who are talking.

--SANDY runs toward the stages and the camera
follows. The camera finds GRIFFIN in his car who is
stopped by WRITER #1. WRITER #1 starts his pitch.
Camera follows GRIFFIN's car as he parks.

--GRIFFIN and WRITER #1 (still pitching) enter the
building. Camera picks up STUCKEL and an OFFICE BOY
who exit the building and bring us to GRIFFIN's
window #1 where we look inside and see WRITER #2
pitching to GRIFFIN.

--JAN escorts WRITER #1 out the side door who we
follow until we pick up STUCKEL and the OFFICE BOY
who lead us back to the stages where we see:

--LEVISON driven up in his limo and greeted by CELIA.
A golf cart passes in the foreground and we hear it
crash into the mail bike. Script pages and post
cards flutter everywhere.

--We pull back as STUCKEL and STUDIO GAPERS
congregate around the crash site.

--SANDY crosses the frame, running to the main
office. The camera follows her to GRIFFIN's Window
#2 where WRITER 3 is pitching.

--BONNIE'S ASSISTANT crosses in the foreground and
brings the camera back to the crash site where the
clean-up is in progress.

--The camera picks up REGGIE's car entering and
parking. REGGIE goes to a bungalow on the stage
side.

--Again the camera picks up the mail guy who takes us
back to the side door where we hold on Window #3 for
WRITER #4's pitch.

--BONNIE enters the foreground, crosses, stops at
GRIFFIN's Window #3 and confirms luncheon date.

--MAIL GUY delivers postcard to GRIFFIN.

A scene breakdown for the eight-minute tracking shot that opens the film. The scene includes actors as well as cameos of
writers, actors, and directors pitching film ideas to studio executives. The script provided an outline from which much of
the dialogue was improvised.
OPPOSITE TOP Tim Robbins (as Griffin Mill) and Greta Scacchi (as June Gudmundsdottir).
OPPOSITE BOTTOM Tim Robbins as Griffin Mill, a studio executive involved in the murder of a writer.

SHORT CUTS

THIS SPREAD Tom Waits and Lily Tomlin, who played Earl and Doreen Piggot, with Altman on the set. Altman divided the shoot by couples, shooting each of them for about one week. During filming, Tom Waits would phone Lily Tomlin at night "in character."

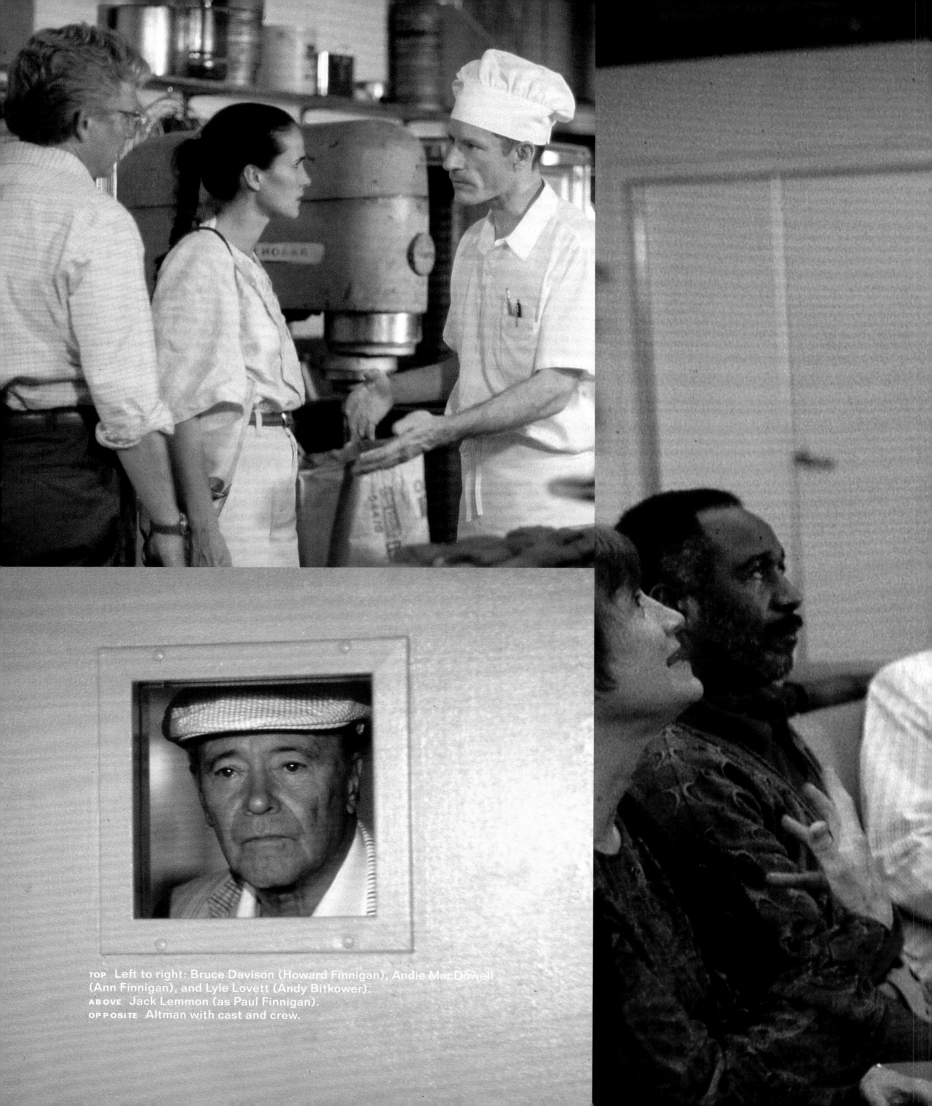

TOP Left to right: Bruce Davison (Howard Finnigan), Andie MacDowell (Ann Finnigan), and Lyle Lovett (Andy Bitkower).
ABOVE Jack Lemmon (as Paul Finnigan).
OPPOSITE Altman with cast and crew.

Portraits of the *Short Cuts* characters by portrait painter Don Bachardy. To preserve *Short Cuts* in a special way, associate producer and marketing executive Mike Kaplan scheduled the cast to spend a full day sitting for Bachardy when they weren't needed on the set during the week they were filming. The final portraits were used in publicity materials and in Kaplan's film about the making of *Short Cuts*, *Luck, Trust & Ketchup: Robert Altman in Carver Country*. The collage above was created for a poster for that film which was never printed.

OPPOSITE TOP Peter Gallagher (as helicopter pilot Stormy Weathers).

OPPOSITE BOTTOM Julianne Moore, Matthew Modine, Fred Ward, and Anne Archer having a dinner party in *Short Cuts*.

PRÊT-À-PORTER

Altman with cast members.

Altman with Jennifer Jason Leigh (as Blondie O'Hara) and Miranda Richardson (as Carolyn Stilton). OPPOSITE: Contact sheet of stills of Jennifer Jason Leigh (as Blondie O'Hara) and Dermot Mulroney (as her husband, Johnny).

Still of the nighttime set of *Kansas City*. In real life, Altman would have been nine years old when the film takes place.
OPPOSITE TOP Steve Buscemi plays Johnny Flynn, getting the vote out in *Kansas City*.
OPPOSITE BOTTOM Hey Hey Club musicians Joshua Redman and Nicholas Payton taking part in an all-night jam session.

GINGERBREAD MAN

COOKIE'S FORTUNE

Altman with Julianne Moore (as Cora Duvall) and Glenn Close (as Camille Dixon).
OPPOSITE Altman directing on the set.

Altman directing Richard Gere as Dr. Sullivan Travis (Dr. T, a Dallas gynecologist with women problems), and Helen Hunt as Bree, a golf instructor who gives him the attention he needs.

BY
KATHRYN REED
ALTMAN

Short Cuts
1992

1–9 *Short Cuts* was another phenomenal breakthrough of Bob's, with an enormous cast of twenty-two principal characters. It was based on nine short stories and one poem by Raymond Carver, and each vignette had a complete cast. I love this page of photos because it shows the energy of the director; he is very much engrossed. You can really see when he's pleased and not pleased.

2 Here's Matthew Modine shooting that great scene with Julianne Moore. In the background is a picture painted by Meg Freeman Harders. She did all the paintings for the character played by Julianne.

6 This is Bob's producer, Cary Brokaw (center), who really got on his nerves. It didn't end well. He certainly was a pleasant man, but Bob had his contentious moments with him. It was all about business.

7 This is his assistant director and friend Allan Nicholls. He was an actor in *Nashville*.

8 Here's Mike Kaplan, who had done all the publicity for *A Clockwork Orange*, which was a phenomenal breakthrough in advertising. He did PR for *Short Cuts* and made a documentary about the film called *Luck, Trust & Ketchup*. He has been very much a part of our lives for many years.

9 Here we have our grandson Christian Reed Altman, who was making his film debut at the age of ten. He was adorable.

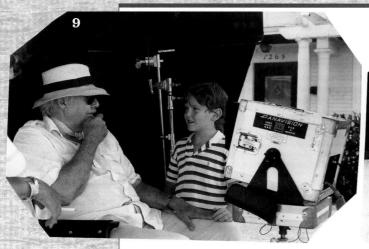

10–12 When Bob shouted, "It's a wrap!" on *Short Cuts,* we immediately went to Chicago, where he was to direct an opera. This was his second opera, after *The Rake's Progress.* This one was called *McTeague.* It was taken from an 1899 book by Frank Norris, which was adapted into an eight- or ten-hour silent film by Erich von Stroheim called *Greed,* starring ZaSu Pitts and Gibson Gowland, in 1924. It was decided at the Lyric Opera of Chicago to make an opera of it, and Bob was suggested by the composer, William Bolcom, to direct and cowrite the libretto. They hired him in a minute. It took about four years for it to finally come together between the other librettist, Arnold Weinstein, and the composer and the director. And then they did only nine performances! After that,

everything went into storage. You always hope that some other opera company will pick it up—the costumes; the scripts; the sets, which were done by Yuri Kuper; and so forth. So far, nobody has, but I guess in the opera world, there's always a possibility they will.

10, **12** Catherine Malfitano, a very prominent diva, was the leading lady, and here she is with her daughter.

=== Film Society of Lincoln Center
=== 1993

13 Every year the Film Society of Lincoln Center presents a tribute to someone. In the past they have honored people like Alfred Hitchcock and Elizabeth Taylor. In 1993 they honored Jack Lemmon, and he had just worked for Bob on *Short Cuts,* so Bob presented him with the award. The following year, in 1994, they honored Bob, and Jack Lemmon presented the award to Bob.

=== The Co-Godfather
=== 1992

14 Here is Bob with Susan Sarandon and Gore Vidal. When Susan Sarandon and Tim Robbins had their second son, Miles, they named Bob and Gore Vidal to share the role of godfather. I think that Tim Robbins was working on *The Player* when Miles was conceived. That's how Bob was chosen.

Tim and Susan were very active politically and very much in agreement with the points of view of Gore Vidal, as was Bob. This picture was taken at the baptism. Bob was very proud of his role as godfather. He was very flattered to be chosen, and of course he admired Gore Vidal so much that it was even more flattering.

Susan would send him a photograph every year with the other two children, which she still does. Bob didn't really follow through as a very good godfather, as godfathers go, but he did send presents and various things for the first few years.

15–**24** In 1993 we took *Short Cuts* to the Venice Film Festival. **21** In this picture, we had gone over to the main part of Venice to watch the regatta on the Grand Canal with Sydney Pollack. **19** And here is Bob's agent, who was in and out of Bob's life, Johnny Planco. They'd fight, and Bob would fire him. Then he'd rehire him, and then they'd fight and he'd fire him again. Overall, a really, really good friend. **15** This is the representative from the studio, Denis Pregnolato. He's a terrific guy, really good company, really watched out for us well.

We had to leave the festival and fly into Paris. Bob was trying to get funding for *Prêt-à-Porter*. Count Volpi, whose father founded the Venice Film Festival, furnished us with his private plane and put us up at the Crillon Hotel.

While still in Paris, we found out that we had won the ensemble acting prize, which made Bob very happy. We went back to Venice for the awards ceremony. After that we went back to the States and tried to get *Prêt-à-Porter* going.

Prêt-à-Porter
1994

It ended up being nine years before Bob was able to get the right script and the right cast for *Prêt-à-Porter*. Finally, Harvey Weinstein just insisted that he do it. They made some sort of deal that wasn't really what Bob wanted, so he went into it a little reluctantly—and he didn't get along with Harvey, which really set up lots of agony. They were both so strong willed. They would scream at each other on the phone for hours. But we finally got settled on location in Paris and got it made.

Pre-production started in 1993, so we had Christmas in Paris. Bob got this great cast, and they shot right through to June. We ended up spending about a year there. It was our last Paris project.

This was the beginning of Bob's weight loss, which ultimately led to his heart transplant. His health was seriously starting to decline on this film—and then he went right into the next one, *Kansas City*. By the end of *Kansas City*, he was very, very sick.

We were big stars in Paris during the shooting of this film, because all the fashion designers were interested in the film and possibly being in the film. We were invited to all the haute couture shows with the top designers like Christian Dior, Gianfranco Ferré, Valentino, Givenchy, Yves Saint Laurent, Thierry Mugler, and so on. So we had great exposure to the fashion world, more than I could have imagined! **27** This is the Valentino show. Isabella Rossellini sat next to us.

25 There are so many vignettes in the movie. Tim Robbins and Julia Roberts had this great scene.

26 Bob started shooting with Danny Aiello, who was excellent in the film.

28 While shooting on the streets in and around Paris, there were certain times when utter frustration was unavoidable, but Bob handled it all very well, as you can see in this picture.

261

29

30

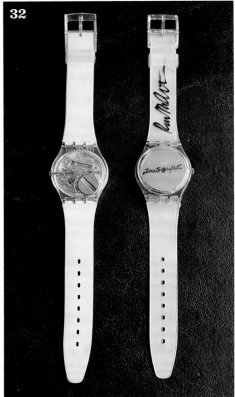

32

29 Bob really enjoyed working with Marcello Mastroianni. He was the perfect actor. His daughter, Chiara, was also in the film and was very good. And Sophia Loren was wonderful, too. What a lovely lady.

30 The last scene in *Prêt-à-Porter* is rather unusual: All the models responded to Bob's direction and did the whole fashion show, the catwalk and all, completely in the nude. It was a real groundbreaker and so tastefully done. Bob had a way with women!

31 One day Denise Breton called and said, "You have to come down to the set." They were shooting at the Grand Hotel, one of the *Vogue*s or some other prestigious magazine was there, and Bob agreed to be photographed on his lunch hour. Denise wanted me to join him. I said, "I can't come today. It's too short notice.

My hair looks like a cat sucked on it. I can't do it. I just look terrible today." But she insisted and made me feel like I'd really blow everything for everybody if I didn't show. So I pulled it together and went down there. I was very nervous. They had the room all set up with lights and scrims, and they had makeup and hair people and this really nice Italian crew. Bob was already there, being lit, and they took me over and sat me beside him. They started shooting and telling me to smile or look over here, look over there. I could tell they knew how uncomfortable I was, and Bob really sensed it, I could tell, but he didn't say anything—he just looked at the camera and took my hand and put it right in his crotch! And that's when I just broke up.

Swatch watch
1994

32 In 1994, during post-production on *Prêt-à-Porter* in New York, the Swatch company asked Bob, Akira Kurosawa, and Pedro Almodóvar to design watches for their Cinema Set. With the help of our granddaughter Signe, who was assisting him at the time, he came up with this design. The hands say, "Time to Reflect," and the watch face is a mirrored surface without numbers. They gave Bob a giant version of his watch, which hung over a door in his office.

31

33

34 We combined the trip with an award he was being given outside Florence, in Fiesole.

We went to Rome first, though. Mr. Pettinari made sure that we were comfortable. We were there for three nights at the Hassler Hotel. **35**, **36** As you can see here, I'm going up the stairs, and Bob is watching me. He was so fond of Bob, this Angelo Pettinari, that he named his racehorse Bob Altman. He had the horse long before we went over there for this event, and while we were there, "Bob Altman" was running. So one day they went to the track, and Angelo and Bob watched Bob Altman run! He didn't win, but the real Bob Altman won the slander suit.

37

Fiesole Festival
1995

33–36 Right after *Kansas City*, when Bob's health was really failing, we had to go to Rome because Bob had to appear in court in a slander suit brought against him by an Italian politician. The politician had a lot of influence with the Italian government's TV agency, RAI, which was putting up the money for a film Bob wanted to do about the life of Rossini. The politician lied a lot, Bob called him names, and it was in the paper, so then he sued Bob for slander. The trial went on and on, but in the meantime, we'd gotten a really wonderful Italian attorney named Angelo Pettinari, who advised that Bob really had to appear in the Italian court in person. It was hard for Bob, but we did it.

34

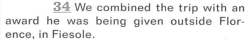

PREMIO FIESOLE
MAESTRI DEL CINEMA
1996
ROBERT ALTMAN

Kansas City
1995

1995 started with pre-production on *Kansas City*, which took us to the Missouri city where Bob had been born and raised. The whole experience was "local boy makes good"—and then comes home to make a film based on his hometown. The whole city was cooperative; Mayor Cleaver supported this project thoroughly, as did the newspaper, the *Kansas City Star*.

37, **38** Bob's immediate family growing up consisted of him and his two younger sisters, Joan and Barbara. Now we had lots of our own children on this movie. Michael, the oldest, worked for a while in pre-production, but personal interests took him elsewhere. Bobby was the main camera operator. Matthew was in props. Stevie was the production designer. Our granddaughter Signe was Bob's assistant. It was a big family affair. Cousins appeared out of nowhere, as did old friends, even one from his kindergarten days. We were surrounded by relatives and caring people. Declining health made things quite difficult. However, by the end

35

36

38

of the year, Bob had a new heart and a renewed enthusiasm for life.

39 One of the great segments of *Kansas City* is the re-creation of the Hey Hey Club, which had really been a club during the thirties. Harry Belafonte portrayed one of the big gangsters of the day, Seldom Seen. Kevin Mahogany portrayed a bartender at the Hey Hey Club. The band was just phenomenal. They were all prominent young musicians, such as James Carter, Joshua Redman, Clark Gayton, Geri Allen, Ron Carter, Russell Malone, Mark Whitfield, Craig Handy, David Murray, Don Byron, Nicholas Payton, Cyrus Chestnut, Victor Lewis, and Curtis Fowlkes, depicting the musicians of the thirties and forties.

Bob called them the Young Lions. They played all the old Count Basie stuff, and they had the cutting scene where one tenor saxophone player tried to play longer and better than the other one. It would go on for hours and hours sometimes.

Heart transplant
1995

The first week of December 1995, as we were getting into bed one night, we got the phone call that the proper heart had been found for Bob. We went to the hospital, and most of our children were there, and it was a very, very successful operation. Bob was home and happy and celebrating by Christmas. He went shopping on Christmas Eve and then celebrated Christmas Day at the beginning of perfect health. **40** We called him "the King," and he had a crown given to him by our very special friend, Jean Bach. It was the beginning of a wonderful, wonderful time of our lives. We felt appreciative, experienced, settled, and happy.

Christmas
1996

41 "King Bob" and his granddaughter Allison. She is the daughter of Michael Altman.

The White House
1990s

We were invited to the White House one weekend. The first night we were there, we went to the estate of Ethel Kennedy, Hickory Hill, just outside the city. She gave this dinner party—not just for us, for a lot of dignitaries, and we happened to be included.

The next night we were invited to some big event at the Kennedy Center. It was raining, and we had to stand in line to go in. **42** Then we did the photo op, which everybody does. You go up on this platform behind the red velvet rope. Then you're introduced to the president and the first lady, and you get in your position to get your picture taken. You say, "Thank you very much," and they move on to the next couple.

Mind you, this was before Monica Lewinsky, so, you know, I had Mrs. America's crush on Bill Clinton like everybody else. In the original picture you could see his fingers peeking out around my waist, and I'd say to people, "That's the best part!" This was the introduction of Photoshop into our lives. Our friend Danielle Weil, a photographer, used Photoshop to block out Clinton's fingers and replace them with Bob's hand, copied from his right hand on the left side of the photo and superimposed on the crucial spot! Bob liked this photo so much, he wouldn't allow the original to be hung in our house. He wanted this in his office and in his home. He just thought it was hilarious. Sometimes people don't get it, or they get it but they just don't know what to say.

=== Honorary Degree, University of Michigan ===
1996

43–45 The University of Michigan gave Bob an honorary doctorate in 1996. He was very honored and humbled by it. We took our grandson Wesley to the event to expose him to the environment, since he was in the process of applying to that school. He ended up entering it a year later and graduated with honors.

45 The other recipients included Johnetta Cole, James Duderstadt, Henryk Górecki, Jesse Hill, John Pickering, Mstislav Rostropovich, Vera Rubin, Nafis Sadik, and Stephen Smale. Another one of them was Sandra Day O'Connor. Bob said he talked to her about relaxing the marijuana laws—and she immediately changed the subject.

They offered him the cap and gown when he left, and he accepted. He was really proud to have that. It hung in his closet the rest of his life.

=== *Kansas City*, Cannes Film Festival ===
1996

46–57 Bob was hoping for a big positive reaction to *Kansas City* at Cannes and was very disappointed when the film didn't get the recognition that he'd hoped it would. It really did not do well at Cannes, and he was very depressed for a while. He stayed in bed at the hotel one whole day, got up to go to dinner, and then stayed in bed the whole next day. I thought that was kind of silly, but he got over it.

48, **54**, **55** In fact, Bob was awarded the Legion of Honor, and it was presented at Cannes by the head of the festival, Gilles Jacob. Afterward, Bob handed me the speech he had written from his pocket, and this is it.

48 Mayor Cleaver of Kansas City attended with his wife. He was so cooperative throughout the shooting of the film and was very much involved with it.

52 This is Roger Ebert—who was the loveliest man and the greatest supporter throughout Bob's entire career—with his lovely wife, Chaz.

49 We attended the big amfAR party honoring Elizabeth Taylor. It was fabulous—until Bob got into a big kerfuffle with Harvey Weinstein! **56**, **57** Afterward we went to the Little Majestic Bar, behind the Majestic Hotel. We were having a drink outside when all of a sudden we were surrounded by all these young, enthusiastic film students. They were asking all kinds of questions, and Bob had so much fun talking to them. He gave them a thrill of a lifetime, and he enjoyed every second of it. And so did the rest of us.

I THANK YOU Gilles -
I THANK The PRESIDENT of the great
  Republic of France
I THANK AND THE people of France
  who have Responded so graciously
  To my WORK.

France has been my mentor
France has been my maiden
France has been my Friend
It is with The greatest Respect
That I Accept this honor
  - VIVA La France

MIDLAND
ROBERT ALTMAN'S
"KANSAS CITY" 7/27
NORTH AMERICA PREMIERE

Kansas City, Venice Film Festival
1996

60–64 Later in 1996 we went to the Venice Film Festival for *Kansas City*. We were traveling with an assistant director of Bob's, Steve Dunn, and a writer, Clyde Hayes. He and Bob were working on a script for Bob's next project, *The Gingerbread Man*. Bob wasn't terribly busy there. He'd do his interviews during the day, and I'd have some glorious lunch or go sightseeing. Then we'd hook up in the evening with Clyde, who had been writing all day, and we'd all go to some nice restaurant or take a water taxi to an island. We were a very good quartet of travelers and very produc-

Kansas City opening, Kansas City, Missouri
1996

58, **59** Shot in 1995, *Kansas City*'s US opening was in Kansas City in July 1996. It was very exciting. All the citizens were enthusiastic. It was quite a great evening at the Midland Theater. Harry and Julie Belafonte were there. Many of Bob's relatives showed up. Everyone was so excited. They had a beautiful party at a private home after the screening. Local boy *did* make good!

tive. The film was very, very well received there. Bob was happy and contented. We had our last visit with Vittorio Gassman. He had been in *Quintet* and *A Wedding* and was a great friend. It was so nice to see him. He died not long afterward.

63

65

64

V. Gassman   R. Altma

66

<u>65</u>–<u>68</u> I've always liked this set of photos by Yann Gamblin. They were taken in our New York apartment. I don't think they were ever used for any particular publication that I can recall. We had great times building and decorating that apartment, and Mr. Gamblin really captured that in these photos. I like the softness of them. Bob loved those masks on the wall that he bought from a guy when we were shooting *O.C. and Stiggs* in Arizona. The guy brought his masks to the set, and Bob bought the whole collection.

67

68

AT Home
IN
New York

69

70

69 Bob liked machines that made things. Way back in the eighties, we were stuck in our pied-à-terre in New York for a whole summer without anyplace to go. He wasn't working that much and was trying to keep his mind occupied, so he bought a pasta-making machine. We had a glass dining table, and I remember we'd sit there and he'd lay out all these strips of pasta. Our boys were kind of in and out, and we'd all make different kinds of sauces. We just made a big project out of it.

This sort of preceded his getting a top-of-the-line bread-making machine. He set it up in his post-production offices. He'd get so excited—he'd come in the morning and turn it on so the bread would be ready around four o'clock. He'd keep going into the kitchen to check on it from time to time. He'd make all different kinds, like rosemary, Irish soda bread, and jalapeño cheddar. He just loved it! As did all of the editors and staff.

70–73 The last time we went to Cannes was in 1997. This time was particularly special because we did not have a film in competition. It was the fiftieth anniversary of the festival, and they invited all the available past winners of the Palme d'Or from the last fifty years, of whom Bob was one for *M*A*S*H*. He had two days of publicity.

The night of the presentation was exciting because Bob had decided to incorporate that trip with time on a yacht. He chartered a yacht right on the new wharf near the Palais des Festivals, where the awards were presented. We went with Joyce and Alan Rudolph, Danielle Weil, and Bob's assistant, Paula Cantu. We had two weeks of just solid entertainment and side trips to Saint-Tropez and Monte Carlo.

73 This is a photograph of Bob's feet plus two of his greatest fans, Steven Soderbergh and Alan Rudolph, and Bob's agent, Ken Kamins.

74–80 The first film Bob did after his heart transplant was *The Gingerbread Man* in 1997. So this was a big milestone in our life, to see Bob back in action. It was very exciting, although he was encumbered by two inexperienced producers who chose to be on the set the entire time. Also, for some reason known only to him, Bob hired a cinematographer who was Chinese and didn't speak one word of English. But Changwei Gu was adorable and did an interesting job.

74 This entire page of photos tells you something about our life at this time. All of these people were dedicated, more or less, to Bob and his projects. Some had worked with him on many films; an exception was Clyde Hayes, a new friend and the writer of the film. David Levy, a close friend since 1978, worked with Bob as an assistant and a producer. Lily Perkins assisted Bob on only this film. Bobby Altman was the camera operator on the film, Stephen Altman was the production designer, Mark

72

73

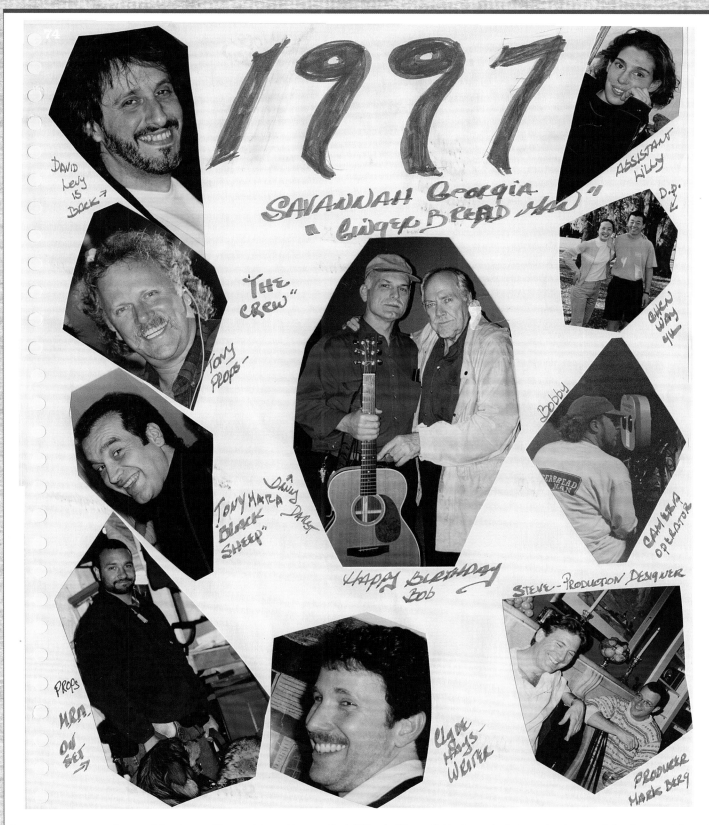

1997

SAVANNAH GEORGIA
"GINGER BREAD MAN"

DAVID LEVY IS DOCK →

ASSISTANT LILLY

D.P.

OWEN ROY 96

'THE CREW"

TONY PROPS

TONY MARA "BLACK SHEEP"

DANNY DARST

BOBBY CAMERA OPERATOR

HAPPY BIRTHDAY BOB

STEVE - PRODUCTION DESIGNER

PROPS MAN ON SET →

CLAUDE HAYS WRITER

PRODUCER MARK BERG

Burg was a producer, Matthew Altman worked in props, Tony Maccario was the property master, and Tony Marra was the key grip—all family or longtime friends and all dedicated to Bob.

Danny Darst was very much a part of our life for about ten years. He's a songwriter and an actor. He would always show up no matter where we were working. He was very laid back, and Bob loved his work. He and Bob wrote a song together called "Black Sheep" that made the charts—"number one with a bullet!" He's a dear friend and a talented man, and he's gone on to make films with our son Michael.

Alan Rudolph had started out as Bob's assistant director on *The Long Goodbye* in 1972, then went on to become Bob's protégé. Bob hated it when I said that, but it's really kind of what it was, because Alan is the first to say that every-thing he learned, he learned from Bob. He is now a prominent director and writer who has done many films.

Savannah was phenomenal. That's where *Midnight in the Garden of Good and Evil* was set. It was popular at the time, so there were tour buses that took you to all the sights—where John Berendt's hero lived, where the Bonaventure Cemetery is, and where Johnny Mercer is buried. Mercer, who had written the title song

for *The Long Goodbye*, is a big name in Savannah.

The picture starred Kenneth Branagh <u>77</u>, who did a magnificent job of assuming an American accent.

Of our many guests in Savannah, one of the most important ones to me was Stephen Shadley <u>78</u>, who had been responsible for the interior design of our New York apartment.

As with so many of Bob's films, *The Gingerbread Man* had very low distribution and many troubles getting edited and released as it should have been. However, it's a work of art.

81

82

84

83

Troops' party
1997

81 This is one of our favorite party photos. We were at a great party at the home of Cindy and Richard Troop, our neighbors.

Christmas, NYC
1997/98

82–84 It's so difficult to find a place for the Christmas tree in our New York apartment. I've tried everything through the years.

In 1997 I came up with the idea of using one of Bob's favorite works of art, a sculpture of an easel by Yuri Kuper. I bought some garlands, thinking we could use them somehow, and had Bob and Alan Rudolph execute my plan. They smoked a joint and discussed very seriously how they were going to decorate with the garlands. So these pictures show them having the best time hanging these garlands on the sculpture. They had the best rapport—they were like girlfriends. We made a whole evening of it. Bob was always wonderful about Christmas and decorating. He really got into it.

Cookie's Fortune
1998

85–89 In 1998 we went to Holly Springs, Mississippi, which is about twenty minutes from Memphis, Tennessee, and twenty minutes from Oxford, Mississippi, where Ole Miss is and where William Faulkner lived. It was a great location. **87** This is our house.

We had lots and lots of parties there. The town was small, and the occupants were thrilled to have us. Many of them had to move out or go stay with each other so that we could have houses to rent. Bob and I lived in a house owned by a lovely couple, Francis and Tubby. Glenn Close **88** (center) was so comfortable there that she ended up riding her bike through the town, and everybody would wave to her. There was no restaurant in town, just a coffee shop, and everybody knew everybody.

89 Liv Tyler was in it, and she was just great. Lyle Lovett, Julianne Moore, and Glenn Close were also great to work with and visit with. And it's such a good movie—I love that movie! And Patricia Neal **88** (right): It was just about her last film—her first in a while and almost her last.

The music was done by Dave Stewart, a British contemporary composer who is an expert in the Delta blues. **85, 86** These are some great pictures of Dave and Bob.

90

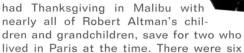

92

Killer App
1998

After _Cookie's Fortune_, Bob did a pilot written by Garry Trudeau called _Killer App_, nobody knew what "app" meant in those days. Now, of course, it's a household word. Bob would try to explain it to me—and at the same time he was trying to explain it to himself. It was fun to be in Vancouver again.

90 Instead of in a screening room, because it was television, we would have dailies in our apartment in the Sutton Place Hotel. Tommy and Janie Thompson and I would get food and drinks, and—as always—we made it a celebration.

Afterward, when the pilot didn't sell, we threw a great party in Malibu for everyone.

Thanksgiving
1998

91 This was a monumental achievement on my part, I have to say. In 1998 we had Thanksgiving in Malibu with nearly all of Robert Altman's children and grandchildren, save for two who lived in Paris at the time. There were six children, seven grandchildren, and three great-grandchildren.

ASC Award
1999

92–93 This was our first social event after Bob's knee replacement. It was the American Society of Cinematographers Board of Governors Award. 93 Mark Rydell, who is a longtime friend and the funniest guy ever, was the presenter. Mark was introduced and made a nice speech, then introduced Bob. Bob got up from our table, which was in the front row, and walked up the steps without any help and without a cane, with his new knee. I was holding my breath! And so was he! He gave a great speech.

93

91

<u>94</u>–<u>97</u> Bob gave me two surprise birthday parties. The first one was for my thirty-ninth birthday. It was in the sixties, and the idea was that we were going down to Malibu to have dinner and drinks with two writer friends of Bob's, David Moessinger and Ed Waters, with whom he was working at Universal Pictures, and their girlfriends. We were very close with them at the time, which happens on different projects: It's like you've known them all your life, and then all of a sudden it's all over and you're involved in another project.

So we were figuring out where we were going to go for dinner, and Ed got a phone call. He said that Laurence Olivier happened to be at a house down the beach with someone we knew, and they would like us to stop by. So that's what we all did. When we got to the house, I knew something was up because I saw some familiar cars. We walked into this condo on the ocean with a great big deck, and the first person I saw was the caterer from all of Bob's television shows. Then I rounded the corner, and there were all our friends! And Bob turned to me and handed me the keys to this condo for a month! That was my birthday present.

In 1999, Bob threw the second surprise birthday party for me. We were in New York, and a driver picked us up. I said, "What in the world do you have in

94

95

mind?" Bob said, "Just don't worry." The driver took us over to the Hudson River. We got off at the pier, and I was led down the gangplank onto this gorgeous boat among fabulous guests. We went down to the Statue of Liberty, had dinner on the boat, and danced. Bob made this terrific toast to me, and I joined him at the mic and we hugged. All of our close friends were there—among them, Harry and Julie

Belafonte; our cousin and lawyer Jerry Walsh <u>96</u>; Sam Cohn <u>97</u>, Bob's agent off and on forever, whom Bob depended on for so much and who did some great things for Bob's career, and Sam's wife Jane Gelfman.

96

97

98

<u>98</u>–<u>101</u> In 1999 we were in Dallas for *Dr. T & the Women*.

Jeanine Cazalas-Fleming was the medical adviser, because we had a birth scene. She and her husband were always on the set, and they were really nice. They lived in Plano, which is right outside Dallas. They had a new home and gave this Christmas party. At one point, Jeanine took Bob upstairs to show him the view. While she was up there, her husband passed out all these masks he had made of Bob's face and had everyone hold them up in front of their own faces. When Bob came down the stairs, he just saw this sea of his own face! It was really effective. Here are three Bobs <u>98</u>!

99

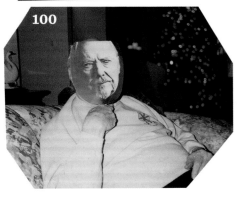

100

101

After the shoot in Dallas wrapped, there was one scene left to shoot in California. Bob took a skeleton crew—his beloved associate director Tommy Thompson, Bobby Altman, and Stevie Altman, among others—to Barstow. As they were driving back to the motel from the location, Bob and Tommy called me. They were exhausted and said they were going right to their rooms.

Bob later saw all this commotion around Tommy's door. It seems that Tommy had gone back to his room, then walked over to the service station to call his wife because his cell phone wasn't working in the motel. He walked back to his room then, and just dropped dead!

Later, at Tommy's memorial, Bob said, "We said, 'Goodnight,' and he just fell off the planet." Bob said I had to call his wife. He couldn't do it, so I did.

Bob did that once before to me, when were shooting *California Split* in 1974 in Reno. Barbara Ruick, who had been a well-known star in her day and then retired

to have children with her husband, John Williams, was making a comeback with her part in *California Split*. We wrapped one night for the weekend and she said she'd meet us later for dinner, but she died in her room that night. Bob could not tell her husband, so I did.

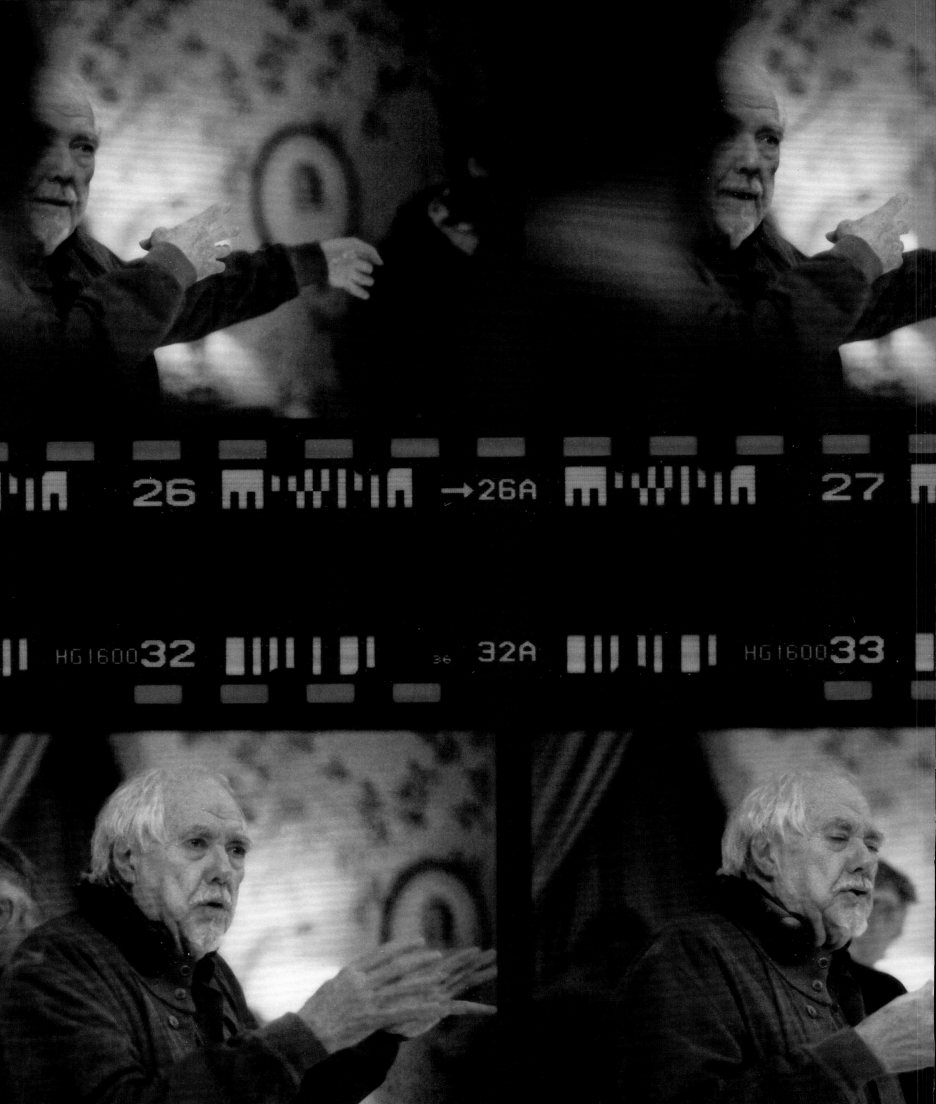

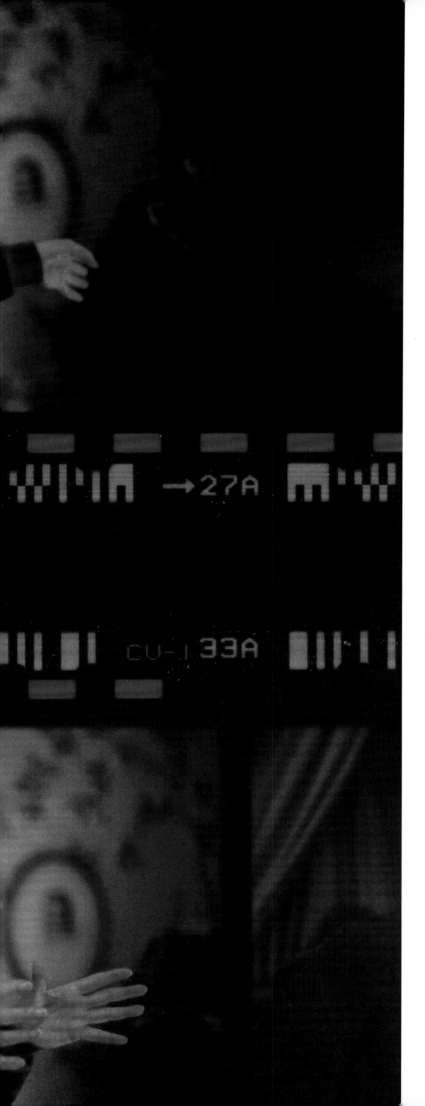

7

THE

AUGHTS

BY GIULIA
D'AGNOLO VALLAN

Ten Little Indians and *The Rules of the Game*, Agatha Christie and Jean Renoir, a whodunit where the murder mystery is secondary to a bigger picture—Altman's next film, an *Upstairs, Downstairs* story deeply rooted in the intricacies of British class relations, is actually a less counterintuitive choice than one might think. The American Midwest and London in the thirties were truly a world apart, but as a child of upper-middle-class Kansas City, Altman had plenty of opportunities to witness the dynamic between servants and masters that he joyfully X-rays in *Gosford Park*. By birth and upbringing he was a product of the upstairs. By heart, and intellectually speaking, he found the downstairs much more interesting.

LEFT Contact sheet of Altman on set of *Gosford Park*, 2001.

With producer Bob Balaban, he asked Eileen Atkins and Jean Marsh, cocreators of the popular British TV series *Upstairs, Downstairs*, to write the script, but they were not available. After trying other name British writers, he settled for one who was unknown and untested but had foolproof upstairs credentials: Baron, and Conservative member of the House of Lords, Julian Fellowes.

As an American filmmaker and a sophisticated satirist, Altman was very conscious of the risk he was taking by venturing into the arcane world of British social conventions. Besides hiring Fellowes as a writer and on-set consultant, he talked to Ismail Merchant and Ruth Prawer Jhabvala, who together with James Ivory had pretty much created the market for a certain kind of literary-inspired period film. Clearly Altman was not envisioning *Gosford Park* as a Merchant–Ivory production, but as always, before breaking the rules of a genre, he had to understand them well. He populated the film with many well-known British actors with strong stage experience. Balaban, who plays a producer of Charlie Chan movies (and who is a figment of Altman's own presence in the film), is virtually the lone Yankee of the party.

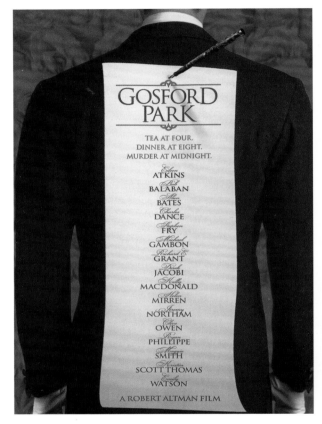

Once again Altman studied a visual solution that would allow him to break the mold and flee the standard preciousness of the well-made, mildewed period drama. By shooting every scene with three cameras at a time (a technique he had already explored in *The Long Goodbye*), the director enveloped *Gosford Park* in continuous, unpredictable movements—their rhythm and focus often not matching the action, or contradicting it altogether.

No matter how sprawling most of Altman's films may be, a certain classical ideal of space-time unity is central to them and intrinsic to his notion of cinema as a way to capture an event or a behavior. By the nature of its settings—the big British country house—and of the spatial metaphor implied in its premise—masters upstairs, servants downstairs—*Gosford Park* is one of the most fulfilled reflections of that ideal.

It is also one of Altman's best-reviewed films and, with *M*A*S*H*, his biggest financial success, bringing his late career a degree of praise and recognition unmatched since the early to mid-seventies. The film won Altman Golden Globe and New York Film Critics Circle Awards for Best Director. Julian

Robert Altman

With a new pic generating the best buzz since 'The Player,' the iconoclastic filmmaker bounces back

'PARK'S PLACE: *Based on Julian Fellowes' original screenplay, "Gosford Park" was envisioned by the filmmakers as "Ten Little Indians" meets "Rules of the Game."*

Genre bender

A whodunit as comedy of manners, 'Gosford Park' signals a return to form

BY ROBERT KOEHLER

HOLLYWOOD During an early meeting with screenwriter Julian Fellowes, who had been hired by Robert Altman and producing partner Bob Balaban to write "Gosford Park," the discussion naturally came around to the plot.

It had to: This was, after all, a murder mystery set at an English country estate in 1932, strictly organized along the class differences of the landed aristocracy upstairs and the servants downstairs. Nothing here was far afield from Agatha Christie's world of murders in the manor.

"I don't think there was a chance with (Altman) at the helm that anything was going to be formulaic, though," Balaban says. "So when we were meeting with Julian, Bob mentioned to him, in Bob's own casual way, 'By the way, I'm not really interested in the mystery.' Bob even considered for awhile not even revealing who did it."

For all the seeming differences from past Altman films, "Gosford Park" is actually a pure-bred work from the director, whose signature is to take familiar material and themes, usually involving a large ensemble of actors, and transform them.

"People may be surprised that Bob would be at all interested in a British period story," adds Balaban, "since he has never done anything before in that realm. But internally it's exactly what all his films are like. He stays true to what interests

Turn to page A8

ACTOR'S HELMER: *In characteristic fashion, Robert Altman offers guidance, and latitude, to "Gosford's" Emily Watson.*

Fellowes won the Oscar for Best Original Screenplay at the 2002 Academy Awards. But *Gosford Park* was passed over in all the other categories in which it had been nominated (*A Beautiful Mind* and Ron Howard took home the statuettes for Best Picture and Best Director).

It would take four more years for the Academy to finally pay its dues to Robert Altman. Still, his sixth decade in the business started on a very high note and, professionally speaking, would be characterized by an almost unprecedented degree of serenity.

Since his years at Calvin, Altman's cinema had entertained a continuous conversation with the documentary form. That conversation became even more intimate and explicit in his next project, *The Company*, a film so steeped in patient, detailed observation that it brings to mind Frederick Wiseman's hypnotic portrait of the American Ballet Theater, *Ballet* (1995). The idea for it came to Altman from actress Neve Campbell and his old collaborator Barbara Turner. A classically trained dancer, Campbell wanted to make a film about the ballet. Over a period of three years, the two had been gathering material for a script mostly based on the Joffrey Ballet in Chicago. Campbell wanted to be in it but was determined not to take a starring role; she would simply be playing a dancer in the company. That notion suited Altman very well. In

OPPOSITE
RIGHT Poster for *Gosford Park*, 2001.
BOTTOM Photo collage of Altman scouting a location for *Gosford Park*.

ABOVE Full page article about Gosford Park in *Variety*, December 10, 2001.

281

AN INTERVIEW WITH
JULIAN FELLOWES
GIULIA
D'AGNOLO VALLAN

BELOW Altman on the set of *Gosford Park* with Ryan Phillippe, Kristin Scott Thomas, and Julian Fellowes in the background.

How did you meet Altman? What was your first encounter like?

I had written a spec script for Bob Balaban, an adaptation of Trollope's *The Eustace Diamonds*, and he was working with Altman on what would eventually become *Gosford Park*. They were looking for a writer and had already gone to Tom Stoppard, Christopher Hampton, and all those people, but for some blessed and sacred reason no doubt organized by my late mama, none of them were able to do the job. So Balaban and Altman were a bit stuck, and they met to have lunch and talk about it. Suddenly Balaban remembered he had my script of *The Eustace Diamonds* in his briefcase. That was why he suggested me. He said that there's this guy and he's never had a feature film made and you won't have heard of him, and then he rang me. I was in the kitchen, and he said, "Would you like to write a film for Robert Altman?" All I had written that actually got made were some TV children's shows. It was quite extraordinary.

Anyway, we then had this conference call with Balaban in New York, Bob in Dallas, and me in London. It was a terrible line. I kept not hearing the second half of sentences, and I felt I couldn't just say, "Shall we dial back and get a better line?" because it made me sound like such a loser. So I kept faking that I'd heard what they were saying, which of course I hadn't really. Anyway, we ended up with my being asked to send over a few character sketches with some ideas for the people who might be involved in this story.

Bob Altman told me later that he never believed it would happen. The truth was I didn't think it was going to happen, either. The whole thing just seemed so unlikely, like a Judy Garland–Mickey Rooney musical: "Let's put on a show!" But then I thought, "What if it does happen and you haven't given it your best shot?" So I ran out and bought every single Altman film I could find and watched them all. I knew then that he was happiest in the genre of multi-arc, multi-strand storytelling where you have stories that go right through the movie, others with less overreaching spans, and some quite short that would be told in two or three scenes.

In other words, I deliberately and consciously structured the screenplay to feel like an Altman film, using that template—but at the same time taking it away from his home territory of the Middle West and setting it in the arcane society of English country-house living before the war.

Were you surprised that such a quintessential American director like Altman would want to make a film in such detail about the British class system?

If the director had been English, we would never have made the film. Because the great thing about Bob was that he was outside the system. He was curious about it, and he wanted to get it right, but he was neither elevated nor diminished by any of it. If a British writer had pointed out any details that were wrong in the handling by a British director, he or she would have felt so undermined by the fact that they didn't know, they would have protested that it was a matter of opinion. Of course, it's not a matter of opinion, it's a matter of fact. But they could never have conceded it was a fact to which they were not privy. Whereas Bob was a real investigator. He approached the whole thing as someone making a study of the genus Englishman thirties.

In fact, he asked me to be on the set the whole time, which is very rare for a writer. So inevitably I became a kind of "no" figure, because every time I opened my mouth it was to say he'd never be in the dining room, the lady's maid wouldn't do that, the groom wouldn't wear gloves, and so on, which at times drove Bob crazy. But finally, because he was essentially an anthropologist, he wanted to get the detail right. Best of all, he wanted not to have that kind of generalized BBC servant acting, where they walk around with a tray. You think, "What's on that tray? Where are they taking that tray? What are they doing?" That was what he was trying to avoid.

David [Levy], his producer, said to me, "We've had this letter from the professor of sociology at something or another university, and he'd love to come on as adviser." But I didn't want an academic. I wanted some servants. And so they found these three old people. One had been a footman with the Londonderry family before the war, one had been a kitchen maid at Elveden for the Countess of Iveagh, and one had been a housemaid at Chequers for Winston Churchill. Of course, they were great. Bob would say, "What would she be doing now?" They would ask, "What time of day is this scene set?" "They're going to be eating in about three scenes," or whatever it was. Well, what they might be doing is this, and they might be chopping that, and they might be sharpening the other. It was all absolutely time-of-day, specific-duty detail. That was thrilling, really.

I wouldn't say we never argued, because we did. We were both pretty peppery people. But he never once said, "Look, I am a world-famous film director who has made fifty films. Nobody on this set has ever heard of you," which was perfectly true and which he would have been completely entitled to say. I didn't really notice that at the time, because we were just these two fat men arguing behind the camera, but I admire him for it now very much. I think it was a tremendously gentlemanly position for him to take. He conferred on me a kind of pseudo equality with him while we were working.

Altman was himself a child of a fairly prominent family in Kansas City. Did his own class background ever enter your conversations about the film?

He talked about the whole business of servant awareness, and I was very interested by that. For the purposes of the film, he would describe his childhood in class terms. It was one of the reasons he was intrigued by the subject, because he had known an American version of it. Of course, he liked to present himself as a good old boy, but he wasn't really a good old boy at all in origin. His family was very distinguished in Kansas City, and he grew up among the upper echelons of that society. His experience as a boy and as a young man was to be at the top of the tree. I think that was an element of him that a lot of people are not perhaps aware of, and I don't think he would have been as interested in the project as he was if he hadn't had some personal experience of it.

It's interesting that you mentioned the word "anthropologist." It seems to me that Altman, especially in the later part of his career, seemed more and more determined to explore

JULIAN FELLOWES is a British actor, author, screenwriter, and director. He is best known for his Oscar-winning screenplay for Altman's *Gosford Park* (2001) and as the creator of the acclaimed TV series *Downton Abbey*.

worlds that were alien from his own. Even before *Gosford Park*, he had done *Prêt-à-Porter* about the Paris fashion industry.

I think you're right. He did seem to get more curious about foreign territory later in his career, although there were differences. In *Prêt-à-Porter*, where he investigated the fashion world, he decided to have an improvised script. Bob always enjoyed the idea that he just sort of turned up and made a film. And in *Prêt-à-Porter*, he really did that. But he took a different approach to *Gosford* and decided he not only wanted a script but also a guide to this strange world, someone to work pretty closely with, and that was me.

I know I must have driven him mad, fussing on about this and that, but I hope I also gave him a kind of freedom. He told me once that I was there to make sure he didn't make a mistake by accident. He might choose to make a mistake on purpose, of course, but by having me there, he gave himself the freedom to know the difference.

What kind of notes did he give you when you were in the writing process?

I always remember him saying: "This isn't a whodunit, it's a who-cares-who-dunit. I don't want the murder on the front ring." I sent him the original draft and he read it and, for the first time, as he told me later, he thought there might be a movie. It was his wake-up moment. He then invited me over to L.A. to spend three or four days with him, and that seemed to me proof of serious intent, even if I was given a third-class ticket.

The main change, for me, that Bob made, which I thought was absolutely brilliant, was the introduction of Ivor Novello, who hadn't been in it before. Bob wanted some practical music instead of just having a score, and in order to do that, he suggested we should make Novello a character, especially since, as it happens, he felt Novello's music was very underrated. He thought we might make him Sylvia's cousin, but it felt more

real to me to make him William McCordle's cousin. Anyway, that was how we decided to do it, and I flew home.

Initially I thought Novello was going to be the Big Star bore among the characters, but I was wrong, and this had to do with the time we had set the story in. We decided on November 1932 for the date of the movie because we wanted it to be as late as possible before the war, but we needed a country house ritual for it all to turn on, which meant hunting or shooting, and hunting was impractical. Pheasant shooting runs from October to 1 February, but Bob didn't want Christmas and neither of us wanted the Nazis. Since Hitler burned down the Reichstag in January 1933, we thought November 1932 was the last moment before Christmas decorations went up when people wouldn't have talked about what was happening in Germany.

Did the characters change much during the shoot?

I don't think he changed any of them really, although sometimes he had a different physical vision. For example, I had imagined Mabel as rather a lump, and Bob had initially been interested in an actress who was quite a big lump—who shall be nameless, obviously—but she couldn't do it for some reason, and then he had the idea of Claudie Blakley, who is quite petite. I remember going to a dinner that he and Kathryn gave for the cast at their flat just before filming began, and this woman came up and said, "I want to introduce myself. I'm playing Mabel," and I thought, "Are you?" But when I was on the set and she arrived for her first day, she was so perfect and she hit the note so precisely that the initial physical vision I'd had of Mabel just evaporated. I suppose Bob could understand the important elements of a character, as opposed to the superficial ones.

Tell me a little bit about your role on the set.

I would come in every morning and go to see Bob, and he'd say, "We'll be running

these two scenes together," or "We're losing the scene on the staircase, but we do need these lines of dialogue." I would then hide in a room, jigger it all about, and make what he wanted happen. But my main job was to stop him making mistakes in the detail, which the critics would have punished him for.

When we were shooting the first scene, which was in fact, unusually, the first scene in the film, there was one moment when he said to the actors, "Oh, well, if you got anything else you want to say, say it." But he was forgetting that the way people talked in the 1930s—certainly the upper-class characters, although these weren't among them—was very particular. There was a style to it and a rhythm and so on. Anyway, I thought, "If I don't say anything, then I might as well go home," so I took him aside and said: "Nothing has been said so far in this scene that could have been spoken before the middle of the 1970s. It's all modern slang." Of course, he was annoyed, for which I don't blame him at all, but I think he must have thought, "I'm here to do this film, let's do it." In other words, that was his moment of decision. There wouldn't have been any point in having me there, or indeed in having got me to write the script, if we were going to go off and do something else. People often ask me, "Wouldn't you rather have been successful ten years earlier?" And of course the short answer to that is yes. But the long answer is that if I had been much younger, I wouldn't have dared intervene in that way. I would just have bitten my lip and kept silent, but at fifty I was old enough to know that if this chance didn't work for me, there would never be another on the same level.

When I think about it now, I must have driven him absolutely mad. And this is when Kathryn really helped. It is, of course, a truism that behind every great man there is a great woman, and in my business there are really two kinds of spouse for the successful: the ones who make everything worse and borrow their partner's power to stir things up in order to reinforce their own position, and the peacemakers who try to smooth away difficulties and get rid of any roughness. Kathryn is one of those. She would come to the set, and she would squeeze someone's arm and joke with this head of department and that member of the camera team, and visit the different trailers and chat with the actors and so on, until everything was back on track. She saw that as her job. Of course, he knew what she was doing. Her work was to make his work happen, and so the films belonged to both of them. That's what I saw. They were a very, very close couple, really a team. I know lots of people say that, but I think it was what they truly had.

With me as well, whenever I felt I'd been pistol-whipped, she would hear about it, often from her stepson Steve, who was our designer. She'd come down to the set and cuddle me and stand with me by the camera and so on, and after that I'd be fine. But even when he was tough, one always forgave Bob. The thing about him was that he was very charismatic. He had an atmosphere around him that was literally hot. When you were near him, you felt something was happening and you were part of it. I'm sure that was true on every set he mastered, and usually the movie justified it. Even when it didn't, that's what it felt like to make a picture with him.

Among Altman's previous films, which one was the most important for your approach to this particular script?

The Player, mainly, although I liked *A Wedding*, too, and that had certain reverberations in *Gosford*. Some of Bob's films have a kind of resolution and some just don't, and I suppose I found that I preferred the ones that are resolved. With *The Player,* you felt that you had gone on a journey with this guy, and at the end he understood Hollywood in a way he had not understood it at the beginning, and so did you, the audience. When I was watching it, I remember hoping that the picture was going to be one of those where we've gone somewhere and things are different at the conclusion from the

way they were at the start. *The Player* delivered that, and I wanted *Gosford* to deliver it, too, which I believe it did.

Bob used to think this need for resolution was a bit sentimental on my part. There was a scene he cut at the very end, when Maggie Smith's character, Lady Trentham, is driving away, and she takes out a Thermos but she can't open it. She is about to lean over and knock on the glass to ask for help, as she did in the film's first scene, but then she decides to have another go, and she opens the stopper and pours herself a cup of coffee. He thought it sentimental and so he gave it the elbow, but I was sorry he cut it. I liked the implicit parable that the whole story had been a learning curve for all the characters.

How much would you say the experience of writing *Gosford Park* has influenced your approach to *Downton Abbey*?

Very much. *Downton* is the child of *Gosford*. In fact, I was approached by Gareth Neame, who said, "Would you consider going back into *Gosford Park* territory for television?" Of course, we realized at once that the subtext of *Gosford* is that it's all about to come to an end, for most people anyway, and the war is about to change everything, all of which was in the script. *Downton*, if it was going to have any life, had to start earlier, so we dropped back twenty years, from 1932 to 1912, to have the whole last sweep of that way of life.

What I also learned from Bob's work is the whole business of the multi-arc, multi-character, multi-narrative kind of storytelling, so you have one or two plotlines that go right through a series, and then you have others that complete within the episode, and alongside them, smaller plots that may only take three scenes, and so on. That is all Altman-esque, a direct result of Bob's influence. And, in fact, I now find that when I am writing something in a straight linear narrative, it feels quite narrow and limiting. I've got used to having different tunes, some funny, some sad, some old,

some young, all going at the same time.

The truth is, it was an extraordinary relationship, for me, anyway, and it changed my life. Lots of people come across individuals who do them a good turn, but I have much more than that to be grateful to Bob for. I have a career now because of him. Think of it: When he hired me, the studio had never heard of me, and when they, perfectly reasonably, wanted to protect their investment by putting in an experienced writer, he just wouldn't allow it. They tried to say it was only "for a polish," but we all know a so-called polish is always a rewrite, and he wouldn't allow it. He told them to get lost. Now, (a) the number of people in the industry who have the power to do that is very limited; and (b) the number who have the guts to do it is even fewer, because normally, in the end, when the studio goes on and on, they throw you to the wolves. In some ways Robert Altman could be something of a grizzly bear, no question. But it makes sense to have a grizzly on your side when you're engaged in a fight.

That's why I was alone on the stage on Oscar night. I do feel I owe him literally everything.

285

fact, for this film—except for Malcolm McDowell, in a role modeled on Joffrey's legendary director, Gerald Arpino, and James Franco, as Campbell's chef boyfriend—he almost avoided actors altogether. Instead he picked forty-four actual dancers and spent a couple of months with them before filming started, showing the same curiosity, appreciation, and genuine interest he had manifested toward the fashion world. A director deeply fascinated with performers all through his career, Altman loved exploring the dancers' rigorous practice and discipline. He did not give them copies of the script, instead describing their scenes as the shoot progressed. Campbell produced the film and was instrumental in choosing the ballets it featured. Altman often said this was really her project. In fact, it is a deeply Altmanesque one, from its concept to the elegant precision of its visual solutions. For the first time in a feature, Altman decided to forgo film in favor of high-definition video, using three or four cameras at a time. Never one to fear new technologies, he found the process quite exciting.

Right after the 1988 Democratic convention in Atlanta, Altman and Garry Trudeau had tried to no avail to convince HBO to extend *Tanner '88*, shooting more episodes as the national election progressed. After having lost the nomination of his party, Jack Tanner would have run as an independent. In 2004, a new primary election gave them the opportunity to bring back their candidate. Together with Altman's Sandcastle 5, the Sundance Channel (which had recently broadcast a very successful rerun of *Tanner '88*) produced a new four-part series, *Tanner on Tanner*. Sixteen years after the original one, its subject would shift from politics (as entertainment) toward its representation. Making a filmmaker of Jack Tanner's daughter, Alex (played again by Cynthia Nixon), and having her make a movie about her dad's political career, *Tanner on Tanner* revolved even more specifically around the notion of documentary itself. It also touched on how the emerging digital technology impacted cinema.

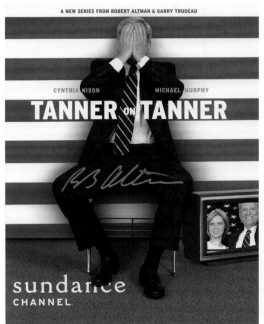

"I love filmmaking. It has given me an entrée to the world and to the human condition, and for that I'm forever grateful," said Altman in his acceptance speech at the 2006 Academy Awards, where he was presented with the Honorary Oscar for Lifetime Achievement. Loyal to his preference for dissonant, unpredictable notes, he chose that ceremony to reveal to the world that he had had a heart transplant—ten years earlier.

Just a few nights before, his staging of Arthur Miller's play *Resurrection Blues* had opened at the Old Vic in London. His new film, *A Prairie Home Companion*, would be released on May 25.

The chronicle of a last broadcast of a public-radio show, *A Prairie Home Companion* brings to Altman's dry spirit Garrison Keillor's more elegiac tones. The building where the show is held (the actual theater where Keillor's program is produced, in St. Paul, Minnesota) is about to be torn down by an evil,

ALTMAN

JAMES FRANCO

I first met Robert Altman at a Golden Globes after-party. I had just won for portraying James Dean in Mark Rydell's film, and Altman had won for *Gosford Park*. Rydell and Altman were old director friends, but Rydell had also played the indelible Marty Augustine in Altman's *The Long Goodbye*: "Everyone take off your clothes, everyone take off your clothes"—a young Schwarzenegger was in that scene, in a yellow Speedo (he looks right into the camera), although Bob told me later that Arnold never acknowledges that he was in that film. Or the scene where Rydell as Augustine cracks his mistress across the face with a bottle and says to Elliott Gould's Marlowe,

"Now, that's someone I love! And you, I don't even like!"

At that point I knew Altman's *M*A*S*H* (a favorite of my parents) and maybe *Nashville*, and definitely Altman's resounding comeback, *The Player*.

═══════════════════

In his young days, Altman had made a documentary about James Dean called *The James Dean Story*, which, I was told by a distributor, Altman subsequently tried to discontinue because he thought it was juvenile work. I don't know if it's true, and if it is, Altman was misguided. There are some funny parallels made between Dean and a dead seagull, but that aside, it is one of the most valuable documents about Dean, because Altman made it so soon after Dean's death and thus he was able to get interviews with people who

never appear in later documentaries: Dean's aunt and uncle back on the farm in Fairmount, Indiana; his former fraternity brothers from UCLA before he dropped out; a waiter at a Italian restaurant that Dean frequented. I think it was Altman's first or second film after he came back from flying bombers in the war and got done with all his industrial, instructional films and cut his teeth on television shows like *Combat!* This film, more than any of the other books and movies about Dean, gave me a sense of the embodied young man, the guy who actually walked around Los Angeles and had relationships with people and tried to make his way in the world. Because the interviews were conducted before the Dean legend had been formed, their sense of Dean is more pure, less adulterated by awareness of Dean's greatness.

═══════════════════

So, not long after meeting Bob at the party, he asked me to be in a

---

JAMES FRANCO is a writer, director, and Oscar-nominated actor who starred opposite Neve Campbell in Altman's ballet movie *The Company* (2003). He has also appeared in such films as *Spider-Man* (2002), *127 Hours* (2010), and *Spring Breakers* (2012).

dance film, starring and produced by Neve Campbell, called *The Company*. The idea was that he would use the actual dance company—the Joffrey Ballet—as the actor-dancers, and Neve, Malcolm McDowell (as the company director), and I would be the only actor-actors. I think Eva Marie Saint was also mentioned at the time, but she didn't end up in it. I met Bob and his young assistant at a coffee shop somewhere on Beverly Drive before it turns into Beverwil. He was very easy: "So, you'll play Neve's boyfriend. You're a chef. But here's the thing: I'm using real dancers for all the other parts. So I want to shoot the whole movie as if it were a dance—not just the dance scenes, but the whole film—the dance of behavior. I'm using real dancers for the other parts, so I don't want to have them do all their dance stuff and then have you and Neve and Malcolm come on and it's 'the

actors' time to do their thing.' I want it all to feel like a dance." It sounded like a good idea, but I wasn't sure exactly what he meant. He also said, "You can design your character however you want, as long as it feels natural to you. If you want him to have an eye patch and a peg leg, that's fine with me, as long as it feels natural. I want you to create this character. I want actors to be able to do what they got into acting to do: to act, to create their characters, to be free."

He might not have said that last part in our first meeting, but it was the underlying impression he implied when talking to me, and I heard him say it many times over the subsequent years. And it's damn true: He loves the actors to be creators, to find their own characters, to be free; this is why he mics everyone with wireless lavs, so he can catch every spontaneous bit of action and dialogue.

One other thing I heard him say often that has been very important to me is that "making films is like making sand castles: You get all your friends together, and someone brings the shovels and someone brings the sandwiches and someone brings the drinks, and you all come together and make something beautiful, and then you stand back and watch the sea take it away."

I think there are two points of emphasis here: that human artistic achievement is often transitory, but, more important, filmmaking is a collaborative medium. For Bob, the cast and crew of a film were family, to the extent that he included his actual family (his son Bobby was a longtime operator on his films, and another son, Stephen, was often his production designer).

Bob's dailies screenings were famous. At the end of each shooting day, he would invite *everyone* to have pasta and wine and watch the previous day's work on a big screen; with the Joffrey Ballet, these screenings were particularly boisterous and enjoyable, as they all commented on each other's moves on screen. Here was the *family* coming together as a group. Yes, Bob had a firm influence as the father-director—an Altman film is always clearly an Altman film—but he got to choose the families he wanted to help him build his sand castles, and once those families were chosen, he wanted them to *play*, not conform to his dictatorial demands.

There is a reason his company was called Sandcastle 5 Productions.

When I got to Chicago to shoot *The Company*, the production had already started. I arrived on a Sunday, and Bob invited me to his room to watch college football with a gang of regulars. As a young actor I felt like I had no time to follow sports, but I loved that Bob loved football. It was as if he knew about everything: sports (the football scene in *M*A*S*H*, the interrogation scene in *The Long Goodbye*), war (*M*A*S*H*), comedy (everything he did), politics (*Secret Honor, Tanner '88*), music (*Nashville,*

ABOVE Poster for a film, *Paint*, that Altman was developing just after the release of *The Company* in 2003. Jeffrey Lewis had written the script and the film was set to star Salma Hayek and James Franco, but it was never made.

Kansas City), the Old West (*McCabe & Mrs. Miller, Buffalo Bill and the Indians*), the Depression (*Thieves Like Us*), literature and plays (*Fool for Love, Beyond Therapy, Short Cuts, The Long Goodbye, The Player*), and the weirdness of human beings (*Brewster McCloud, 3 Women*). I popped my head into the football viewing party that first Sunday; there were four fat joints on the coffee table.

I started filming. There had been a script—I think the writer spent two years following and researching the Joffrey Ballet—but on set, I never saw Bob use it. He had little cards that detailed what the scenes were about, but he hardly ever had us say the lines. I remember one scene in the script where Neve was supposed to deliver a two-page monologue about how she started dancing when she was five and has devoted her life to it and doesn't know anything else. When we got to the set, Bob had set up the four cameras about the small apartment. He said to Neve and me: "Forget the script. Neve, you'll be over there in the bathroom taking a bath. James, you'll come in, maybe you'll hang up your coat, then go over and kiss her hello in the bath, and then go over to the couch, and there will be a tape in the VCR; pop it in, and it will be the video of Neve dancing when she's five. Then Neve will come over with her towel on and sit by you on the couch, you'll watch the video for a bit, maybe she says something or other about it, and you laugh about it. Then maybe you kiss and end up sideways on the couch." And that was it. We probably only did it two or three times, because he had four cameras rolling. It was all about the movement around the apartment and the behavior. The dialogue was unnecessary because we got everything about her history by having the characters watch the old video of her. All behavior, and all more or less spontaneous.

I think a bunch of writers got angry with Bob over the years, but he also helped quite a few of them win Oscars.

He had me train with a chef to learn how to cut vegetables like a pro, so we could turn the scene of making Neve breakfast into its own kind of dance.

I remember when I slipped in the lane during the bowling scene, he made me do it again, because it was the kind of moment he loved.

He said the ending of the film was uncharacteristically happy: My chef character had a bad burn on his hand and she had a dance injury, but they were in love. Neve and I kissed backstage as the dance performance ended.

When I directed my first film, I tried to direct like Bob. I gave my actors a lot of freedom. It was chaos. What I didn't realize is, Bob's seemingly free-form approach takes a lot of skill and control. You need to know how to set certain parameters so the freedom can have direction. Alan Rudolph told me that after Bob made *The Company*, he became obsessed with minimalist acting, or the idea that actors just live in front of the camera; they don't need to *perform*. I think this must have come from his experience with the Joffrey dancers, who were not actors and were just playing versions of themselves. But in order to make such minimalistic acting work, the director needs to frame such performances in a particular way so that the drama still rises, so that tension is still present. Part of this is having a strong pictorial sense of drama, that one can tell a story simply through images. And part of this is guiding performers like water, so they flow naturally in the directions they are inclined to move in.

Later, Bob asked me to be in a film about the New York art world. We went around to a bunch of artists' studios to prepare for the film. Bob wanted the different characters to represent different types of artists. I was going to be a conservative painter from the Midwest; my character's brother was a contemporary artist who made very slick conceptual paintings. There was going to be a

Gordon Matta-Clark kind of character who painted swimming pools, and Selma Hayek was going to play a video artist whose work would be designed by Tony Oursler. So Bob and his team and I met all kinds of artists. I remember meeting the great Mark Grotjahn at this time, right before his abstractions became famous.

The gallery Blum and Poe in L.A. gave me a lot of help, but they thought we wouldn't be able to capture the art world as it is. Maybe we wouldn't have; maybe the art world loses its energy when represented in another medium. In the film, my character becomes so jealous of his successful art-world brother, he murders him. Then he starts to forge his brother's paintings, the paintings that he hates because they represent an art market that has no interest in his conventional work. But he needs to make money, and no one will buy his paintings. The movie was going to be called *Paint*.

Then Bob called me one day and said that the movie was off. I think he didn't like the script; I'm not sure. I wanted to ask why he cared about the script, because he seemed to improvise everything anyway. But maybe that was only with the dance film, where behavior was everything. I don't know why I didn't ask.

Later he offered me a part in his fictional rendition of *Hands on a Hard Body*. It seemed like it was right up his alley: Southern, ensemble, a great way to get a bunch of different, wacky characters together. It was going to have Meryl Streep (they had just done *A Prairie Home Companion*) and Hilary Swank and The Rock.

His office called on a Friday to make sure my dates worked for the new film. I think he died on the following Monday. He was truly working until the end. Making sand castles with the people he loved. The problem with his metaphor is that his sand castles won't be washed away. I think Bob showed us ourselves at our most interesting and our most terrible. His films stand as some of the best and most original the world has ever seen.

Scripture-quoting capitalist played by Tommy Lee Jones. A blonde angel of death (Virginia Madsen) haunts the backstage, chased by romantic detective Guy Noir (Kevin Kline). Meanwhile, Lola (Lindsay Lohan) writes a poem about suicide. From this apocalyptic scenario, Altman extracted a tender twilight, bathed in warm, glowing light by Ed Lachman's photography as well as by the performers' relaxed mix of fun and sadness. It may be the last show, but the Johnson Sisters (Meryl Streep and Lily Tomlin) and singing cowboys Lefty and Dusty (John C. Reilly and Woody Harrelson) are having the time of their lives.

Radio, a stage not unlike *Nashville*'s, an ever-moving camera, built-in unity of time and space, music, a group of great actors, the Midwestern soul—so many Altman things come together in *A Prairie Home Companion* that one could call it the perfect ending.

But Robert Altman never liked tidy, perfect endings. He was just about to start shooting his next film, *Hands on a Hard Body*, when he died, on November 20, 2006.

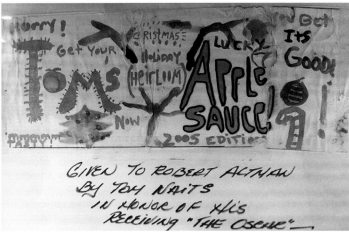

LEFT Poster for *A Prairie Home Companion*, 2006.
TOP A letter and envelope from Tom Waits to Altman congratulating him for his 2006 Academy Honorary Award.
ABOVE Altman on the set of *A Prairie Home Companion*.

OPPOSITE Meryl Streep and Lily Tomlin as the singing sisters Yolanda and Rhonda Johnson in *A Prairie Home Companion*.

BOB
GARRISON
KEILLOR

Back in 2004, when he had decided to make a picture with me, Mr. Altman and I went to lunch at Orso in New York, and he told me that he had bladder cancer and that he'd had a heart transplant ten years before. "You have a right to know that," he said. I said, "Are you sure you want to do this?" He said, "I want to go out with my boots on." And then the food came: I believe he had linguini and sausage.

He was seventy-nine, and of course I knew him by reputation, but we hadn't spent much time together. I knew that his wife, Kathryn, liked *A Prairie Home Companion*, and that was a big reason he was interested in the show. Altman said he usually watched basketball on TV in the next room, and if he heard her laughing, he'd walk in to see what was so funny. He never said he liked the show, only that Kathryn did, and I liked that there was no flattery from this guy. It meant that I didn't have to talk about how much I loved *Nashville*, which, as a matter of fact, I didn't. I liked *Gosford Park* more, and *Popeye*. But it doesn't matter. I knew he'd be good to work with. He was candid, he was eager, and his wife, whom he adored, was a fan of mine.

During lunch I asked him about World War II, and I think it was a subject not many people brought up with him. It took some direct questioning to get him rolling.

He was sixteen, a Kansas City boy, when Pearl Harbor was bombed, and at the age of eighteen he joined the Army Air Force. He went through ten months

GARRISON KEILLOR is the author of several books including *Lake Wobegon Days* (1985). He is also a humorist and the radio personality behind the long-running Minnesota Public Radio show, *A Prairie Home Companion*. He wrote the screenplay for Altman's final film, *A Prairie Home Companion* (2006).

of basic and flight training, got his pilot's stripes, and shipped over to the Pacific in 1944 to join the 307th Bombardment Group, in a squadron of twelve B-24 Liberators. He joined them in Guadalcanal, and then the squadron shifted to Indonesia, then called the Dutch East Indies, where it carried out raids against Japanese airfields, warships, refineries, and naval bases in the Philippines, Borneo, the Solomons, and all over the Pacific.

The B-24 Liberator was a four-engine bomber with the power of ten semis and the weight of one. It could carry a five-thousand-pound bomb load 1,700 miles at 25,000 feet, cruising at about 278 miles per hour. It carried ten crewmen, including six gunners, a pilot and copilot, navigator, and bombardier, and it was known as a very tough plane to fly. It wasn't pressurized or insulated, and at 25,000 feet the temperature is around thirty below. The wind whistled in around the gun turrets and through the bomb bay doors, and it was as loud as a steel foundry. The Pacific is a big place, and navigation back then was by the stars, by a navigator who'd been trained just as quickly as you had, and if you missed the little island you were looking for, you would run out of fuel in a bad place. Every cubic foot was used for fuel or weapons, and there wasn't much space for survival gear. The B-24s were a big target for enemy fighter planes and antiaircraft guns. America lost twelve thousand big bombers in the war, the B-24s and the B-17s. Only 30 percent of the crewmen survived thirty missions. These men were gamblers. Bob Altman survived almost fifty.

He was twenty years old, flying around the Pacific in this boxcar, and he grew up awfully fast. And that, I decided, is how you get to die old and honored and beloved in California, by being awfully lucky when you were nineteen and twenty. Once you've flown in this screaming-loud, freezing-cold, cramped boxcar in the sky, with people shooting at you, then what do you have to fear in the movie business? And he was fearless. He was the daddy of the indie film movement, older than the others and also braver (or more reckless, depending on how you look at it), who fought with studios and collaborators and the money guys and did his work and didn't waste time worrying about his career and what might happen two years from now. And that was my permanent impression of Altman, that a person is so lucky to be able to create things—music, dance, film, writing, comedy—so be lucky and enjoy the work. Compared to flying a B-24 and bombing the bejesus out of people and dodging their flak, it is a darned good life. Ironic that the man who directed a great antiwar movie should have derived so much good from the experience of war.

He hated unemployment, sickness, retirement—all dreadful, unspeakable. He sat at his big desk in New York, anxious to get the show on the road and start shooting. When I saw him in New York, he was an old man dealing with serious infirmity, and when I saw him in St. Paul, sitting at a bank of monitors, headphones on, talking to cameramen, he looked twenty years younger. He loved talking about moviemaking, and at various times Woody Harrelson and Meryl Streep and Paul Thomas Anderson sat in the canvas chair next to him, and he expounded while VB [Vebe Borge, first assistant director] wrangled the cast for the next shot.

He took a nap in a dressing room every day while the rest of us had lunch; he disappeared sometimes for (I was told) chemotherapy; he worked around the complicated schedules of his cast, some of them only available for a day or two of shooting; and he finished with an all-night shoot outdoors at Mickey's Diner in downtown St. Paul. An old railroad car diner with neon and all, and he wanted it for the opening scene: Kevin Kline (as private eye Guy Noir) leaving a curved Hopperesque counter and exiting the diner, stopping, striking a match on a window frame, lighting a smoke, exhaling, and walking across a rain-soaked street. We had shot the last scene of the movie inside the diner, which was Meryl's last scene, and she kissed everybody good-bye around 1:00 A.M., and then Bob got to work setting up Guy Noir's walk. He sat on his high canvas chair, with his monitor bank, on the northeast corner of the intersection, and he enjoyed that scene more than anything—the lighting, the wetness of the street, Kevin's moves, the counterman in the diner wiping his grill, the two other patrons. Bob knew that the sun would rise in a couple hours and then he couldn't shoot nighttime anymore, and he savored every bit of the business until they told him to stop. It was the last scene he shot, and all of us who were there watching will remember how much he loved it.

2001

GOSFORD PARK

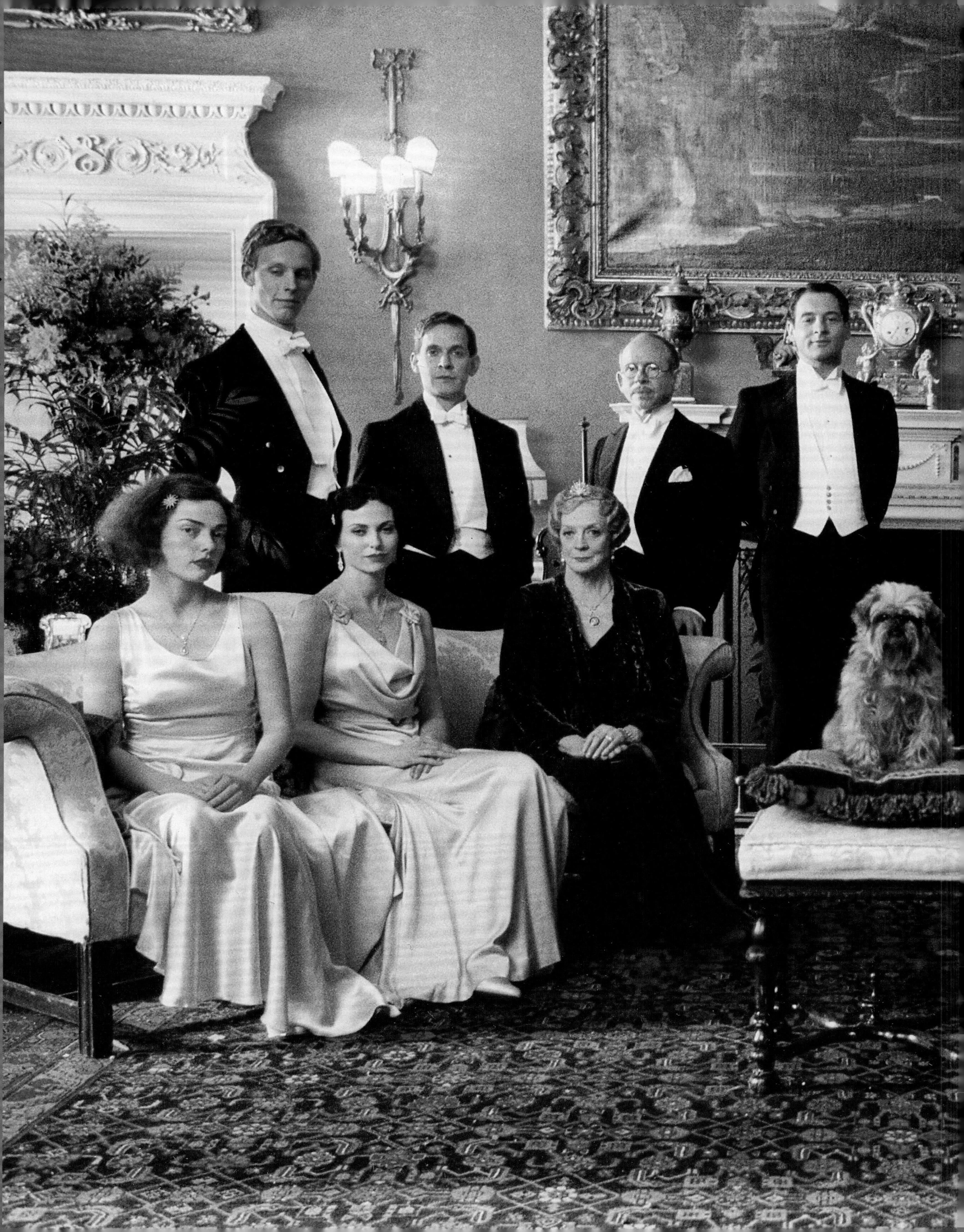

The "upstairs" cast, including Michael Gambon, Kristin Scott Thomas, Bob Balaban, Maggie Smith, Jeremy Northam, James Wilby, Claudie Blakley, and Geraldine Somerville.

LEFT Altman and Emily Watson (as Elsie).
RIGHT TOP Emily Watson (as Elsie) with Jeremy Northam (as Ivor Novello) and Maggie Smith (as Constance Trentham).
RIGHT BOTTOM Emily Watson (as Elsie) serving Michael Gambon (as William McCordle).
OPPOSITE Altman with Maggie Smith (as Constance Trentham) and Kelly McDonald (as

The cast of *Gosford Park*.

OPPOSITE The *Gosford Park* house staff (top) and weekend guests (bottom)

THE COMPANY

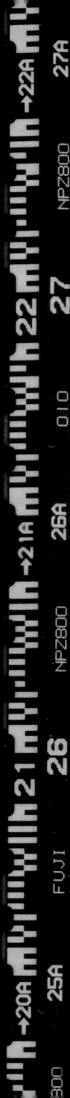

OPPOSITE Contact sheet of photos of the dancers.
TOP Altman directing.
BOTTOM Neve Campbell with Brian McSween, one of the many members of the Joffrey Ballet who appear in *The Company*.

2004

TANNER ON TANNER

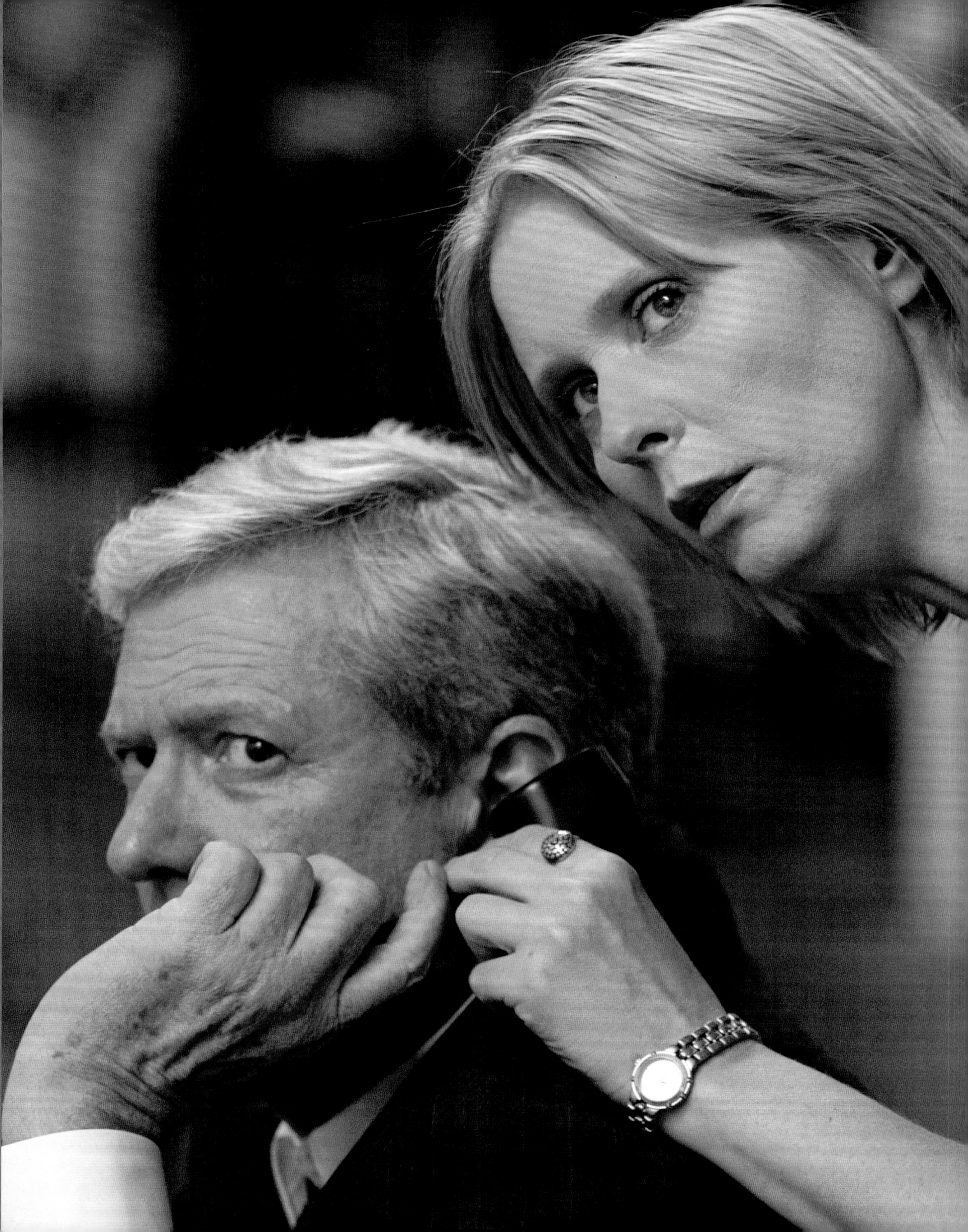

OPPOSITE Michael Murphy and Cynthia Nixon (as Alex Tanner).
TOP Altman with Al Franken and Michael Murphy.
BOTTOM Pamela Reed (as J.T. Cavanaugh) and Michael Murphy (as Jack Tanner).

A PRAIRIE HOME COMPANION

OPPOSITE TOP Altman on the set.
OPPOSITE BOTTOM Kevin Kline as private detective Guy Noir, a character well known to listeners of Garrison Keillor's radio show).
TOP Woody Harrelson and John C. Reilly (as cowboy singers Dusty and Lefty).
BOTTOM The cast.

THE AUGHTS

BY
KATHRYN REED
ALTMAN

Deauville Film Festival
2000

3 We went to the Deauville Film Festival in 2000. Deauville is a wonderful little town on the water in northwestern France. It was originally a noncompetitive festival, so the tempo was really cool. It's always nice to be invited to go there. You have to take a project, and this year I think we took *Jazz '34*. This is Ruda Dauphin (center), the U.S. representative of the festival.

Twins' first Halloween
2000

4 Of all the pictures that Bob had in his office, none of them had been personal or of family except for one showing the three generations of my granddaughter, Signe; my daughter, Konni; and me. But he just absolutely flipped over this picture of our twin grandsons', Reed and Parker's, first Halloween, and it got the place of honor!

Altman documentary
2000

1 The Fox Movie Channel did a documentary on Bob called *Altman on His Own Terms*. They took a billboard ad on the Sunset Strip. Some of us piled in a car and had a photo shoot in front of the sign.

Backgammon
2000

2 This is Bob waiting for someone to play backgammon with him on a summer Sunday in Malibu.

5

Gosford Park
2001

5-8 I don't have many photos from the set of *Gosford Park*, as that was when cell phone cameras and digital cameras were really getting popular. So what I do have is pretty telling. **5** Here is one shot of Bob in action—very much so—in the belowstairs section of the film, which is the kitchen area and where the help lived.

6 This was an interesting day. I joined Bob for lunch in the commissary, where people kind of came and went between wardrobe fittings and various meetings, so not everybody was in there at the same time. As we were sitting there, Helen Mirren walked through in her wardrobe. There had been some difference of opinion, of which I wasn't really aware, in terms of how Bob was going to end the picture. He looked at Helen as she went to her table, and then Eileen came in, and then I realized that Bob was no longer listening to me. As you can see here, I think I got the picture that I'd lost him completely. At that moment he realized how much those two look alike and how perfect it would be to make those characters sisters and pick up the plot from there.

Stephen Frears is a very prominent British director, and because of Bob's age and his health at this time, the insurance company made him have a standby director so that if he got sick or was unable to direct, this standby would immediately be able to take over. The standby had to be approved by everybody. And Maggie Smith, who is a big, big star, had a reputation for really being tough to work with. Directors were afraid of her, and so were other actors. She and Eileen Atkins hadn't spoken in years, but that was all resolved during this picture. So anyway, Stephen Frears hardly ever came around, but once it was official that he was to be Bob's standby, he said, "All I hope is that if Bob's going to croak, he does it after he's finished with Maggie."

6

7

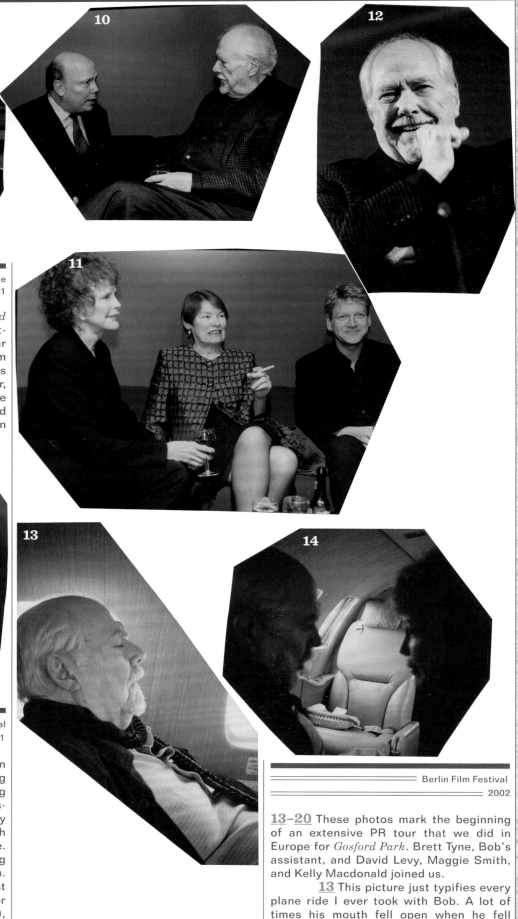

Gosford Park, Patrick Doyle
2001

<u>8</u> The composer of the score of *Gosford Park* was Patrick Doyle, a most interesting, fun, gracious man. This particular day, they were recording Jeremy Northam doing his piano part for the movie as his character, Ivor Novello. Jeremy's brother, a distinguished pianist, did a lot of the backup music for Jeremy. I always wished that Patrick had been nominated for an Oscar.

The National
2001

<u>9–12</u> When we first got to London to begin work on *Gosford Park*, we were just settling into our residence in this terrific building called the Thorney Court, right in Kensington. The British Film Institute, a very prestigious organization, honored Bob with its Fellowship at the National Film Theatre. This was the night we were all gathering prior to the presentation, in the greenroom. <u>10</u> This is Julian Fellowes, who had just started working with Bob on the script for *Gosford Park*; <u>11</u> Glenda Jackson (center), who had done *HealtH* and *Beyond Therapy* with Bob; and Kenneth Branagh (right), who had done *The Gingerbread Man*.

Berlin Film Festival
2002

<u>13–20</u> These photos mark the beginning of an extensive PR tour that we did in Europe for *Gosford Park*. Brett Tyne, Bob's assistant, and David Levy, Maggie Smith, and Kelly Macdonald joined us.

<u>13</u> This picture just typifies every plane ride I ever took with Bob. A lot of times his mouth fell open when he fell asleep. Luckily, it hadn't yet at this time.

<u>14</u> I love this. I cut this out and put it on the refrigerator in New York. It's

such a great photo. We are really communicating on some level.

15 (far left), **16** (center) This is Dieter Kosslick, the head of the Berlin Film Festival. Through Dieter we were invited to the Berlin city hall for some sort of dedication to Bob. The mayor of Berlin, Klaus Wowereit **15** (far right), **18** (left), **16** (far left) was our guide through this beautiful building. Bob made his speech and then they invited him to sign this book. **16** Then they invited me to sign the book, which was very touching. The scarf I'm wearing is the one that we gave as crew gifts to everyone on *Gosford Park*.

19 Something happened that made us laugh in this picture. We were trying to suppress our laughter; it wasn't working. Oh, how I wish I could remember what set us off!

We went to Berlin in the first place because Bob was to receive the Honorary Golden Bear Award. Here they are presenting it to him **20**. As we were leaving, David Levy, our producer, was holding up the plane because he was on the phone getting the news that *Gosford Park* had been nominated for seven Oscars! We were nominated for Best Director, Best Picture, Best Art Direction, Best Costume Design, Best Supporting Actress for both Helen Mirren and Maggie Smith, and Best Original Screenplay. As it turned out, *A Beautiful Mind* took Best Picture and Best Director, and *Moulin Rouge* took Best Art Direction. But Julian Fellowes won for his screenplay.

21–25 This is a birthday party for Bob in the same room where I had given him a surprise birthday party seventeen years earlier, for his sixtieth. Same room, same venue, but this time we had a band.

21–23 Bob used to say, "I like to change my temperature when the sun goes down." These three photographs, in sequence, illustrate that. **24** Lois Smith was such an important part of the last fifteen years of Bob's career. She was a marvelous, highly respected publicist, loved and adored by many. **25** And Sam Cohn (right) was a highly respected agent, loved—and not so loved—by many.

26 In our New York apartment, I used to take this same photograph over and over, because I could stand on the second-floor balcony and look down into the living room.

32–33 We went to Chicago to make a film called *The Company* with the Joffrey Ballet. It was written by Barbara Turner from an idea by Neve Campbell, and it starred Neve as a dancer who was working in and among the Joffrey Ballet dancers. We had this great exposure to the inner workings of a ballet company. It was quite phenomenal, all the wonderful things that happen when a filmmaker is taken into the world of the subject he is filming.

Special thanks to the dedication and persistence of Joshua Astrachan for helping pull this film together. Josh worked with Bob for many years, producing *The Company*, *Gosford Park*, and *A Prairie Home Companion*.

32 Malcolm McDowell was the star of the film, along with Neve. We used the entire Joffrey Ballet company as dancers, so there were very few actual actors. We stayed close friends with Malcolm and his wife, Kelley.

27–31 We moved into our new Sandcastle 5 offices in New York in 2002. We'd been in our other office for twenty-six years, from 1976 to 2002. For the first nine years, though, our New York space had been a pied-à-terre for us; then we turned it into an office, which it was for another seventeen years. It was great until Donald Trump took over the building and remodeled it completely into another Trump Tower. So we moved to these terrific new offices on the West Side, in an area north of Chelsea. **30** This is a picture of Bob on his first day in the office: the boss!

31 These are posters that hung on the long, long wall. We had posters of every film that he made—for some, more than one. **27**, **28** And here are some of his oil paintings that he had done in 1959.

315

==
================= 44th anniversary
================= 2003

34–37 Bob loved boats and loved to fish, and so do his sons. Matthew, Bob, and I joined Bobby in Florida to go fishing and celebrate our forty-fourth wedding anniversary. It was kind of funny: **37** We were in a small town called Delray Beach, and our anniversary dinner was in a Chinese cafeteria.

==
================= Bob and Harry Belafonte
================= 2003

38 Bob and Harry Belafonte had a really special relationship. They met kind of late in life, and they just took to each other. They only did one film together, *Kansas City*, but they talked about and worked on other projects that never came to fruition. They always had such a good time together. They seemed to inspire and stimulate each other and laugh a whole lot. It was great to be around them.

39–47 Bob gave me a big, fabulous party at Elaine's, a restaurant in New York, for my birthday in 2003. There were close to one hundred people there. As the night went on, everybody ended up mingling. We had many photographs, because we put throwaway cameras on all the tables. And digital photography was really coming to the forefront, so many people had cell phone cameras, too.

Guests made speeches and sang songs to me. **40** Harry Belafonte sang "Try to Remember." Cynthia Adler read a poem she'd written. Arnold Weinstein sang "You Must Have Been a Beautiful Baby." Bud Cort sang "The Darktown Strutters' Ball." Charles Michener and Coco Brown gave toasts. **43–45** And Bob sang "The Rabbit Rhapsody." Prior to our ever meeting, Bob had written this song with Bob Eckton. It was a funny parody because it was written to the tune of about four different previously existing songs. It was very rare that Bob would perform it, but he did it this night, and it was terrific. He got up and he said, "Ladies and gentlemen, this is a gift to my wife. It's the first time that I've ever sung in public, and I can guarantee you it's going to be the last!" He was so nervous.

Annie Ross helped him and had to cue him. They had even rehearsed earlier that afternoon. There is only one recording of Bob doing "The Rabbit Rhapsody," and it's because Stephen Shadley filmed this performance on his little cell phone, so it's not the best quality. But it was my best birthday present!

47 Sally Kellerman's birthday is also June 2, and as often as possible, since 1976, we have celebrated them together. Bob asked me what I wanted for my birthday, and I said to spend it with Sally, so he sent for her and she was very much a part of the festivities that night. Fabulous event!

48 We hosted a small evening for John Kerry when he was running for president. We held it at the office. We were very much behind Kerry and very disappointed when he lost. Bob is standing in front of the Polish poster for his film *3 Women*.

In 2000 the composer William Bolcom contacted Bob regarding his film *A Wedding*. Bolcom had been commissioned by the Lyric Opera of Chicago to write an original opera. His choice was to write it based on *A Wedding*, with Bob to direct. It would be four years until opening night. It was wonderful. **49** This is Bob with his diva, Lauren Flanigan. **51** And this is Bob with (left to right) William Bolcom, choreographer Patricia Birch, and L.A. theater producer and director Gordon Davidson. **50** This is costume designer Dona Granata and divas Catherine Malfitano and Lauren Flanigan. **52** Opera music coordinator Scott Griffin and me.

53 Bob was most comfortable at his office—he always had wonderful offices. He knew just what he wanted and where he wanted it, starting with his first office in the early sixties. Lion's Gate in Westwood, California, was warm and open, with no interior doors. He had the perfect colors, and all the paintings, carpets, and furnishings were his choices.

When we did the Broadway production of *Come Back to the 5 & Dime, Jimmy Dean, Jimmy Dean*, there was this great big neon sign, which was one of the props. He took that and put it behind his desk in his office.

54

55

Bob just hated to shop. Sometimes he'd go into a clothing store and just buy all kinds of stuff to get it over with. If he saw a shirt that he liked, he'd get three of them. The days of the men's haberdashery is when he grew up. The one in Kansas City where he and his father went was called Jack Henry. He got the full service. He was very particular about his clothes, and he loved the personal service. Today, the haberdashery for men is gone—but Bergdorf's for men is not! This time he took Dona Granata, his costume designer on several projects. **54, 55** Here he is modeling some of the things he bought that day.

53

56

New York terrace
2004

56 This is our terrace in New York. Many, many lovely hours have been spent out there at the end of the day and early evening.

Paul Thomas Anderson
2004

These pictures were taken in our New York apartment in 2004. **58** This is Paul Thomas Anderson, a very prominent director who was also a big fan of Bob's and a good friend. **57** This is his partner, Maya Rudolph. They now are the parents of four children. Paul played a very important part in Bob's last film, *A Prairie Home Companion*: Paul was right there at Bob's elbow and doing all the running around that needed to be done. He assisted Bob in a terrific way, and she was an actress in the film. We all became very good friends.

Bob and Signe
2004

59 This is Signe, the first of the four granddaughters, and in some ways the closest because she stayed with us a lot as a child and was close to us during her college days. She worked as a production assistant on a few films over the years, then assisted Bob during the *Kansas City* production. It was a very special relationship.

Revlon commercial
2004

60 Bob was experiencing failing health when he was invited to direct a Revlon commercial with Halle Berry, Susan Sarandon, Julianne Moore, and Eva Mendes. He was being treated in the hospital at the time and had to have continuous shots of antibiotics. He worked it out to have a nurse accompany him to the set so that he could continue treatment during the day while shooting—but he didn't want anybody to know he had a nurse with him, so he dressed her as an assistant, and he pulled that off beautifully.

Tanner on Tanner
2004

61–65 Originally, Bob made *Tanner '88* for HBO. Then he made *Tanner on Tanner* in 2004 for the Sundance Channel. I think we did four episodes. This idea came from Garry Trudeau, the famous cartoonist and liberal Democrat **64**. He and Bob had their ups and downs, but they did very well.

In both of these series, we wound it up by shooting at the conventions. For *Tanner '88* it was when Dukakis was nominated. We finished *Tanner on Tanner* by shooting at the convention in Boston, when our candidate, John Kerry, was nominated. This convention was very exciting. It was where Obama gave the keynote address and the world became aware of him.

65 Robert Redford is the man who started the whole Sundance world, and he was so interested in this project. He visited the set and actually appeared in one of the segments, which we shot at Lincoln Square Cinemas in New York.

Actually, the funny thing about this association with Robert Redford is that in the sixties when Bob was doing episodic television, an episode of *Bus Stop* was shot at Fox and Robert had a small part in it. They used to kid about it, about how many years ago he directed Robert in that episode. It was a show about a kidnapping, and Bob called it a "training film for kidnappers!"

66–71 This is a man at work. All of these expressions are meaningful to me, because I can see how his mind is working. On the last several pictures that Bob did, the insurance company required that he have a backup in case he became ill and couldn't finish it. It was difficult, because the insurance company had to approve Bob's choice. He asked for Alan Rudolph on every one, but they wouldn't approve him. Paul Thomas Anderson was living with Maya Rudolph, whom Bob had already cast in the film. And then the production got shut down before it even got started. By the time it picked up again, Bob called the people he had cast and Maya said, "I'm pregnant." Bob said, "That's OK, I'll work it into the script." Paul wanted to come on location with her and write his next movie, which he did. It was *There Will Be Blood*. So it worked out perfectly that Paul would be the backup. **70** He assisted Bob on this picture and was as much involved as Bob, as you can see in this photograph.

71 This second picture I find remarkable for some reason. The involvement of each crew member is so all-consuming, it gives me chills.

Prior to shooting, Bob spoke to Garrison Keillor, whose script this is and whose radio show this is based upon, and told him that he was being treated for cancer and that he'd have to continue treatment throughout the production of the film. It was a real plus to have Paul there with us because of that. He was really able to help Bob. So we had all these transfusions and injections and trips to the hospital going on behind the scenes, but as soon as Bob stepped on the set, you wouldn't know that he had anything going on at all. Associate producer Lowell Dubrinsky and I would take him to the hospital in Minneapolis, about a forty-minute drive from where we were in St. Paul, Minnesota. Thinking back, people were just stunned that he was going through that, though it was never openly discussed. He never missed a day, and they never rolled the camera without him. It was tough, but he never complained. At one point he had gout, which lasted about two days, and they were going to be shooting at night. That was the only time he ever said it was hard for him.

70

72 We were on a boat at Cannes with several friends of ours. I think it was Alan Rudolph who was telling Bob a joke, and you can see from this picture series how he's responding to it from beginning to end. They were taken by a friend, the photographer Danielle Weil. It's just so Bob! She named it after one of Bob's favorite expressions: "Giggle and give in!"

71

73

Elaine's Oscar party
2006

Elaine Kaufman of Elaine's restaurant was a close friend. She gave a party for Bob honoring his 2006 Oscar. **73** Here's Bob with Robin Williams—probably discussing Popeye's arms!

72

74

We have always prided ourselves on the number of grandchildren we have. We tried to do the best we could for them, to include them as much as possible in all of our various Thanksgivings and Christmases. Three of them were raised in Nebraska and two in France. Our son Bobby is the one child of ours who never had any children of his own until 2006. **74**, **75** After twenty years of marriage, he and his wife adopted our twelfth grandchild, and here she is with her grandfather. Her name is Cora.

75

Last photograph together
2006

76 This was our last photograph together, and we had no idea it was being taken. A young man named Yuichi Hibi, a photographer who was a friend of our son Bobby, asked if he could take some pictures of our home and of Bobby and his family. Later, he was taking some more pictures in the living room, and I didn't even realize he was there. It was a special day, and it was near the end of Bob's life. I think it's a very special picture.

76

A trendsetter always
Robert Altman 1925 - 2006

ROBERT ALTMAN

77 This is the night of the Oscars when Bob was presented with the Lifetime Achievement Award. He gave a great speech—it was just terrific. He initially resisted the award. He didn't want to do it, because he always said it was the "Old Man's Award," given to the artist who has retired. He had just finished *A Prairie Home Companion*. So he said he'd accept the award on condition that they would show clips from his upcoming film; that's the only way he'd do it. He had Meryl Streep and Lily Tomlin introduce him, and he told them to just keep talking and overlapping each other's dialogue. Then he came out, looking absolutely gorgeous, and he discussed his movie and told the world that he'd been working for the last eleven years with a heart transplant. We, his family, were all sitting in a box watching. He threw me a kiss and told me that he loved me.

After the Oscars, we went to the *Vanity Fair* party. **78** This photograph was taken by Jonathan Becker of *Vanity Fair* magazine. We had a nice time there, and then we went on to Paul Thomas Anderson and Maya Rudolph's home and had a blast until 6:00 A.M.

79 *Variety* seemed to like this particular expression—borderline perturbation, I'd say. I like it a lot!

FILMOGRAPHY

FILM

(1957) THE DELINQUENTS
DISTRIBUTION United Artists
PRODUCER Robert Altman
SCREENPLAY Robert Altman
CINEMATOGRAPHY (B/W) Charles Paddock
EDITOR Helene Turner
MUSIC Bill Nolan Quintet Minus Two
SONG "The Dirty Rock Boogie" (Julia Lee)
PRODUCTION DESIGN Chet Allen
71 mins

(1957) THE JAMES DEAN STORY
DISTRIBUTION Warner Brothers
PRODUCERS Robert Altman, George W. George
SCREENPLAY Stewart Stern
CINEMATOGRAPHY (B/W) Louis Lombardo
PHOTOGRAPHS Dennis Stock, Roy Schatt, Frank Worth, Weegee, Edward Martin, Dick Miller, Peter Basch, Carlyle Blackwell Jr, Tom Gaffrey, Jack Delano, Murray Garrett, Paul Gilliam, Fred Jordan, Russ Meyer, Don Ornitz, Paul Popesil, Charles Robinson, Jack Stager, Phil Stern, William Veercamp
EDITORS Robert Altman, George W. George
MUSIC Leith Stevens
SONG "Let Me Be Loved" (Tommy Sands)
PRODUCTION DESIGN Louis Clyde Stoumen
NARRATOR Martin Gabel
82 mins

(1964) NIGHTMARE IN CHICAGO
(expanded version of TV film *Once Upon a Savage Night*)
PRODUCTION CO. Roncom/Universal
PRODUCER Robert Altman
SCREENPLAY Donald Moessinger, based on the novel *Death on the Turnpike* by William P. McGivern
CINEMATOGRAPHY (B/W) Bud Thackery
EDITORS Danford B. Greene, Larry D. Lester
MUSIC John Williams
81 mins

(1968) COUNTDOWN
PRODUCTION CO. William Conrad Productions for Warner Brothers
PRODUCERS James Lydon, William Conrad
SCREENPLAY Loring Mandel, based on the novel *The Pilgrim Project* by Hank Searls
CINEMATOGRAPHY (PANAVISION) William W. Spencer
EDITOR Gene Milford
MUSIC Leonard Rosenman
PRODUCTION DESIGN Jack Poplin
101 mins (cut to 73 mins for UK distribution)

(1969) THAT COLD DAY IN THE PARK
PRODUCTION CO. Factor-Altman-Mirell Films Ltd/Commonwealth International
PRODUCERS Donald Factor, Leon Mirell
SCREENPLAY Gillian Freeman, based on the novel by Richard Miles
CINEMATOGRAPHY Laszlo Kovacs
EDITOR Danford B. Greene
MUSIC Johnny Mandel
PRODUCTION DESIGN Leon Ericksen
110 mins
(cut to 105 mins for UK distribution)

(1970) M*A*S*H
PRODUCTION CO. Aspen/20th Century Fox
PRODUCER Ingo Preminger
SCREENPLAY Ring Lardner Jr, based on the novel by Richard Hooker
CINEMATOGRAPHY (PANAVISION) Harold E. Stine
EDITOR Danford B. Greene
MUSIC Johnny Mandel
SONG "Suicide Is Painless" (Ahmad Jamal)
PRODUCTION DESIGN Jack Martin Smith, Arthur Lonegan
116 mins

(1970) BREWSTER MCCLOUD
PRODUCTION CO. An Adler-Phillips/Lion's Gate production for MGM
PRODUCER Lou Adler
SCREENPLAY Doran William Cannon
CINEMATOGRAPHY (PANAVISION) Lamar Boren, Jordan Cronenworth
EDITOR Lou Lombardo
MUSIC Gene Page
SONGS "Brewster McCloud"; "Lift Every Voice and Sing," "White Feather Wings" (Merry Clayton); "Last of the Unnatural Acts," "The First and Last Thing You Do," "I Promise Not to Tell" (John Phillips)
PRODUCTION DESIGN Preston Ames, George W. David
105 mins

(1971) MCCABE & MRS. MILLER
PRODUCTION CO. An Altman-Foster Production for Warner Brothers
PRODUCERS David Foster, Mitchell Brower
SCREENPLAY Robert Altman, Brian McKay, based on the novel *McCabe* by Edmund Naughton
CINEMATOGRAPHY (PANAVISION) Vilmos Zsigmond
EDITOR Louis Lombardo
SONGS "Sisters of Mercy," "The Stranger Song," "Winter Lady" (Leonard Cohen)
PRODUCTION DESIGN Leon Ericksen
121 mins

(1972) IMAGES
PRODUCTION CO. Lion's Gate Productions (Dublin) for the Hemdale Group
PRODUCER Tommy Thompson
SCREENPLAY Robert Altman
CINEMATOGRAPHY (PANAVISION) Vilmos Zsigmond
EDITOR Graeme Clifford
MUSIC John Williams, Stomu Yamash'ta
PRODUCTION DESIGN Leon Ericksen
101 mins

(1973) THE LONG GOODBYE
PRODUCTION CO. Lion's Gate Films for United Artists
PRODUCER Jerry Bick
SCREENPLAY Leigh Brackett, based on the novel by Raymond Chandler
CINEMATOGRAPHY (PANAVISION) Vilmos Zsigmond
EDITOR Lou Lombardo
MUSIC John Williams
SONG "The Long Goodbye" (The Dave Grusin Trio, Jack Sheldon, Clydie King, Jack Riley, Morgan Ames' Aluminium Band, The Tepotzlan Municipal Band)
111 mins

(1974) THIEVES LIKE US
PRODUCTION CO. A Jerry Bick-George Litto Production for United Artists
PRODUCER Jerry Bick
SCREENPLAY Joan Tewkesbury, Robert Altman, Calder Willingham, based on the novel by Edward Anderson
CINEMATOGRAPHY Jean Boffety
EDITOR Lou Lombardo
SONGS "Massah's in the Cold, Cold Ground," "Just a Song at Twilight," "I Love You Truly," "Deep River," "It's Somebody's Birthday Today," "In the Five and Ten Cents Store," "Baby, Take a Bow," "She'll Be Coming Round the Mountain When She Comes"
VISUAL CONSULTANTS Jack DeGovia, Scott Bushnell
123 mins

(1974) CALIFORNIA SPLIT
PRODUCTION CO. Won World for Columbia Pictures
PRODUCERS Robert Altman, Joseph Walsh
SCREENPLAY Joseph Walsh
CINEMATOGRAPHY (PANAVISION) Paul Lohmann
EDITOR Lou Lombardo
SONGS Phyllis Shotwell
PRODUCTION DESIGN Leon Ericksen
109 mins

(1975) NASHVILLE
PRODUCTION CO. American Broadcasting Corporation for Paramount
PRODUCER Robert Altman
SCREENPLAY Joan Tewkesbury
CINEMATOGRAPHY (PANAVISION) Paul Lohmann
EDITORS Sidney Levin, Dennis Hill
MUSIC SUPERVISION Richard Baskin
SONGS "200 Years," "For the Sake of the Children," "Keep-a-Going" (Henry Gibson); "Be the One," "I Never Get Enough" (Gwen Welles); "Sing a Song" (Lily Tomlin, James Dan Calvert, Donna Denton); "The Heart of a Gentle Woman" (Dave Peel); "Bluebird" (Timothy Brown); "The Day I Looked Jesus in the Eye," "Memphis," "Rolling Stone," "I Don't Know if I Found it in You" (Karen Black); "Tapedeck in His Tractor (The Cowboy Song)," "My Idaho Home," "Dues" (Ronee Blakey); "Old Man Mississippi" (Misty Mountain Boys); "One, I Love You" (Henry Gibson, Ronee Blakey); "I'm Easy," "Honey" (Keith Carradine); "It Don't Worry Me" (Barbara Harris); "Since You've Gone," "Trouble in the USA," "Swing Low, Sweet Chariot," "Rose's Café," "My Baby's Cookin' in Another Man' Pan"
161 mins

(1976) BUFFALO BILL AND THE INDIANS, OR SITTING BULL'S HISTORY LESSON
PRODUCTION CO. Dino de Laurentiis Corporation/Lion's Gate Films/Talent Associates-Norton Simon
PRODUCER Robert Altman
SCREENPLAY Alan Rudolph, Robert Altman, based on by the play *Indians* by Arthur Kopit

CINEMATOGRAPHY (PANAVISION) Paul Lohmann
EDITORS Peter Appleton, Dennis Hill
MUSIC Richard Baskin
PRODUCTION DESIGN Tony Masters
123 mins
(cut to 104 mins for European distribution)

(1977) 3 WOMEN
PRODUCTION CO. Lion's Gate Films for 20th
Century Fox
PRODUCER Robert Altman
SCREENPLAY Robert Altman
CINEMATOGRAPHY (PANAVISION) Charles Rosher
EDITOR Dennis Hill
MUSIC Generald Busby
VISUAL CONSULTANT J. Allen Highfill
123 mins

(1978) A WEDDING
PRODUCTION CO. Lion's Gate Films for 20th
Century Fox
PRODUCER Robert Altman
SCREENPLAY John Considine, Patricia Resnick,
Allan Nicholls, Robert Altman, from a story by
John Considine and Robert Altman
CINEMATOGRAPHY (PANAVISION) Charles Rosher
EDITOR Tony Lombardo
MUSIC John Hotchkis, Tom Walls
125 mins

(1979) QUINTET
PRODUCTION CO. Lion's Gate Films for 20th
Century Fox
PRODUCER Robert Altman
SCREENPLAY Frank Barhydt, Robert Altman,
Patricia Resnick, from a story by Robert Altman,
Lionel Chetwynd, Patricia Resnick
CINEMATOGRAPHY (PANAVISION) Jean Boffety
EDITOR Dennis M. Hill
MUSIC Tom Pierson
PRODUCTION DESIGN Leon Ericksen
118 mins

(1979) A PERFECT COUPLE
PRODUCTION CO. Lion's Gate Films for 20th
Century Fox
PRODUCER Robert Altman
SCREENPLAY Robert Altman, Allan Nicholls
CINEMATOGRAPHY (PANAVISION) Edmond L. Koons
EDITOR Tony Lombardo
MUSIC Tom Person, Tony Berg, Allan Nicholls
SONGS "Somp'ins Got a Hold on Me" (Tomi-Lee
Bradley, Steven Sharp); "Hurricane" (Ted Neeley
and Keepin' 'Em Off the Streets); "Week-End
Holiday" (Ted Neeley); "Won't Somebody Care,"
"Lonely Millionaire" (Marta Heflin, Steven
Sharp); "Love Is All There Is" (Heather MacRae);
"Searchin' for the Light" (Tomi-Lee Bradley);
"Fantasy" (Heather MacRae and Keepin' 'Em Off
the Streets); "Let the Music Play" (Keepin' 'Em
Off the Streets); "Goodbye Friends" (Keepin'
'Em Off the Streets, including Renn Woods)
PRODUCTION DESIGN Leon Ericksen
112 mins

(1980) HEALTH (H.E.A.L.T.H.)
PRODUCTION CO. Lion's Gate Films for 20th
Century Fox
PRODUCER Robert Altman
SCREENPLAY Frank Barhydt, Robert Altman, Paul
Dooley
CINEMATOGRAPHY Edmond L. Koons
EDITORS Tony Lombardo, Dennis M. Hill, Tom
Benko
MUSIC Joseph Byrd, Allan Nicholls
SONGS "Exercise the Right to Vote," "Health"
(The Steinettes); "Chick and Thin"
PRODUCTION DESIGN Robert Quinn
96 mins

(1980) POPEYE
PRODUCTION CO. Paramount/Walt Disney
PRODUCER Robert Evans
SCREENPLAY Jules Feiffer, based on characters
by E. C. Segar
CINEMATOGRAPHY Giuseppe Rotunno
EDITORS Tony Lombardo, John W. Holmes, David
Simmons
MUSIC Harry Nilsson, Van Dyke Parks, Tom
Pierson
SONGS "I'm Popeye the Sailor Man," "I Yam
What I Yam," "He Needs Me" "Swee' Pea's
Lullaby," "Sweethaven," "Blow Me Down,"
"Everything is Food," "Sailin," "It's Not Easy
Being Me," "He's Large," "I'm Mean," "Kids"
PRODUCTION DESIGN Wolf Kroeger
114 mins
(cut to 96 mins for European release by Disney,
with Altman's approval; three songs were
omitted—"Sailin," sung by Popeye and Olive Oyl,
and "It's Not Easy Being Me" and "Kids," sung
by Poopdeck Pappy)

(1982) COME BACK TO THE FIVE & DIME, JIMMY DEAN, JIMMY DEAN
PRODUCTION CO. A Sandcastle 5/A Mark
Goodson presentation in association with Viacom
PRODUCER Scott Bushnell
SCREENPLAY Ed Graczyk, based on his own play
CINEMATOGRAPHY Pierre Mignon
EDITOR Jason Rosenfield
SONGS "Sincerely," "If It's a Dream," "Seems
Like Old Times," "It May Sound Silly," "You'll
Never Know Till Monday," "Are You Looking for
a Sweetheart?," "I'm in the Mood for Love,"
"The Last Dance," "Miss You," "Answer Me My
Love," "Kid's Stuff," "Moon Love"; "Melody of
Love" (The McGuire Sisters); "Keep on Walkin'"
(Jo Ann Harris); "How Long Has it Been?" (The
Statesmen Quartet); "Must Jesus Bear the
Cross Alone?" (Allan Nicholls)
PRODUCTION DESIGN David Gropman
110 mins

(1983) STREAMERS
PRODUCTION CO. Streamers International
Distributors
PRODUCERS Robert Altman, Nick J. Mileti
SCREENPLAY David Rabe, based on his own play
CINEMATOGRAPHY Pierre Mignot
EDITOR Norman Smith
SONGS "Boy from New York City" (The Ad Libs);
"Boys in the Attic" (Ellie Greenwich); "What a
Guy," "Let's Go Together," "The Kind of Boy You
Can Forget" (The Raindrops); "I'm Gonna Make
You Mine" (Alan Braunstein)
PRODUCTION DESIGN Wolf Kroeger
118 mins

(1984) SECRET HONOR
PRODUCTION CO. Sandcastle 5 in cooperation
with the University of Michigan (Department of
Communication) and the Los Angeles Actors'
Theatre
PRODUCER Robert Altman
SCREENPLAY Donald Freed, Arthur M. Stones,
based on their own play
CINEMATOGRAPHY Pierre Mignot
EDITOR Juliet Weber
MUSIC George Burt
PRODUCTION DESIGN Stephen Altman
85 mins

(1985) FOOL FOR LOVE
PRODUCTION CO. Cannon
PRODUCERS Menahem Golan, Yoram Globus
SCREENPLAY Sam Shepard, based on his own play
CINEMATOGRAPHY Pierre Mignot
EDITORS Luce Grunenwalkdt, Steve Dunn

MUSIC George Burt
SONGS "Let's Ride," "It Comes and Goes,"
"God Rosa," "You Lied Your Way," "Call Me
Up," "Love Shy," "First and Last Real Cowboy,"
"Why Wyoming" (Sandy Rogers); "Honky Tonk
Heroes," "Black Rose" (Waylon Jennings)
PRODUCTION DESIGN Stephen Altman
108 mins

(1987) O.C. AND STIGGS
PRODUCTION CO. Sand River Productions for
MGM/UA
PRODUCERS Robert Altman, Peter Newman
SCREENPLAY Donald Cantrell, Ted Mann, based
on a story by Todd Carroll, Ted Mann
CINEMATOGRAPHY Pierre Mignot
EDITOR Elizabeth Kling
MUSIC King Sunny Ade & His African Beats
PRODUCTION DESIGN Scott Bushnell
109 mins

(1987) BEYOND THERAPY
PRODUCTION CO. New World Pictures/Sandcastle
5 Productions
PRODUCERS Roger Berlind, Steven Haft
SCREENPLAY Christopher Durang, Robert Altman,
based on the play by Christopher Durang
CINEMATOGRAPHY Pierre Mignot
EDITORS Steve Dunn, Jennifer Ague
MUSIC Gabriel Yared
SONGS "Someone to Watch Over Me" (Yves
Montand)
PRODUCTION DESIGN Stephen Altman
93 mins

(1987) ARIA
(Compilation film, with other episodes directed
by Nicolas Roeg, Charles Sturridge, Jean-Luc
Godard, Julien Temple, Bruce Beresford, Franc
Roddam, Ken Russel, Derek Jarman, Bill Bryden)

(1987) LES BORÉADES
PRODUCTION CO. Boyd's Co. Film Productions for
Lightyear Entertainment, Virgin Vision
PRODUCER Don Boyd
SCREENPLAY Robert Altman
CINEMATOGRAPHY Pierre Mignot
EDITOR Jennifer Auge
SONGS "Lieux desoles," "Suite des vents,"
"Jouissons! Jouissons!" from Rameau's Les
Boréades, performed by Jennifer Smith,
Anne-Marie Rodde, Philip Langridge, Monteverdi
Choir, and English Baroque Soloists conducted
by John Eliot Gardiner
PRODUCTION DESIGN Scott Bushnell, John Hay
89 mins (complete film)

(1990) VINCENT & THEO
PRODUCTION CO. Belbo Films (Paris), Central
Films (London)
PRODUCERS Ludi Boeken, David Conroy, Emma
Hayter
SCREENPLAY Julian Mitchell
CINEMATOGRAPHY Jean Lepine
EDITORS François Coispeau, Geraldine Peroni
MUSIC Gabriel Yared
PRODUCTION DESIGN Stephen Altman
140 mins (TV version: 200 mins)

(1992) THE PLAYER
PRODUCTION CO. Avenue Entertainment
PRODUCERS David Brown, Michael Tolkin, Nick
Wechsler
SCREENPLAY Michael Tolkin, based on his own
novel
CINEMATOGRAPHY Jean Lepine
EDITOR Geraldine Peroni
MUSIC Thomas Newman
SONGS "Snake," "Drums of Kyoto" (Kurt

Newman); "Precious" (Les Hooper); "Tema Para Jobin" (Joyce, Milton Nascimento)
PRODUCTION DESIGN Stephen Altman
124 mins

(1993) SHORT CUTS
PRODUCTION CO. Spelling Films International in association with Fine Line Pictures, Avenue Pictures
PRODUCER Cary Brokaw
SCREENPLAY Robert Altman, Frank Barhydt, based on writings by Raymond Carver
CINEMATOGRAPHY (PANAVISION) Walt Lloyd
EDITOR Geraldine Peroni
MUSIC Mark Isham
SONGS Cello Concerto No. 2 by A. Dvorak, Cello Suite No. 5 by J. S. Bach, "Schelomo" by E. Bloch, "Berceuse" from The Firebird by I. Stravinsky (Lori Singer and others); "I Don't Want to Cry Anymore," "Punishing Kiss," "I Don't Know You," "Conversation on a Bar Stool," "I'm Gonna Go Fishin'" (Annie Ross and The Low Note Quintet); "Blue," "Nothing Can Stop Me Now," "Full Moon," "These Blues," "Those Blues," "Imitation of a Kiss" (The Low Note Quintet)
PRODUCTION DESIGN Stephen Altman
188 mins

(1994) PRÊT-À-PORTER (READY TO WEAR)
PRODUCTION CO. Miramax Film International
PRODUCER Robert Altman
SCREENPLAY Robert Altman, Barbara Shulgasser
CINEMATOGRAPHY Pierre Mignot, Jean Lepine
EDITOR Geraldine Peroni
MUSIC Michel Legrand
SONGS "Here Comes the Hotstepper" (Ini Kamoze); "Here We Come" (Salt-N-Pepa); "'70s Love Groove" (Janet Jackson); "These Boots are Made for Walking" (Sam Philips); "Martha" (Eric Mouquet, Michel Sanchez); "Keep Givin' Me Your Love" (Cece Peniston); "Supermodel Sandwich" (Terence Trent d'Arby); "Style Is Coming Back in Style" (John Pizzarelli); "I'm Too Sexy" (Right Said Fred); "My Girl Josephine" (Supercat); "Natural Thing" (M People); "Jump on Top of Me" (The Rolling Stones); "Pretty" (The Cranberries); "Close to You" (The Brand New Heavies); "Get Wild'" (NPG); "Lemon" (U2); "I Like Your Style" (Tower of Power); "Got the Bull by the Horns" (k.d. lang); "Dopest Ethiopian" (Asante); "Ruby Baby" (Bjork); "Be Thankful for What You Got" (William DeVaughn); "Addicted to Love" (Robert Palmer); "Unchained Melody" (The Righteous Brothers); "Blackjack" (Donald Byrd); "As" (Dag); "Abat-jour" (Henry Wright); "Twiggy, Twiggy" (Pizzicato Five); "Raga" (Jah Wobble); "How Long Dub" (Soul II Soul); "Reste sur moi" (Patricia Kass); "Third Time Lucky" (Basia); "Same Brown Earth" (Latin Players); "Violent and Funky" (Infectious Grooves); "Swamp Thing" (The Groove); "L'accordeoniste," "La Coulante du pauvre Jean" (Edith Piaf); "Transit Ride" (Guru); "Here We Go" (Stakka Bo); "La Vie en Rose" (Grace Jones); "Concerto for Trumpet and Strings by Torelli," "Bararolle" (Offenbach); "The Pirates of Penzance" (Gilbert and Sullivan)
PRODUCTION DESIGN Stephen Altman
133 mins

(1996) KANSAS CITY
PRODUCTION CO. Ciby 2000/Sandcastle 5 Productions
PRODUCER Robert Altman
SCREENPLAY Robert Altman, Frank Barhydt
CINEMATOGRAPHY Oliver Stapleton
EDITOR Geraldine Proni
MUSIC Hal Willner, Steven Bernstein
SONGS "Hosts of Freedom" (The Lincoln College Preparatory Academy Band); "Indiana," "Blue in the Dark," "Pagin' the Devil," "Froggy Bottom," "Lullaby of the Leaves," "Queer Notions," "Tickle Toe," "Moten Swing," "I Surrender Dear," "I Left My Baby," "Yeah Man," "Lafayette," "Solitude" (musicians of The Hey-Hey Club)
PRODUCTION DESIGN Stephen Altman
115 mins

(1998) THE GINGERBREAD MAN
PRODUCTION CO. Polygram Filmed Entertainment presents an Island Pictures/Enchanter Entertainment production
PRODUCER Jeremy Tannenbaum
SCREENPLAY Al Hayes, based on an original story by John Grisham
CINEMATOGRAPHY Changwei Gu
EDITOR Geraldine Peroni
MUSIC Mark Isham
PRODUCTION DESIGN Stephen Altman
114 mins

(1999) COOKIE'S FORTUNE
PRODUCERS Robert Altman, Etchie Stroh
SCREENPLAY Anne Rapp
CINEMATOGRAPHY Toyomichi Kurita
EDITOR Abraham Lim
MUSIC David A. Stewart
PRODUCTION DESIGN Stephen Altman
118 mins

(2000) DR. T AND THE WOMEN
PRODUCTION CO. Initial Entertainment Group presents a Sandcastle 5 production
PRODUCERS Robert Altman, James McLindon
SCREENPLAY Anne Rapp
CINEMATOGRAPHY Jan Kiesser
EDITOR Geraldine Peroni
MUSIC Lyle Lovett
SONGS "You've Been So Good Up to Now," "She's Already Made Up Her Mind," "Ain't It Something" (Lyle Lovett)
PRODUCTION DESIGN Stephen Altman
122 mins

(2001) GOSFORD PARK
PRODUCTION CO. Capitol Films and The Film Council present in association with USA Films a Sandcastle 5 production in association with Chicagofilms and Medusa Film
PRODUCERS Robert Altman, Bob Balaban, David Levy
SCREENPLAY Julian Fellowes, based on an idea by Robert Altman, Bob Balaban
CINEMATOGRAPHY Andrew Dunn
EDITOR Tim Squyres
MUSIC Patrick Doyle
SONGS "What a Duke Should Be," "Nuts in May," "The Land of Might-Have-Been," "And Her Mother Came Too," "I Can Give You the Starlight," "Why Isn't it You?," "Keep the Home Fires Burning" (Jeremy Northam as Ivor Novello); "Waltz of My Heart," "Glamorous Night" (Christopher Northam); "The Way it's Meant to Be" (Abigail Doyle)
PRODUCTION DESIGN Stephen Altman
137 mins

(2003) THE COMPANY
PRODUCTION CO. Capitol Films presents in association with CP Medien a Killer Films/John Wells production in association with First Snow Productions and Sandcastle 5 Productions
PRODUCERS David Levy, Joshua Astrachan, Neve Campbell, Robert Altman, Christine Vachon, Pamela Koffler
SCREENPLAY Barbara Turner, from a story by Barbara Turner and Neve Campbell
CINEMATOGRAPHY Andrew Dunn
EDITOR Geraldine Peroni
MUSIC Van Dyke Parks
SONGS "My Funny Valentine" (Elvis Costello, Lee Wiley, Chet Baker, Kronos Quartet)
BALLETS "Tensile Involvement" (Alwin Nikolais); "Suite Saint-Saens" (Gerald Arpino); "Trinity" (Gerald Arpino); "Light Rain" (Gerald Arpino); "My Funny Valentine" (Lar Lubovitch); "Creative Force" (Laura Dean); "La vivandi e re pas de six" (Arthur Saint-Leon); "White Widow" (Moses Pendleton); "Strange Prisoners" (Davis Robertson); "The Blue Snake" (Robert Desrosiers)
PRODUCTION DESIGN Gary Baugh
112 mins

(2006) A PRAIRIE HOME COMPANION
PRODUCTION CO. Picturehouse in association with GreenStreet Films in association with River Road Entertainment. Co-production with Sandcastle 5 Productions/Prairie Home Productions
PRODUCERS Robert Altman, Wren Arthur, Joshua Astrachan, Tony Judge, David Levy
SCREENPLAY Garrison Keillor, from a story by Garrison Keillor and Ken LaZebnik
CINEMATOGRAPHY Edward Lachman
EDITOR Jacob Craycroft
MUSIC Garrison Keillor
PRODUCTION DESIGN Dina Goldman
106 mins

TELEVISION

(1953) PULSE OF THE CITY (plus co-creator, co-producer)

(1957) SUSPICION
"Heartbeat" (production consultant only)

(1957–58) ALFRED HITCHCOCK PRESENTS

(1958) M SQUAD

(1958–59)
WHIRLYBIRDS
THE MILLIONAIRE

(1959) HAWAIIAN EYE

(1959–60)
THE TROUBLESHOOTERS
U.S. MARSHALL (SHERIFF OF CONCHISE)
SUGARFOOT

(1960)
THE MAN FROM BLACKHAWK
THE GALE STORM SHOW (OH! SUSANNAH)
BRONCO
MAVERICK
WESTINGHOUSE DESILU PLAYHOUSE

(1960–61)
THE ROARING 20'S
BONANZA

(1961)
LAWMAN
SURFSIDE 6
PETER GUNN
ROUTE 66

(1961–62) BUS STOP

(1962)
CAIN'S HUNDRED
THE GALLANT MEN

(1962–63)
KRAFT MYSTERY THEATRE
COMBAT!

(1963–64)
KRAFT SUSPENSE THEATRE

(1964)
THE LONG, HOT SUMMER

(1968)
A WALK IN THE NIGHT (plus co-producer, story, and co-script)

(1982) TWO BY SOUTH:
PRECIOUS BLOOD AND
RATTLESNAKE IN A COOLER
PRODUCTION CO. Alpha Repertory Television Service
PRODUCERS Scott Bushnell, Joseph Butt
SCREENPLAY Frank South, from his own plays
CINEMATOGRAPHY (VIDEO) Lloyd Freidus
EDITORS Gary Princz, Max K. Curtis
MUSIC Danny Darst
PRODUCTION DESIGN John Kavelin
Precious Blood 60 mins
Rattlesnake in a Cooler 57 mins

(1985) LAUNDROMAT
PRODUCTION CO. A Byck/Lancaster production of a Sandcastle 5 film
PRODUCERS Dann Byck, David Lancaster
SCREENPLAY Marsha Norman, from her own play
CINEMATOGRAPHY Pierre Mignot
EDITOR Luce Grunenwaldt
SONGS "Common Folk," "Somebody's Daddy," "Can't Make a Livin' on the Road" (Danny Durst); "Downhearted Blues," "Some Sweet Day," "I'm Having a Good Time," "Black Man," "The Love I Have for You," "My Castle's Rockin," "I Cried for You," "My Handy Man Ain't Handy No More" (Alberta Hunter)
PRODUCTION DESIGN David Gropman
57 mins

(1987) THE DUMB WAITER
PRODUCTION CO. Secret Castle Productions/ABC
PRODUCER Robert Altman
SCREENPLAY Harold Pinter, from his own play
CINEMATOGRAPHY Pierre Mignot
EDITOR Jennifer Auge
MUSIC Judith Gruber-Stizer
PRODUCTION DESIGN Violette Daneau
60 mins

(1987) THE ROOM
PRODUCTION CO. Secret Castle Productions/ABC
PRODUCER Robert Altman
SCREENPLAY Harold Pinter, from his own play
CINEMATOGRAPHY Pierre Mignot
EDITOR Jennifer Auge
MUSIC Judith Gruber-Stitzer
PRODUCTION DESIGN Violette Daneau
49 mins (*The Dumb Waiter* and *The Room* were also combined as a double bill called *Basements*)

(1988) TANNER '88
PRODUCTION CO. Zenith and Darkhorse Productions/Home Box Office
PRODUCER Scott Bushnell
SCREENPLAY Garry Trudeau
CINEMATOGRAPHY (VIDEO) Jean Lepine
EDITORS Alison Ellwood, Ruth Foster, Mark Fish, Sean-Michael Connor
MUSIC Allan Nicholls
PRODUCTION DESIGN Stephen Altman, Jerry Fleming
300 mins
(*Episode 1*: 60 mins; *Episodes 2–9*: 30 mins each)

(1988) THE CAINE MUTINY
COURT-MARTIAL
PRODUCTION CO. The Maltese Companies, Inc. in association with Wouk/Ware Productions and Sandcastle 5 Productions
PRODUCERS Robert Altman, John Flaxman
SCREENPLAY Herman Wouk, based on his own novel and play
CINEMATOGRAPHY Jacek Laskus
EDITORS Dorian Harris
MUSIC Dan Edelstein
PRODUCTION DESIGN Stephen Altman
100 mins

(1992) THE REAL MCTEAGUE: A
SYNTHESIS OF FORMS (concept and creative supervision only)
PRODUCTION CO. A production of WTTW/Chicago in association with Thirteen/WNET and Lyric Opera of Chicago
PRODUCER Geoffrey Baer
COORDINATING PRODUCER Frank Barhydt
OPERA SEGMENTS DIRECTED FOR TELEVISION Kirk Browning
SCREENPLAY James Arntz, Geoffrey Baer
EDITOR Paul Thornton
60 mins

(1993) BLACK AND BLUE
PRODUCTION CO. The Black and Blue Company in association with Thirteen/WNET, Japan Satellite Broadcasting, and Reiss Media Productions, Inc.
PRODUCER David Horn
COORDINATING PRODUCER John Walker
SUPERVISING PRODUCER Scott Bushnell
EDITOR Brent Carpenter
CONDUCTOR Leonard Oxley
THE SINGERS Ruth Brown, Linda Hopkins, Carrie Smith
THE HOOFERS Bunny Briggs, Lon Chaney, George Hillman, Bernard Manners, Jimmy Slyde, Dianne Walker
115 mins (US version)

(1997) JAZZ '34
PRODUCTION CO. Sandcastle 5 Productions/CiBy 2000
PRODUCERS James McLindon, Matthew Seig, Brent Carpenter, Robert Altman
SCREENPLAY Robert Altman
CINEMATOGRAPHY Oliver Stapleton
EDITORS Brent Carpenter, Susan Jacobs, Steven Bernstein
SONGS "Tickle Toe," "Indiana," "Solitude," "Blues in the Dark," "Prince of Wails," "Froggy Bottom," "Harvard Blues," "King Porter Stomp," "Lafayette," "Lullaby of the Leaves," "Piano Boogie," "Pagin' the Devil," "Moten Swing," "Queer Notions," "Yeah Man"
PRODUCTION DESIGN Stephen Altman
75 mins

(1997) ALL THE PRESIDENT'S
WOMEN
PRODUCTION CO. Kusher-Locke Company/Sadwith Productions/Sandcastle 5 Productions
PRODUCERS James Sadwith, Robert Altman, Rob Dwek, Donald Kuchner, Peter Locke
SCREENPLAY Anne Rapp
CINEMATOGRAPHY Roy H. Wagner
EDITOR Dorian Harris
MUSIC Roy Hay, Mike Burns
PRODUCTION DESIGN Bernt Capra
45 mins

(2004) TANNER ON TANNER
PRODUCTION CO. The Sundance Channel presents a Sandcastle 5 production
PRODUCERS Matthew Seig, Wren Arthur

CINEMATOGRAPHY (VIDEO) Tom Richmond, Robert Reed Altman
EDITOR Jacob Craycroft
MUSIC House of Diablo, Allan Nicolls
PRODUCTION DESIGN Dina Goldman
120 mins (4 episodes, 30 mins each)

IMAGE CREDITS

PREFACE
Courtesy of Sandcastle 5 Productions, Inc.: 6; courtesy of Kathryn Reed Altman: 10, 11.

CHAPTER 1
Courtesy of Richie Sarafian: 15, 17 (top & bottom), 18 (right); courtesy of Silvio Francesco Rizzi: 19 (top left); courtesy of Sandcastle 5 Productions, Inc.: 14, 16, 18 (left, center), 19 (top right, bottom), 20, 21, 22, 24–27, 29–33, except 26 (top left) courtesy of Variety; courtesy of Kathryn Reed Altman: 34–39.

CHAPTER 2
M*A*S*H still photographer: Robert W. Full. *The Long Goodbye, Thieves Like Us*, special photography by Jean Pagliuso. *California Split* still photographer: Sid Baldwin. Courtesy of Sandcastle 5 Productions, Inc.: 40–47, 49, 50, 51, 53, 55–83, except 43 (sheet music, top left, middle) courtesy of Michael Altman, 44 *MAD* illustration courtesy of E.C. Publications, Inc.; courtesy of Kathryn Reed Altman: 84–89, except photo no. 23 courtesy of Jean Pagliuso.

CHAPTER 3
Nashville photographers include Joyce Rudolph, Jim Coe; special photography by Jean Pagliuso. Courtesy of Sandcastle 5 Productions, Inc.: 90–93, 95, 97–101, 103, 104, 106–113, 117, except 98 (sheet music top) courtesy of Jonathan Gibson, (sheet music bottom) courtesy of Keith Carradine, 99 (bottom left) illustration by J. William Myers courtesy of the artist, 101 (bottom left), courtesy of Allan Nicholls; courtesy of Allan Nicholls: 114, 115; courtesy of Kathryn Reed Altman: 121.

CHAPTER 4
Buffalo Bill and the Indians still photographer: Bruce Lohmann; additional photography by Joyce Rudolph; special photography by Jean Pagliuso and Lauren Hutton. Special photography on *A Wedding* and *Quintet* by Jean Pagliuso. *A Perfect Couple* photography by Sid Baldwin. *HealtH* photography by Melinda Wickman; special photography by Jean Pagliuso. Courtesy of Sandcastle 5 Productions, Inc.: 122–125, 127–133, 135, 136, 138–157, except 127 courtesy of Jill Krementz, 129 (top, middle, bottom) courtesy of Jean Pagliuso, 131 (bottom) courtesy of Film Society of Lincoln Center; courtesy of Kathryn Reed Altman: 154–161, except no. 17 and no. 22 courtesy of Jean Pagliuso.

CHAPTER 5
Popeye still photographers: Paul Ronald, Melinda Wickman; special photography by Jean Pagliuso. *Come Back to the Five and Dime Jimmy Dean, Jimmy Dean* (Broadway) photographers: Amy Arbus, Jean Pagliuso. *Secret Honor* still photographer:, Debra Eve Lewis. *O.C. and Stiggs* special photography by Jean Pagliuso. *Fool For Love* still photographers: Robert Reed Altman, Ed Klamm. *Beyond Therapy* still photographer: Robert Reed Altman. *Tanner '88* still photographers: Richard Howard (New Hampshire); Dean Dixon (Nashville); Ed Lamb (Detroit); Cliff Lipson (Washington D.C.); Lynn Houston (Los Angeles, Atlanta); Will Hart (Atlanta); special photography by Jean Pagliuso. *Vincent & Theo* still photographers: Micheline Pelletier, Leendert Jansen, Christophe Rouffio. Courtesy of Sandcastle 5 Productions, Inc.: 166, 169 (top right, bottom left), 171, 174–179, 181, 184–206, except 168, 175 (bottom), 191 (bottom right) courtesy of Jean Pagliuso, 169 (top left) courtesy of Cathy Keller, 176 (bottom left) courtesy of *National Lampoon*, 182 © Doug

Marlette Estate, courtesy of the Estate, 207 courtesy of Micheline Pelletier: 207; courtesy of Kathryn Reed Altman: 208–219, except no. 19, no. 20, photographs by Jaime Ardiles-Arce, *Architectural Digest* March 1990, courtesy of *Architectural Digest*.

CHAPTER 6
The Player still photographer: Lorey Sebastian. *Short Cuts* still photographer: Joyce Rudolph. *Prêt-à-Porter* still photographer: Etienne George. *Kansas City* still photographer: Eli Reed. *Gingerbread Man* and *Cookie's Fortune* still photographer: Joyce Rudolph. *Dr. T and the Women* still photographer: Zade Rosenthal. Courtesy of Sandcastle 5 productions, Inc.: 220–224, 226, 227, 229, 232–257, except 244, portraits © Don Bachardy, provided by Mike Kaplan; courtesy of Kathryn Reed Altman: 258–277, except nos. 65–68 courtesy of Yann Gamblin, no. 92, no. 93 courtesy of American Society of Cinematographers.

CHAPTER 7
The Company still photographer: Matt Dinerstein. *Gosford Park* still photographer: Mark Tillie. *Tanner on Tanner* still photographers: Robert Reed Altman, Albert Ferreira, Stuart Ramson, Dina Goldman. *Prairie Home Companion* still photographer: Melinda Sue Gordon. Courtesy of Sandcastle 5 Productions, Inc.: 278–280, 282, 286, 287, 289, 290, 292–305, except 281 courtesy of Variety, 292 (top right) courtesy of Tom Waits, 292 (bottom right)–295, 306–309 courtesy of Melinda Sue Gordon. Courtesy of Kathryn Reed Altman: 310–327, except no. 65 courtesy of Thomas Concordia, 67–71 courtesy of Melinda Sue Gordon, no. 72 courtesy of Danielle Weil, no. 76 courtesy of Yuichi Hibi, no. 77 courtesy of Academy of Motion Picture Arts and Sciences, no. 78 courtesy of Jonathan Becker, no. 91 courtesy of *Variety*, photo © by Mark Tillie.

ACKNOWLEDGMENTS

The authors sincerely thank everyone who contributed the essays and interviews that appear throughout this book, providing historical context and insight into the creative process of Robert Altman: Frank Barhydt, E. L. Doctorow, Chaz Ebert and Elliot Ephraim (The Ebert Company), Donald Farber (Kurt Vonnegut Jr. Copyright Trust), Jules Feiffer, Julian Fellowes, Isabel Flower (*Artforum*), James Franco, Tess Gallagher, Reggie Hui (Library of America), Garrison Keillor, Catheryn Kligariff (Marion Boyars Publishers), Michael Murphy, Annie Ocharek (*Artforum*), Max Rudin (The Library of America), Alan Rudolph, Martin Scorsese, Lily Tomlin, Michael Tolkin, and Stuart Waterman (Curtis Brown, LTD).

Many people graciously responded to our requests to read drafts, verify facts, remember names, and provide and identify images: Robert Reed Altman, Michael Altman, Stephen Altman, Luca Andreotti, Jonathan Becker, Keith Carradine, Konni Corriere, Sarah Eaton (Sundance Institute), John Gibson (Estate of Henry Gibson), Melinda Sue Gordon, Lindsay Jensen, Mike Kaplan, Dave Kehr, Cathy Keller, Jill Krementz, Bill Krohn, David Levy, Patricia McHugh, J. William Myers, Allan Nicholls, Jean Pagliuso, Joyce Rudolph, Brian Sheehan (*Variety* Media), Bridget Terry, Richie Sarafian, Melinda Swearingen, and Ginger Wilmot. Thank you, J. William Myers, for your portraits of the Nashville cast, and Don Bachardi for your portraits of the characters in *Short Cuts*. Thank you, Monica LoCascio, for exploring every lead, and Thea Kerman, for your guidance.

Aside from Kathryn Altman's photo albums, most of the images in this book have been drawn from the Robert Altman Archive, a collection of more than a thousand boxes that dates from his work with the Calvin Company. Many people have cared for this collection since then. Thank you to Robert Altman's final staff at Sandcastle 5 Productions for your stewardship of these records: Wren Arthur, Joshua Astrachan, Tim McDowell, and Lowell Dubrinsky. The Robert Altman Archive is now housed at the University of Michigan in Ann Arbor where it has been indexed, cataloged, cared for, and is available to researchers. At the Special Collections Library, we are grateful for the assistance of Peggy Daub, Philip Hallman, Kathleen Dow, Melissa Gomis, Kate Hutchens, Rosa Moore, and Gregory Brown. Ron Mann spent many weeks at the Archive conducting research for his documentary film, *ALTMAN*, and generously shared his findings with us. It would have been difficult to create this book without his help.

Kathryn Altman's portrait of life with Robert Altman benefited greatly from the assistance of Signe Lohmann. Sandcastle 5 Productions, founded by Mr. Altman in 1981 to produce his films, continues under the oversight of Jerome Walsh and Matthew Seig. Thank you, Signe, Jerry, and Matthew for helping make this book possible.

The team at Abrams is dedicated to the art of books, and they worked hard on this one. Thank you, Eric Klopfer, for your patience, support, encouragement, and guidance, and Chris Nashawaty, for your invaluable last-minute assistance with caption-writing and fact-checking. Thank you to Sheila Keenan for bringing us to Abrams and making this endeavor possible. Thank you, Martin Venezky, for a book design that captures the sensibility and art of Robert Altman so well.

ABOUT THE IMAGES FROM THE ROBERT ALTMAN ARCHIVE

I spent the summer of 2012 digging through the Robert Altman Archive at Special Collections, the University of Michigan Library, Ann Arbor, for a documentary I was planning to make about America's greatest filmmaker. I had no concept of what to expect when I arrived—a few dusty old photographs or faded newspaper clippings that Bob may have kept over his half-century career. Instead I stumbled upon a treasure trove the size of the last scene in *Raiders of the Lost Ark*. Organized by project, each box extensively documented Bob's artistic process—from concept to release. With only a few exceptions, it was all there. Every box was like opening a birthday present. I'd like to think it was a gift that Bob intended to give the world. I planned on being there a week—and stayed six, scanning documents and images continuously. Some of these are included in my upcoming documentary, also titled *ALTMAN*. Many are in this book. I hope you enjoy them.

Ron Mann
Documentary Filmmaker

PROJECT MANAGER ERIC KLOPFER
EDITOR MATTHEW SEIG
DESIGNER MARTIN VENEZKY
PRODUCTION MANAGER DENISE LACONGO
PERMISSIONS COORDINATOR MONICA LOCASCIO
RESEARCH SIGNE LOHMANN
PHOTO RESEARCH RON MANN

Grateful acknowledgment is made to those who supplied additional text to this book, both original and reprinted:
Introduction © 2014 MARTIN SCORSESE
CHAPTER 1
"**Kansas City Bob**" © 2014 FRANK BARHYDT
"**Something Akin to Love**" © 2014 MICHAEL MURPHY
CHAPTER 2
"**Review of *McCabe & Mrs. Miller***" © 1971 THE EBERT COMPANY, LTD. First published in the *Chicago Sun-Times*
"**Love and Coca Cola**" © 1974 PAULINE KAEL. First published in the *New Yorker*. Reprinted by permission of Curtis Brown, Ltd.
CHAPTER 3
"***Nashville***" © 1975 KURT VONNEGUT JR. First published in *Vogue*. Reprinted by permission of the Kurt Vonnegut Jr. Copyright Trust
"**COMING: *NASHVILLE***" by Pauline Kael, from *The Age of Movies: Selected Writings of Pauline Kael*, edited by Sanford Schwartz. First published in the *New Yorker*. Copyright © 2011 LITERARY CLASSICS OF THE UNITED STATES, INC., New York, N.Y. All rights reserved.
"**An Interview with Lily Tomlin**" © 2014 GIULIA D'AGNOLO VALLAN
CHAPTER 4
"**Remarks at the Robert Altman Memorial Tribute**" © 2006 E. L. DOCTOROW
"**Altman After Hours**" © 2014 ALAN RUDOLPH
CHAPTER 5
"**An Interview with Jules Feiffer**" © 2014 GIULIA D'AGNOLO VALLAN
"**Some Thoughts on *Tanner '88***" © 2014 MICHAEL MURPHY
CHAPTER 6
"**Greener Pastures: Michael Tolkin on Robert Altman**" © 2007 ARTFORUM
"**Altman and Barhydt**" © 1993 TESS GALLAGHER. First published as the foreword to *Short Cuts: The Screenplay*.
CHAPTER 7
"**An Interview with Julian Fellowes**" © 2014 GIULIA D'AGNOLO VALLAN
"**Altman**" © 2014 JAMES FRANCO
"**Bob**" © 2014 GARRISON KEILLOR

LIBRARY OF CONGRESS CONTROL NUMBER 2014930546
ISBN 978-1-4197-0777-3
PUBLISHED IN 2014 by Abrams, an imprint of ABRAMS.

PRINTED AND BOUND IN CHINA
10 9 8 7 6 5 4 3 2 1

Abrams books are available at special discounts when purchased in quantity for premiums and promotions as well as fundraising or educational use. Special editions can also be created to specification. For details, contact specialsales@abramsbooks.com or the address below.

THE ART OF BOOKS SINCE 1949
115 West 18th Street
New York, NY 10011
www.abramsbooks.com